White Métisse

KIM LEFÈVRE

White Métisse

translated by

JACK A. YEAGER

University of Hawai'i Press
Honolulu

This work, published as part of a program of aid for publication, received support from the Mission Culturelle et Universitaire Française aux États-Unis, a department of the French Embassy in the United States.

Métisse blanche first published in Paris in 1989.
@ Editions Phébus, Paris, 2008
English translation @ 2018 University of Hawai'i Press

23 22 21 20 19 18   6 5 4 3 2 1

Library of Congress Cataloging-in-Publication Data

Names: Lefèvre, Kim, author. | Yeager, Jack Andrew, translator.
Title: White métisse / Kim Lefèvre ; translated by Jack A. Yeager.
Other titles: Métisse blanche. English
Description: Honolulu : University of Hawai'i Press, [2018] |
Identifiers: LCCN 2017055850| ISBN 9780824872663 (cloth alk. paper) | ISBN 9780824872670 (pbk. alk. paper)
Subjects: LCSH: Lefevre, Kim. | Eurasians—Vietnam—Biography. | Vietnam—Ethnic relations. | LCGFT: Autobiographies.
Classification: LCC DS556.83.L45 A3 2018 | DDC 959.704092 [B]—dc23
LC record available at https://lccn.loc.gov/2017055850

Cover photo: Kim Lefèvre, circa 1949 (author collection).

University of Hawai'i Press books are printed on acid-free paper and meet the guidelines for permanence and durability of the Council on Library Resources.

Design and composition by Wanda China

CONTENTS

NOTES ON TRANSLATION

The French word *métis/se* has no adequate equivalent in English. Suggested dictionary translations such as "mulatto," "half-caste," and "mixed-race" carry too many connotations, while "biracial," if more neutral, does not convey the idea of cloth woven (*tissé*) from two threads, linen and cotton. I have thus chosen to retain the original French word, in italics, throughout this translation.

The edition of *Métisse blanche* used for this translation was published in Paris by Phébus libretto in 2008. The original edition was published in Paris by Editions Barrault in 1989.

TIMELINE

INTRODUCTION

In 1989, Kim Lefèvre published *Métisse blanche*, the memoir of her child-hood and adolescence in Viet Nam spanning two and a half decades from the mid-1930s to 1960. As the biracial daughter of a Vietnamese mother and a French father whom she never knew, she became the target of distrust and rejection in an atmosphere of increasing resistance to the French colonists and rising nationalism during the 1930s in what was then a Viet Nam divided into three parts administered by France: Tonkin in the north, Annam in the center, and Cochinchina in the south. These, along with Laos and Cambodia, made up what the French called Indochine française, or French Indochina.

Emerging from the veils of Hanoi's fog and the depths of her own memory, Lefèvre's story is located from the opening lines in a space that is uncertain and undefinable. She refers to the events of her early life as sketchy and blurry, evoked in the use of terms such as "it seems" and "ephemeral"; time, for her, is not measured chronologically. This uncertainty manifests also in her family situation as well as in the series of names she carries, equally unstable and constantly shifting, common among *métis* children: Tran, the family name of her mother Tran Thi My; Tiffon, that of her French father; Lam, that of her stepfather Lam Khe; Eliane and Thérèse, names given her by the French; 238, the "name" given to her when she was abandoned by her mother. As a child, she lives with various relatives and moves in and out of an orphanage, from one house to another, from one town to the next, from north to south and back again. Put simply, she is always on the move, a mobility that reflects her own shifting racial identity, her *métissage,* her difference.

As a young girl, Kim does not understand the undercurrents swirling around her and even less so the resultant reactions of others to her presence. Why is she treated differently than other children? Isn't she just like them? she wonders. She feels Vietnamese and yet even she is shocked when she sees her reflection in a mirror for the first time. Her situation, we understand, is a complicated one: her face itself shows others the collaboration of the Vietnamese with the colonial enemy, as well as the moral downfall of her mother for being the "*con gái*" of a French soldier, having sex out of wedlock, losing her virginity in a society in which it is highly prized, and for bearing his child.[1] The complex meanings and overtones of Kim's story are thus captured in the title of her narrative, *Métisse blanche, White Métisse*: she is biracial, with the status of white bearing the charge of negativity.

The reactions of others to the biracial child are foreseen even before the little girl is born. Her mother's half-brother Tri, who works clandestinely for the nationalist cause, warns his half-sister that she should hand her child over to "[her] people" as soon as possible after the birth:

> He had the deep conviction that given my heritage, I was a tree that would never bear fruit. "Believe me . . . a snake is growing inside your body, and her French blood will win out no matter how much good you do. She's a bad seed and she'll betray you" ("Il avait l'intime conviction qu'avec mon atavisme j'étais un arbre dont on ne pouvait attendre de fruits. 'Crois-moi . . . tu couves une vipère en ton sein, son sang français prendre le dessus malgré tes bienfaits. C'est de la mauvaise graine, elle te trahira,'" 1:35–36F).[2]

Soon after Kim is born, her mother sees a fortune teller who confirms Tri's prediction, calling her an "unlucky mother." He says, "The ingratitude of this child is marked there, on her face, in her destiny" ("L'ingratitude de cette enfant est marquée là dans son destin" 1:36F). Later her grandmother tells her that her life will be difficult because of her mixed heritage: "You are an alloy, neither gold nor silver" ("Tu es un alliage, ni or ni argent . . ." 1:39F), words that cut the young child like the blade of a knife. These early scenes in the memoir set the stage for the long series of challenges she will face, located at the intersection of being female, mixed-race, and illegitimate.[3] In the course of the narrative, Kim Lefèvre will assume her hybrid identity and gain self-esteem on her own terms, in the context of her pursuit of education, her coming of age, and the discovery of her own sexuality and desire. Her departure for study in Paris at the end of the text, wrenching as it is in the separation from her mother, sisters, and friends, represents in many respects her own personal triumph, a triumph that will lead her to graduate education in France, a thesis at the Sorbonne, a position as a *surveillante* or proctor in a *lycée* in Paris, another as a librarian at the École Normale Supérieure, Rue d'Ulm, and yet another as a teacher of French literature as well as to marriage, motherhood, acting, translating, and writing.[4]

As we see in *Métisse blanche*, Kim is not the only biracial character in her memoir. We encounter what seems to constitute a shadow society in Indochina with, for example, Ba Tu, the mother of four daughters all from different French fathers. And these are far from being the only such characters in *Métisse blanche*. Kim's situation is, thus, not an uncommon one, and as a result, her memoir resonates with the stories of many others who were marginalized, sent away, rejected, misunderstood, or in some cases, as we see in a heartbreaking scene in Chapter 3, torn from their mothers' arms by French fathers returning to France. At the orphanage where she is sent early in her life, all the other girls are *métisse*, for example, and before arriving there, she imagines an ideal place inhabited only by *métis* where she will feel at home. However, when she finds that community at the orphanage, she is shocked and disappointed. Her ambivalence and suddenly shifting emotions in this reaction underscore the sense of instability and uncertainty on other levels of the text but also exemplify the situation of not merely this biracial character but many others. In writing and publishing her memoir, Kim Lefèvre gives voice to them all. As an old friend from the Couvent des Oiseaux says to Kim following the publication of *Métisse blanche*, "You spoke for me" ("Vous avez parlé pour moi").[5]

What we see in Kim's narrative tells us much both about the situation of *métis* in late colonial and postcolonial Viet Nam and the historical backdrop against which her childhood and adolescence unwind. In her essential and timely book *The Uprooted: Race, Children, and Imperialism in French Indochina, 1890–1980*,[6] Christina Elizabeth Firpo provides an in-depth exploration of the history of *métis* children in Indochina and in the three regions of Viet Nam especially during the colonial period and after. The larger outlines of French colonialism from the nineteenth century conquest to the defeat of the French at Dien Bien Phu in 1954 and on through the Viet Nam War to 1980 provide the context for the personal stories of many of her subjects, and by extension for *Métisse blanche*. Children born to married parents inherited the French citizenship of the father, but those who were born to unmarried parents and unrecognized by their French fathers were considered indigenous and enjoyed none of the privileges of French citizenship. As Firpo writes, "Almost all of them lived in poverty with their mothers in the indigenous cultural milieu and had come to identify as Vietnamese, Cambodian, or Lao." In the early chapters of *Métisse blanche*, we see Kim in similar surroundings, considering herself as Vietnamese and not understanding the negative reactions of others. The 1890s brought the creation of "protection" societies by "French citizens and colonial officials acting in a civilian capacity" for fatherless mixed-race children. Although developed independently, these societies collaborated with each other and with colonial authorities, leading eventually to their official takeover in 1938 by the colonial administration. After World War II, the protection societies moved once again to civilian control.[7]

During the colonial period, one overriding goal united the protection societies: their desire to see unrecognized mixed-race children considered as French with the same advantages provided to French children. Although this desire might have been viewed as magnanimous, a deeper motive was clearly to "save" *métis* children from the dangerous influence of both their mothers and the indigenous culture that surrounded them. This rescuing meant removing the children from their mothers and their Vietnamese families, an act of uprooting like no other; colonial officials used an 1889 French law controlling the "moral abandonment" of children, a law bolstered by another from 1897 passed in Indochina declaring that children of unknown parents were French, to carry out these separations, placing the children in orphanages. There were other motives for these forced removals: first, the fear that mixed-race children, and boys in particular, would grow up to resist colonialism and rebel against it; second, that mixed-race girls might marry indigenous men and assimilate into the indigenous population. Taking custody of both boys and girls, if they were considered

French, was seen as a way of stabilizing the colonial population of French people and thus their permanence and power.[8]

In the orphanages children were to speak French only and assimilate to French cultural practices,[9] an expectation that is illustrated in Kim's recollection of her life in an orphanage. In *Métisse blanche* we also see the involvement of the well-to-do colonial community in Sam Son and its "Frenchified" Vietnamese counterparts ("Vietnamiens 'francisés'" 2:65F), who host a Christmas party with a tree and gifts for the orphans at the posh Grand Hotel, an example of the civilian colonial support of the protection societies. Kim, however, was not forcibly removed by the colonial government; in fact, her mother was convinced by her own family to give up her eldest daughter by signing an irrevocable oath. As we see, there were many orphanages to choose from ("Les orphelinats ne manquaient pas," 1:45F), an indication of just how widespread the influence of the protection societies was. Some mothers did eventually have the opportunity to reclaim their daughters, but under the direst of circumstances. Faced with the possibility of being caught in the armed conflict of the Revolution, the nuns considered various alternatives including moving the wards to stay one step ahead of the fighting and evacuation of the orphans to France.[10] However, there were far too many to send abroad, and as a last resort, the sisters contacted the families to propose the option of reclaiming their daughters despite the signed documents. Kim's mother, as we shall see, is one of those mothers who returns to the orphanage and is reunited with a daughter she has not seen in years.

Questions of sexuality, of course, underlie the story of the *métis* offspring of French legionnaires, the foreign soldiers from France stationed in French colonies around the world, and their indigenous girlfriends. Vietnamese moral imperatives around the sanctioned institution of marriage and sex out of wedlock determine Kim's mother's advice to her daughter about remaining a virgin until her wedding day and Kim's obsessive stance as an "impregnable fortress" ("forteresse impregnable" 15:308F). At the moment of her daughter's first period, the mother strongly advises Kim not to commit the same mistakes as she did. Throughout the text Kim is reminded that her very presence recalls her mother's moral failing, the event that sets the narrative in motion. And the mother also knows that the Viet Minh consider the mothers of Eurasian children as prostitutes, which prompts her to hide her *métisse* daughter in a large pottery jar when the Viet Minh soldiers periodically visit the village where Kim and her mother end up after leaving the orphanage together.

The French, likewise, consider the single mothers of biracial children as prostitutes, thus providing the protection societies and colonial officials with further justification for the removal of daughters in particular, to prevent them from following in the footsteps of their mothers. In this setting Kim reaches puberty, discovers her own sexuality and begins to understand the pleasures associated with love while living with a young amorous couple who have bought her from her stepfather. The development of her body and her awareness culminate in a chaste affair with a married music teacher twice her age, which causes a scandal in the coastal city of Nha Trang where the family is living at the time and merely reconfirms the long-standing perspective of others on the dubious morality of mother and daughter. Kim's story thus shares a great deal with those of other *métis* children in colonial Indochina and postcolonial Viet Nam.

Like many of the novels produced by French-Vietnamese writers, Kim's story plays out in the repressive atmosphere of late colonialism which devolves into misery and violence with the invasion of the Japanese in 1940, the devastating famine of 1944–1945, the Japanese coup in 1945 that overthrew the French, and Vietnamese resistance and revolution against the French, considered by many to be the most tumultuous period in Franco-Vietnamese history. The First Indochina War ends in 1954 with the defeat of the French army at Dien Bien Phu, the signing of the Geneva Accords, and the provisional division of Viet Nam into North and South in 1954. These events and more figure prominently in *Métisse blanche*. Early in the war, for example, as the French advance on Tuy Hoa where Kim lives with her family, the communist/nationalist Viet Minh forces holding the coastal town decide to destroy it rather than abandon it to the French. After evacuating the inhabitants, the Viet Minh detonate the fire bombs they had placed in the houses. The townspeople then observe the conflagration as it reduces to ashes the place where they were born and expected to die, where their ancestors were buried, breaking the ties to the land and to the past that are so central to Vietnamese culture. The moving scene of lamentation clearly conveys the trauma of this event, like so many others, during the war (6:81–82).

At the Couvent des Oiseaux, to cite another example of the role of history in *Métisse blanche*, Kim and her friend Dô celebrate the official end of colonialism and the return of independence in Viet Nam upon hearing the news of the defeat of the French army at Dien Bien Phu. However, knowing that the Geneva Accords have stipulated the division of Viet Nam at the 17th parallel, Kim isn't sure if her family, now back in a reconstructed Tuy Hoa, will end up on the north side of the line and thus be inaccessible. As a day student who moves easily to and from the world outside the isolated Couvent, Dô agrees to find out and the next day surreptitiously slips her friend Kim a hand-drawn map showing Tuy Hoa south of the 17th parallel.

In yet another passage early in the memoir, Kim's uncle, her mother's older brother, arrives in Saigon in 1954 to tell the harrowing story of the purges carried out against well-to-do Vietnamese in the north after the victory at Dien Bien Phu and how in their village Kim's grandfather and his second wife were bound and placed on display in the courtyard of their home without food or water in a kind of "public trial," at the mercy of the insults and blows of the villagers. After several days, the grandfather begged for death and was hanged. Subsequently, his wife, once released, jumped to her death down a nearby well. The uncle witnesses these events from a hiding place, then manages to escape to the coast and then by boat to the south.

In these passages and elsewhere, we clearly see the impact of watershed moments in Vietnamese history on the lives of Kim, her family, and her friends. Thus, Kim's story operates on multiple levels: as a personal memoir and coming of age story, as an exemplar of the fate of *métis* in the late colonial period, and as a *mise-en-scène* of well-documented historical events from 1935 to 1960.[11]

Métisse blanche takes its place beside other memoirs of remarkable originality, but I would suggest that it also expands our definition of Vietnamese novels in French. Kim Lefèvre herself has termed this text a novel,[12] and well-known theoretical work on autobiography and fiction tells us that that the lines between these genres, if such lines can be traced at all, are anything but clear, adding yet another level of ambiguity. In other words, Kim Lefèvre's memoir could easily be part of a corpus of texts that includes the autobiographical novels of Pham Van Ky and Ly Thu Ho or the memoirs of Nguyen Manh Tuong and Tran Van Tung.[13] Moreover, in referring to her memoir as a novel, Kim Lefèvre highlights the blurred line between genres that would invite a comparison with the Vietnamese novel in French.

Shortly after the appearance of *Métisse blanche* in bookstores in France in 1989 to warm reviews, Kim Lefèvre appeared on television as part of Bernard Pivot's primetime book discussion, *Apostrophes*. This particular program focused on the theme of humiliation and included Jean-Marie Rouart, Niu Niu, Charles Juliet, and Dominique Fernandez.[14] Sales of the book skyrocketed after this broadcast, and the text has been in print continuously in France since that time. Translated into Vietnamese in 1995,[15] *Métisse blanche* received positive reviews from critics in Viet Nam. The memoir has also been included routinely on the reading lists for French and Francophone courses in Australia, North America, and Europe.

This translation aims to share Kim Lefèvre's memoir with an English-speaking audience at what many would agree is a timely moment. Decades later, the issues it raises still persist—life between racial, linguistic, and cultural worlds; immigration; border crossings and borders becoming fenced and walled; rejection, humiliation, discrimination. Indeed, while set in colonial and postcolonial Viet Nam with an autobiographical backward glance from Paris, *Métisse blanche* will resonate with readers from all walks of life, from all around the globe.

NOTES

1. Like so many words coming from the languages of the colonized (*souk* and *bled* come to mind), the word *con gái*, meaning simply young girl or daughter in Vietnamese, is often pejorative when used in French. The Vietnamese word here takes on the signification of concubine.

2. The page numbers for these citations refer to the latest edition of *Métisse blanche* published in Paris by Phébus libretto in 2008. This edition served as the basis for the translation.

3. See Michèle Sarde's introduction to the 2008 edition of the memoir, p. 11.

4. Conversation with Kim Lefèvre, October 5, 2016, Paris.

5. Kim Lefèvre, *Retour à la saison des pluies* (Paris: Editions Barrault, 1990), 23.

6. Honolulu: University of Hawai'i Press, 2016.

7. Firpo 2–3.

8. Firpo 3–5.

9. Firpo corroborates this situation, 22.

10. Firpo covers these evacuations, 123–131 and 142–143. About 4,000 wards were sent to France between 1945 and 1954.

11. As one might reasonably expect of someone writing from memory, there are a few anachronisms in *Métisse blanche*. The stepfather converts to Catholicism before the Vietnamese victory at Dien Bien Phu and thus before the return and rise to power of Ngo Dinh Diem who would not necessarily have been favoring Catholic businesses before becoming prime minister, then president in the latter half of 1954 (14:262F). Likewise, some references to South Viet Nam, dating from the geographic division of Viet Nam at the 17th parallel as stipulated by the 1954 Geneva Accords, are also anachronistic.

12. During a reading followed by a question-and-answer session at the Viet Nam House (Nhà Việt Nam) on Rue Cardinal Lemoine in Paris, May 28, 1989, Kim Lefèvre referred to her memoir as a novel ("roman"). Likewise, in her preface to the French edition of *Métisse blanche*, Michèle Sarde uses the same term (see the 2008 edition, page 13).

13. See, for example, Nathalie Huynh Chau Nguyen, *Vietnamese Voices: Gender and Cultural Identity in the Vietnamese Francophone Novel* (Dekalb, IL: Northern Illinois University Press, Southeast Asia Publications, 2003); Karl Ashoka Britto, *Disorientation: France, Vietnam, and the Ambivalence of Interculturality* (Hong Kong: Hong Kong University Press, 2004); Ching Selao, *Le roman vietnamien francophone: orientalisme, occidentalisme et hybridité* (Montréal: Les Presses de l'Université de Montréal, 2010); Sharon Lim-Hing, "Vietnamese Novels in French: Rewriting Self, Gender and Nation," Diss. Harvard University, 1993; Michael O'Riley, "Discerning the Empire's Other: Literary Interventions in the Culture of French Modernity," Diss. University of Oregon, 1998; Lily Chiu, "Alter/Native: Imagining and Performing the Native Woman in Francophone and Vietnamese Literature," Diss. University of Michigan, 2004; Pamela Pears, *Remnants of Empire in Algeria and Vietnam: Women, Words, and War* (Lanham, MD: Lexington Books, 2004); Michèle Bacholle-Boškovic, *Linda Lê: L'écriture du manque* (Lewiston, ME: Edwin Mellen, 2006); Julie Assier, "Des écrivaines du Viêt-Nam en quête d'ancrage: Linda Lê, Kim Lefèvre et Anna Moï," Diss. Université de Cergy-Pontoise, 2013; Leslie Barnes, *Vietnam and the Colonial Condition of French Literature* (Lincoln: University of Nebraska Press, 2014); Nguyen

Giang Huong, *La littérature vietnamienne francophone* (Paris: Classiques Garnier, forthcoming); and my *The Vietnamese Novel in French: A Literary Response to Colonialism* (Hanover, NH, and London: University Press of New England, 1987).

14. This broadcast on Antenne 2 from April 7, 1989, is available at: http://www.ina.fr/video/CPB89003895. Many interviews with Kim Lefèvre are also available online.

15. Dương Linh and Hoàng Phong translated the original French text into Vietnamese, published by NXB Hội Nhà Văn in Hanoi as *Cô gái lai da trắng*.

White Métisse

∽ 1 ∾

Wandering

I was born in Hanoi, or so it seems, on a spring day, shortly before the Second World War, from the ephemeral union of a young Annamite woman[1] and a French man.

I have no tangible proof of this; no birth certificate was drawn up until I was fifteen. Besides, I didn't try to find out. It had no importance, neither for me nor for others. We lived in a society in which the notion of quantifiable time did not exist. We knew that our lives were divided into major phases: childhood, the moment of the first period—a sign of the ability to have children and thus of an approaching marriage, motherhood, and then of being a mother-in-law when you finally had acquired the right, if luck had given you a son, to rule over a fearful daughter-in-law who came to live in your house. Four or five years more or less didn't matter much.

I don't know what my biological father looked like. My mother never spoke about him. On my gloomier days, I liked to imagine him as a legionnaire, not "my handsome legionnaire" from the popular song, but an arrogant, detestable colonial, a man from the other side. I nurtured an intense hatred for this unknown father as only deeply wounded children can.

I was called a series of names that marked the pivotal moments of my life. First my mother's—Tran, at the moment when she found herself alone and responsible for a child. Panicked by the full extent of the consequences of my existence on her life, she entrusted me to a wet

---

1. Considered by many to be pejorative, "Annamite" and "Annamese" were words used during the colonial period to refer to all Vietnamese.

1

nurse before fleeing far away, all the way down to Saigon, an unknown world to her but where she hoped to rebuild a future. After that, the name of my biological father—Tiffon, at a time when, pressured by everyone in her family, my mother tried to get me placed in an orphanage in order to "give me back to my race." Because, truth be told, I was considered a monstrosity in the very nationalist milieu in which I lived. My uncle had been a member of the Viet Minh since 1941, holding meetings regularly in the forests of Tuyen Quang.[2] Everything about me offended my relatives: my physical appearance as someone of mixed race, and my unpredictable character, difficult to understand—in a word, not very Vietnamese. They attributed everything that was bad in me to the French blood circulating in my veins. And that's what prevented people from feeling any real affection for me. I understood them, and I agreed with them. I also detested the blood inside me. As a little girl, I would dream of providential accidents that would rid me of this tainted blood, leaving me as pure Vietnamese, reconciled with those around me and with myself. For I loved that country, its rice fields, the green bamboo hedges, and the ponds I would splash around in with other children my own age.

I have no memory of the first years of my life, except for the feeling early on that I was out of place and a foreigner everywhere. I suffered greatly from it, experiencing it not as an injustice but rather as the result of an existential defect within myself.

My childhood is a long, dark night in my memory, a night of drifting. I have fragmented images of going from one place to another, like a package without an addressee. The old nurse, whom no one had paid for some time and who thus couldn't keep me any longer, carried me on her back in search of an old uncle, and an old aunt, or any other member of the family upon whom she could unload her burden.

It was an autumn night in Hanoi. I remember the penetrating coolness of the drizzle—that fine, misty rain typical of Tonkin,[3] and

---

2. Tuyen Quang, outside Hanoi, was known as a town with a military base and for having a large population of non-recognized *métis* children. It was known as one of the so-called "international provinces" in Indochina because of the presence of many French legionnaires and their mistresses (Firpo 64, 98).

3. During the colonial period the French divided Viet Nam into three parts: Tonkin in the north, Annam in the center, and Cochinchina in the south.

the smooth sensation of the nurse's bare back, her skin at once flabby and accommodating. Clinging to her flesh like a warm and silky hammock, I savored the happiness of the endless road. I would have liked my whole life to resemble that voyage without destination, suspended against the warm skin of my nurse with my own exposed to the Tonkinese drizzle.

In the depths of my memory, like a Chinese painting obscured by mist, appears the lake in Hanoi. What year was that? I can't say precisely. Young girls were walking, long jet-black hair down their backs, their light *áo dài*[4] floating in the wind. Children were playing on the grass. People were selling green rice: creamy, scented with fresh herbs and wrapped in a lotus leaf.

I see the kindergarten where each morning little Vietnamese children were all lined up and would sing at the top of their lungs *Maréchal, nous voilà* [Field Marshal, here we are] . . . in front of the French flag.[5] We were taught the superiority of intelligence over brute force. I still remember a song about little Tom Thumb who triumphed over the ogre by simply saying these words to him:

> Let me pass, bandit!
> For I am not afraid of you.
> You can do nothing to me.
> At school, I'm learning, I am,
> but you, you will stay ignorant.

The marvelous power of knowledge whose cult I still venerate.

At the time, I was living with one of my mother's aunts, an old, infirm lady of great beauty. It was said that she had broken her pelvis falling off a ladder. Since that accident she was immobilized in her armchair, with a keen eye and an alert mind, an eternal and formidable goddess. When Fate brought me to her house, she must have been about sixty-five. But the oval shape of her face showed no signs of sagging and

---

4. The *áo dài* is a long Vietnamese garment. Women's *áo dài* feature a fitted bodice and long skirt, split on both sides to the waist. Long trousers are worn underneath. In the original text, the word "tunic" is used to refer to the *áo dài*.

5. This was a chant of the Vichy government in France.

her fine features still retained a stunning youthfulness. She was proud of her miraculously smooth skin, which she washed in milk. That was the secret of her beauty, or so she told us. Her only flaw was without doubt her unusual and sickly pallor, like plants that wilt for lack of light. Ba Pho had no tenderness for my mother or for me. In fact, she rather inspired a kind of terror. I would often contemplate her on the sly, my heart pounding for fear of being caught.

Before her accident, she had led a life of luxury in the company of a French officer. A daughter born of that union was my mother's cousin, her elder by a few years. Aunt Marcelle stayed in her mother's house while she was pregnant. She gave birth to a son, entrusting him right away to her mother before leaving to live in France. She understood early on that her only chance in life would be not to stay in Viet Nam. I believe it was about then that my mother met my father, although I'm not certain, and no one ever said anything to me about it.

Ba Pho professed an idolatrous love for her grandson. He was a young boy of about fifteen whom everyone called "Monsieur Yves." He reigned over the household like a tyrant, supported and encouraged by my grandmother. He was overweight almost to the point of obesity with soft, pinkish skin. In our Asiatic world, he represented the "man with the big nose," according to the popular expression used to refer to the French. We lowered our eyes in his presence. Like the master of the house, he ate his meals at a table while we would eat on a mat at his feet. Sometimes he would throw us some table scraps.

I was very afraid of my cousin, Monsieur Yves. He nurtured a perverse interest in me and was quick to seize upon any weakness or mistake that might allow him to punish me. I still remember my terrified screams as he held me over an anthill. My mistake hardly deserved such a punishment: he had heard that I wasn't very well-behaved at school. In spite of everything he wanted to exercise his authority, making me uncover my knees so that he could put them in the middle of the busy ants. Since I wasn't tied up, I could have fled. But instead, I stayed there, yelling and crying until I lost my voice; that was how fascinated I was with his power.

Twenty years later someone suggested that I see him again. At the time he was an engineer for an oil company in Saigon, where I was a young French teacher in a Vietnamese secondary school. After much hesitation, my own curiosity outweighed my apprehension and I accepted. The cyclo driver let me off in front of his villa, located in the residential neighborhood. From the gate I could see a path lined with tamarind trees and a lawn dotted with hibiscus groves. I turned around and went home. And so the doors to my past remained closed, the doors behind which the evil spirits from before would continue to terrify a little girl.

Our relationship was ambiguous. During the day, I was part of the staff of domestic help. At night, my cousin and I slept in the same bed, a French bed high off the floor. For me it was a strange bed that I was unaccustomed to. But it was also a dreaded and hated universe where each night I would lie down next to the person who would torture me during the day. Frozen with fear, I would keep my eyes closed, attentive still to the slightest movement from my cousin. I would wait for him to fall asleep in order to be able to let myself drift off as well. We would spy on each other. But more often than not, my own fear made me more vigilant than his perversity made him, and he would give up first. Only then would I manage to fall asleep.

I hated that big bed. When I was beaten, I would take advantage of my crying to urinate deliberately on the white sheets. I would feel a kind of perverse joy in seeing the soiled bed and my cousin's fury. Those rare feats avenged my terror at night, when, awakened suddenly, I would find my hand in the big, soft hand of my cousin who would place it on his penis. I would be suffocating under the shroud-like sheets, paralyzed with disgust. A deadly coldness flowed through my veins, and I wanted to die. I must have been about four or five.

With the return of day, I would rediscover my taste for life. The fragrance of coriander and ginger of the morning *phở*,[6] and the clatter of bowls and spoons from breakfast would reach me from the kitchen, an entire world of its own that was both familiar and reassuring.

My great-aunt's house included a main building opening onto an interior courtyard with a well in the middle. On the other side of the well was a row of bedrooms, all alike, which she had rented to her "protégées": adolescent girls who had come in straight from the rice fields and who were destined to become the concubines of the French

---

6. Noodle soup, commonly eaten for breakfast.

officers who frequented the house. They had left the countryside to spare their families another mouth to feed and had nothing of value but their youth and their beauty. What could have been simpler than to sell your body? They were not, however, prostitutes, having neither their qualities nor their faults. Naturally timid, virgins both emotionally and physically, they gave themselves to these men they didn't know, with shudders as though they were swallowing some distasteful potion. It was a difficult moment to get through. They really didn't have enough of a sense of their own individuality to feel affected. Besides, didn't respectable women have to submit to the same fate on their wedding day? It was simply their condition as women. As for love, they never even dreamed about it, and even less so with these men whose height, hairy bodies, and superior position in our country filled them with apprehension. All they wished for was to avoid their displeasure. They promised themselves to be docile and undemanding concubines provided that they could keep the secrets of their interior Annamite universe.

I liked one of them in particular. She was a frail young girl endowed with hair so long it brushed the floor when she was sitting down. Her affection was gratifying to me. In order to look like her, I would copy her way of walking, I would adopt her poses, and I would wrap my head in a long towel to imitate her hair. Sometimes I would follow her to her bedroom, a small room cluttered with men's clothing. Once, diving down under the bed, she brought out a box for me. Inside the box were hairpins on which you could see a bird taking flight, an embroidered handkerchief, and a little change in a small purse. It wasn't a large sum but she counted on using it if by some misfortune she fell ill. The concern of having a little bit of money hidden away was very common among Asian women, whose traditional education was based upon the precept of submission. Submission to the father while she was a child, to her husband when she got married, to her eldest son when destiny made her a widow. She knew that she was not safe from being mistreated or possibly repudiated. Her destiny was entirely in the hands of her master of the moment. If he were good, she could thank the gods; if he weren't, the stash of money would let her purchase offerings so that Buddha could give her a happier fate.

I always saw my mother conceal a small amount, a guarantee of her security in case of misfortune.

Mother, I was so close to you during those pitch-black nights when we walked with muffled steps, the oil lamp sheltered under your conical hat. We could see only our bare feet and the small space around them. You were afraid you would not be able to find the spot where you had buried your treasure. The rasping croak of the frogs made me jump. Sometimes a firefly would rend the dark night with its fleeting glow. I would think about the wandering souls with no grave, and I imagined the insects' faint glimmers as their silent moaning. I would have preferred that the earthenware jar be buried at the ends of the earth and that we be leaving in search of it, abandoning for good all that was behind us.

My life in Hanoi with my great-aunt and my cousin was brief. They got tired of me very quickly. Besides, I had thought for some time that there was something deep inside me that was not likable, even disagreeable and unpleasant, something that discouraged even the best intentions and made the fervor others might feel for me seem without promise. I didn't know that people got rid of me every time my mother stopped sending the money they needed to support me. The proof of it this time was that I was sent once again to Saigon to be with my mother.

I don't remember which year it was or anything about the trip that took me to the capital of South Viet Nam. I might have been about four or five. My mother lived with her husband in a house located somewhere in the suburbs. A small passageway separated the kitchen and the main house where the ancestral altar sat imposingly. It was there that she would light sticks of incense and become lost in prayer on her most discouraging days.

She was pregnant and continually in tears.

Her cold-mannered husband was markedly older than she and neither handsome nor charming. He never spoke to us directly. She never loved him and for a long time she led him on. She explained to me once that he was trying to avenge the difficulty he had had in convincing her to marry him. So, she lived in his house, sheltered and fed, but alone.

Each month he would give the cook the necessary expenses for food and the upkeep of the house. Later on, she admitted to me that she had never had even the money to buy a needle to mend the clothes.

But at the time I was unaware of this situation. I would hang around during those interminably boring afternoons, my only distraction the lost turtle who had taken refuge under the wardrobe. I spent long hours watching it, calling out to it softly, always surprised by the extreme slowness with which it would stick out its head from its shell. It had a tiny head streaked with gold. I knew it was fearful and kept myself from touching it. We slowly became friends; otherwise I would never have been able to hold it in my hand.

One evening, the turtle escaped, and I took off to find it. It was dark. Here and there the faint yellow light of the oil lamps glimmered. I ventured further and further away, but the turtle was nowhere to be found. I then tried to retrace my steps, but everything seemed unfamiliar; I didn't recognize any house or street. Alarmed, I began to run and only ended up getting more lost. I screamed for my mother, my face turned toward the sky, surprised to see so many stars above. An old lady surprised me like that. She took me home, where I was beaten for my disobedience. There was no justice for me.

That period of my life had one aspect that dominated everything else: emptiness. My mother had no relationships or friends. No one came to see us, and we never invited anyone in. My stepfather lived his life elsewhere. Contrary to the neighboring houses, where there was always noise, laughter, and arguments, ours was stunningly silent, a house abandoned.

Our solitude was accentuated by the fact that my mother was from Tonkin. She had retained the accent of people from the North, wore a turban instead of a chignon—so many handicaps in a context where regional hostilities were alive and well. In Cochinchina, in the south, people thought that northerners were stingy and lived only for their representation in society, for face. Laughing, they would say that when visitors arrived, even the most destitute would hastily put a wooden fish on a plate to make them think they had the means to fix a decent meal.

My mother was always sad. Tired of being shunted around, she got stuck in a loveless marriage out of a need for social recognition and material security. In linking her own life to that of a man without any appeal, she had hoped to conjure up an acceptable past, attain a respectable life, and maybe even take me back to live with her. But she soon realized her error. As the days passed she took the full measure of the lingering grudge of the man who had been wounded by her initial indifference. Thus, she was set on sending me away, back to Hanoi once again.

This departure didn't prompt any particular feelings on my part. The short time I'd spent with a mother completely turned inward upon her own pain did not allow me to strengthen our bonds. The love she may have had for me was rarely expressed. As for her husband, my stepfather, I remember only a periodic and hostile presence.

I left without sadness, emotionally numb.

At the train station, the platform was swarming with people. With all the strength of my five years, I trotted along behind the lady I had been entrusted to, vaguely conscious that from then on, I would have only her. Gripping onto the panel of her brown *áo dài*, I was determined not to lose her. Around us, men with bundles on their backs pushed through the crowd. Children screamed. Tea sellers, holding their trays high above their heads with one hand as the other swung their aluminum teakettles, swayed with the rhythm of the jostling crowd. Sellers of custard apples, bananas, cakes, and candy all hawked their wares at the same time. And the arguments and cries of terror of the children who had lost their parents in the crush . . . it seemed like open warfare and a festival all at the same time. I wrapped the panel of the *áo dài* around my waist and ran after her as fast as I could.

In front of the steps that led up into the train car, the pressing crowd was at its height. We were jostled, then pushed roughly, then lifted into the car by the crowd. Inside there were no seats left; third class was packed, as usual. Passengers were sitting down right on the floor, each group with its mat, belongings, and baskets of provisions. People were saying hello to each other and engaging in a bit of conversation while the flood of travelers continued to flow into the car. Feeling ill from the lack of fresh air and fatigue, I lay down in a ball on the corner of a mat, trying to repress the strong urge to vomit.

"For goodness' sake, you're as white as a sheet!" my guardian cried out. "Go get some fresh air at the window."

I got up, reeling, and tried to step over the tightly packed mass of bodies; then I was carried aloft by their arms and finally put down in front of the window. The train was gathering speed. I took in deep breaths of fresh air, slowly settling the spasms shaking my insides.

In front of me, fields of rubber trees, trunks aligned like checkerboards, each bearing a white, oozing wound, flew by at high speed; sparks from the locomotive burst forth in showers, then burned out as quickly as shooting stars. From time to time a spark would get caught in my hair, giving off a pleasant burning smell. I closed my eyes, my head resting on my arms, rocked by the monotonous rhythm of the train.

When I opened my eyes, night had fallen. I've always liked the night, its caress and its feeling of calm solitude that fills the soul. In the train car coconut oil lamps had been lit. The outlines of the travelers were projected on the ceiling in dark shapes, giant shadows making huge gestures. Enormous hands grabbed rice balls and cut them into outsized slices. I was given my share and then tasted it slowly, chewing on a mouthful of rice, then one of meat. How can I describe the sheer pleasure of having something to eat when hungry? I let the two flavors mix in my mouth, chewing slowly to make the pleasure last.

After dinner, the men got out their water pipes, passing them from one to another, each taking in a long breath in turn with his eyes closed, before exhaling a long curl of smoke, his head thrown back. As for the women, they were chewing betel. Little by little their lips turned red and when they smiled, the light glinted on the shiny surface of their lacquered teeth. Every now and then they would lean out the window, spitting out long streams of saliva the color of blood.

Some of the old women were already hanging up their hammocks for the night. The atmosphere was relaxed and peaceful. You could hear only the gurgling of the water pipes and the squeaking of ropes as the hammocks swung back and forth. In a solemn voice, an old man intoned *The Song of the Soldier's Wife,* a long poem whose theme and many passages were known to everyone. He sang of the pain of separation, the loneliness of a wife continually looking toward the battlefield where her husband raised his sword for the glory of the sovereign and in the service of his realm. From the first lines, the hammocks stopped moving, and the water pipes fell silent. We were no longer in a dirty, crowded train car but at the side of the warrior on a dusty road leading to the border, in the midst of the sound of the drums, the arrows, and the flags. The complaint of the wife brought tears to the eyes of the women:

> Plum trees were still wind-shy when you went forth
> and promised you'd come back as peaches bloomed.
> Peach blossoms now have fled with their east wind—
> Beside the river, roses fall to shreds.
> [. . .]
> You're galloping your horse on cloud-wrapped trails—
> I'm shuffling slippers through moss-covered paths.
> Day after day the spring winds brought no news—
> How many balmy seasons we have missed![7]

I, too, listened, filled with a feeling of complete security. How I loved to be on the way somewhere. What did it matter that I had left the South to return to the North? I was leaving a place without happiness, and nothing good seemed to wait for me at the end of the road. I was perfectly happy on the moving train. My whole life was there, in that warm atmosphere, in that community with no tomorrow, protected by strangers who would be my guardian angels for as long as the trip lasted.

Once in Hanoi I was taken to Ba Tu's house, the fourth sister of my maternal grandfather. When she was young, she had lived with a number of French officers. They would drift in and out whenever their military transfers would allow; now she was living alone with her four daughters, all from different fathers.

---

7. Đặng Trần Côn and Phan Huy Ích, *The Song of the Soldier's Wife* [*Chinh Phụ Ngâm*], translated by Huỳnh Sanh Thông, bilingual edition in Vietnamese and English, Lạc Việt Series, No. 3 (New Haven: Council on Southeast Asia Studies, Yale Center for International and Area Studies, 1986), 27, 61.

I was a little afraid of her house, where everything seemed incomprehensible to me. It was as if I had changed countries. The four young girls were like whirlwinds, lively and impertinent. They had an abrupt way of talking to their mother that was disarming. They intimidated me. They almost never heard me speak and hardly saw me. Self-effacing and undemanding, I didn't bother anyone.

The life of my four aunts was like some meteoric dance, a fascinating display I never got tired of that took my mind off my own isolation. Their beauty, elegance, sparkling laughter, and deafening arguments revealed a world as yet unknown to me. Up to then I had only seen Vietnamese women who were like my mother, discreet and silent, women who didn't dare ask for their share of satisfaction from life. Hardship was common for them and they didn't complain about it.

Ba Tu's daughters opened my eyes to an unexpected universe, one in which you could aspire to individual happiness. Aunt Suzanne, Aunt Odile, Aunt Germaine, and Aunt Sophie . . . I admired them all and my admiration was boundless. I loved to watch them spin around in their full skirts. Fascinated, I would witness the infinite amount of time they took in the meticulous care of their makeup and nails. With incredible grace and concern, they would tend to their toenails, filing them, cleaning them, and treating them carefully as if they were precious objects. Their bodies seemed like rare things destined for the highest calling, and they cared for them with great passion. They represented what I was not but that which I would have hoped to become. My position of inferiority hit me like a blinding and painful bolt of lightning.

Every afternoon Ba Tu went to friends' houses for a card game. My aunts Suzanne and Odile would earn their living working at white collar jobs while their younger sisters were taking classes in secondary school. Left to myself, I would invade the forbidden realm of my aunts' bedrooms with much excitement. I would admire the cast-iron beds with their winding patterns of ivy, the dressing tables whose mirrors would reflect your face a dizzying number of times. But what attracted me the most was Aunt Suzanne's collection of nail polish. There was the intense pink of bougainvillea petals, the dazzling red of hibiscus flowers, and the pale pink, so pale it seemed almost white.

On the walls were photographs of French women with huge eyes bordered with lashes so thick you could hardly believe it. Their mouths, outlined in lipstick in the shape of hearts, seemed to smile at me with imperceptible irony.

I would look into the mirror quizzically and came out on the short end in comparison to them. I found myself ugly. I hated my straight hair, and by extension all Vietnamese hair. I thought my complexion was too dark and that my eyelashes were too sparse, my eyes too small, my nose too flat, and my lips too thick. I, too, dreamed of being French. Well, I was French, in fact, but only half; still, enough so that people could tell the difference between me and a Vietnamese girl but not enough to take me for a European. In any case, not enough to find me beautiful like the extraordinarily attractive images that stared down at me scornfully from their frames high up on the wall.

The notable event from my stay at Ba Tu's was the meal we all ate together twice a week on Thursdays and Sundays, the only times I was allowed to eat with my aunts. I would leave my chopsticks behind with regret for the knife and fork they thought were more noble eating utensils. All through dinner I was under strict supervision, because teaching me proper manners was close to my aunts' hearts. I was the clumsy student in front of a panel of harsh judges; I really wanted to do well but was overwhelmed by insurmountable feelings of demoralization. My awkwardness exasperated my aunts:

"Hold your knife more lightly. That's not a hatchet you're using!"

"Put your hands on the table. I said your hands, not your elbows."

I made every effort to cut the piece of meat—never very tender in Viet Nam—trying to prevent the knife from scraping on the plate. I learned to chew with my mouth closed, without a sound, even when I was eating a raw carrot. In a word, I learned to eat without seeming to, as if food were the least of my worries, as if I were an abstraction, without a stomach, without saliva. Completely preoccupied with my manners, I was no longer even aware that I was swallowing. With my throat in a knot, I thought about a Vietnamese meal, when eating was a pleasure and not a code of conduct.

Once the meal was finished, we would go out on the veranda for some air. My aunts would tell each other stories in low voices, stories that would provoke rippling laughter, a distinctive, yet unusual kind of laughter. Annoyed, their mother would get up and leave quickly. Sitting away from them, I would look up into the night sky and try to guess the topic of their mysterious chattering, full of innuendo. The night was damp. My aunts had hiked up their skirts and, with their legs apart, were fanning the insides of their thighs. I would hear them ranting about the heat before giving a curt order to the maid:

"So, what are you waiting for? Fan us!"

Chị, or "elder sister" as we called her in the kitchen, would wave the fans she held in each hand with all her might. Sighing with relief, my pretty aunts would raise their arms up high so that their wet underarms would get some of the fresh air, too.

Forgotten in the shadows, I would look at the stars. The heavy fragrance of the jasmine grove nearby was almost unbearable. My head felt heavy.

"So, cat got your tongue as usual?" mocked Aunt Odile. "We're wasting our time with you; you'll never be anything more than a little Annamite!"

I didn't answer. I had learned to keep quiet. However, an image crossed my mind, the image of an explosion of words from a wide-open mouth, harsh and bruising words, like a rockslide.

Chị came over to me. "Don't listen to them. Go to bed and sleep."

From my bed, I could hear the voices of my aunts drowning out the music of the crickets. Ba Tu came back to rejoin her daughters.

"So, are you getting rid of that kid for us?"

"I'm wondering if she's completely stupid. She never says anything and is quite content to look at you with those empty eyes like she can't see you."

"If you dislike her so much, I'll send her to my sister's in Tuyen Quang," answered Ba Tu.

"The sooner, the better," they all sighed together.

I didn't manage to fall asleep. I was thinking about Tuyen Quang and Ba Tu's sister, whom I had never met. Would she think I was stupid, too?

Ba Tu's sister had almost a dozen ovens to make wood into charcoal for household use. She lived in a two-story house on a busy street. I would have been perfectly happy there were it not for my Uncle Tri, the son of my grandfather's second wife, and thus my mother's half-brother.

He was convinced that there was nothing to be done with me and that the best solution was to hand me over to "my people," that is, the French. He had the deep conviction that, given my heritage, I was a tree that would never bear fruit. "Believe me," he would say to my mother before I was born, "a snake is growing inside your body, and her French blood will win out no matter how much good you do. She's a bad seed and she'll betray you."

These predictions upset my poor mother who, deep inside, had never really doubted it herself. Hadn't the fortune teller she went to see shortly after my birth vaguely grimaced when he saw me? "You're an unlucky mother, madame!" he had told her. "The ingratitude of this child is marked there, on her face, in her destiny."

Ba Tu's sister, whom I affectionately called Grandmother, went early every day out to her charcoal operation in the forest. I would still be sleeping. She would leave a little money next to my pillow to buy rice cakes for my breakfast.

I loved these mornings alone, lazing in bed dreaming about my life, a better life. What would have been better than having a mother who loved me? I tried to imagine my own, not the one I hardly knew and whose image was blurry in my mind, but another one, invented according to my wishes and whom I sketched with new features each time I thought of her, always dissatisfied with the portrait I had just drawn.

Free of supervision during the day, I lived as I pleased. Usually I would take advantage of being alone to sleep in. With my elbows leaning on the windowsill, I would watch with some amusement the kids who were late, running to school. They would call out to me, urging me, "Hurry up or you'll get yourself punished!"

"I'm sick," I would cry out to them.

And then I would go back to bed. It was a moment of deep satisfaction, something that resembled happiness, I guess. Safe from disappointed or hostile looks, I didn't have the burden of my background to bear anymore; I was no longer Eurasian, I was just simply me. The world seemed good to me. How I loved that country, Viet Nam, my country; its familiar people, their coppery skin, and my Uncle Tri's almond-shaped eyes, eyes that were black, shining, and intelligent. And the way my grandmother would hold her chopsticks suspended in the air, saying, "mmm . . . mmm," when the food was to her liking. Or the swaying walk of our neighbor, carrying her two buckets of water on a stick bending across her shoulders, her teeth clenched, regularly spaced and lacquered as black as the seeds in a custard apple. I promised myself that I would have teeth as beautiful as hers when I was old enough to tint them. I knew that it was a delicate process that had to be undertaken with care. The hardest part was finding a good lacquer, one that would be in the form of a black, oily paste. My grandmother would doubtless help me choose one. You would coat the surface of the teeth with the paste, taking care to cover them afterwards with a light piece of cloth. For days on end your teeth were out of commission in order to give time for the lacquer to penetrate the enamel. You would have to be content with swallowing some nutritious fluids, but with great care and even then, not very often: the longer the fasting period, the darker your teeth. As for the time it would take, I had no doubts about my capacity for endurance nor about the end result. My mother would be proud of me.

My mother . . . People had told me she was gentle. She had lost her own early when she was still a child. Her father, a rich property owner, had two concubines, one of whom was a former domestic servant, thirty years his junior. My mother did not have a happy childhood; in her father's household, there were too many rivalries and power struggles. On top of that, she was a daughter, that is, worth less than nothing. As the old saying goes, "A hundred daughters cannot equal a son." She was lucky not to have been smothered as soon as she was born. She had an older brother who might have defended the children of my father's first wife, but he became addicted to opium when he was young. Little by little, his life was reduced to the ivory pipe whose smoke would give him a few illusory moments of nirvana.

We met up with him in Saigon in 1954. He had come in with the wave of refugees leaving the North at the time of the division of Viet Nam into two, leaving wounds on both sides.[8] He was tall and extremely thin, like most opium smokers, emaciated but still handsome, to my great surprise. I had expected to see an aged uncle, stooped and wasted from the drugs. Even when he was in withdrawal, he was able to

---

8. This is a reference to the 1954 Geneva Accords, which divided Viet Nam at the 17th parallel and allowed those who wanted to migrate to cross from one side to the other for a period of two years.

maintain his noble bearing, which would trump any feelings of pity for him. On several occasions, he had tried the treatments for drug addiction, but he had smoked opium since he was sixteen and now he was fifty. The doctor he saw said it was too late and that he could not quit smoking without dying from withdrawal.

At those moments when he felt well, he would tell us about the public trials that were held in his village in the North and how my grandfather and his second wife were handed over to the people's revenge. They were tied up, then abandoned without food and water in the courtyard of their own house. For several days, they were subjected to the accusations and insults of the villagers who would walk through the house all day long, looking with some envy upon the scandalous riches of the people in whose presence they always had to lower their eyes. Then they would return to the courtyard, overflowing with hate, and beat this couple of "leeches who had fed on the blood of the people." My grandfather was already an old man and his wife was scarcely any younger. Exhausted by hunger, thirst, and the beatings, he begged to be put to death. His prayers were answered; he was hanged before a vehement crowd. Out of grief, his wife threw herself into the nearby well.

Knowing that the same fate awaited him, too, my uncle hid in the bushes. He stayed there, tortured by not having any opium. Finally, he managed to join his sister who lived in the village nearby. Together, they fled, walking by night and hiding by day thanks to everyone's help, for my aunt was beloved in her village. Finally, they made it to Haiphong where they boarded a boat for Saigon.

It was the end of 1954. In Saigon, that meant the advent of Ngo Dinh Diem, a Catholic president who was fiercely anti-Communist. An anti-Communist who found some positive resonance with the refugees coming from the North, the majority of whom remembered well persecutions similar to those my family members had undergone.

In Tuyen Quang, I led a life that was a bit wild, on my own, at least until six o'clock in the evening when my grandmother returned home from the forest. We would have dinner, just the two of us, in the absence of my uncle who was always absorbed in his political activities. I loved listening to her talk about what happens in life.

"Here we are, you and me, both alone, for you know I'm like you: I don't have anyone else either," she would say tenderly to me. "But you're still a young bamboo shoot and the future belongs to you. You, like everyone else, will have easy times, but you will also cringe when the storms come; bend if you must, but never break."

I smiled back at her: "Do you think I'll have a good life?"

My question hung in the air for several moments. In the silence, we could hear the clucking sounds of the geckos, those translucent lizards in the tropics that gobble up insects.

"My little one," she finally answered, "if you worry your pretty little head too much about that, there won't be any life that will seem good enough to you." And then, after a moment of thought, "You are like an alloy, neither gold nor silver, and so your life will be difficult. But the man who is looking for something rare will be happy to find someone like you."

Her words wounded me like the blade of a knife. I burst into tears in spite of myself. I didn't want to be a mixture. I didn't want to be different from her or from the ones I loved. She caressed my hair softly with her hand: "There . . . there . . . What a silly little girl you are! Why are you crying anyway?"

And then she told me about her hard life in the forest, about having to supervise constantly the workers who took care of the charcoal ovens. She talked about how giving orders was a delicate task that required understanding and courage.

"Ah, my sweet little one, you know that in every man there's a tame animal and a wild one. You have to respect the wild animal in them; never humiliate those inferior to you or you will risk unleashing their dark and untamed forces against you."

Her face, round like the full moon, with its complexion tanned from working outside, was illuminated softly in the light, and all her wrinkles were like so many well-worn paths. She had her hair carefully rolled up in a turban of black velvet that she had fashioned into a crown around her head. Looking at her calmed me down. I would have liked to stop time right there and keep that moment of pure happiness forever.

"It's late," she said, getting up.

I stayed awake for a long time in my bed, getting worked up about my plans for the future. I would ask for her permission to accompany her each day into the forest. I would take care of the charcoal ovens and manage the workers according to her advice. And when she got too old to work, I would take care of her and watch over her. And I would be at her side when she died. Everything seemed simple to me. My life would be like a river that had hollowed out its bed. All that was left for me to do was to follow it to the end.

Those lazy days ended with the return of my Uncle Tri. A man of discipline, he made me go regularly to the local school. Not that he wanted to make something of me—on that score he had a firm opinion: only another snake could come from the womb of a snake. No, it was a natural thing he did out of the generosity of his spirit. But school started to bore me very quickly. Racking my brains was of no use, and laboring away stubbornly over the difference between a "j" or an "a" spotted in passing, I found reading to be an ordeal that was beyond my strength. I got discouraged. In the beginning the school teacher was very solicitous toward me, but then she began to suspect me of who knows what kind of diabolical unwillingness. She ended up punishing me at every opportunity, with an almost patriotic conviction, as if by lighting into me she were saving the entire country from the venom of colonialism. These repeated humiliations became poisonous; I dug in my heels and just stopped listening to her. I would fall asleep more and more often during class time. So, the teacher's contempt was added to her antipathy toward me. I was dismissed.

I decided not to go back to school anymore. One morning, instead of taking the hallway leading to the classroom, I stealthily dropped out of line, turned to the left, and found myself in the yard behind the building. Out there, vines had grown up to meet each other, creating an arch that protected a sandy trail. I lay down in the sand as if on a soft bed, my school bag wedged under my neck. I could hear the droning of the good students as they recited a stanza of poetry together.

From that time on, the marvels of playing hooky were opened up to me. As the days passed, I discovered the town and its surroundings, and the cemetery where I would take refuge in the cool shade of the tombs, collecting the multicolored pearls that had become detached from the metal funerary wreathes, rusted by the inclement weather. I would make them into bracelets, earrings, and even a tiara. Like a princess without a realm, I would invent a genealogical tree for myself, subjects, a history. I would imagine myself held captive. I would invoke the court in distress and the sorrow of the queen mother, inconsolable at having lost me. I would go around in a kind of exquisite sadness through the maze of tombs, intoxicated by the silence and the solitude. No sound came from the town, making one believe that it had disappeared into thin air. "And what if I died?" Solemn and stiff, I would lie down on a tombstone, holding my breath.

The noon siren would rip through the silence. It was the moment when school let out. I would grab my bag in haste and run to rejoin the group of schoolchildren.

Imperceptibly, from peregrination to peregrination, my steps would take me further and further away, toward clearings covered with delicate moss, up onto the high branch of a banyan tree, or even into vegetable gardens far from any houses. But however far I'd gone, I was always careful to return at the exact time when the other children returned from school, exhausted from my long escapades. My uncle would notice my tiredness with a satisfied look; he thought he'd cowed me, once and for all. So, I would play along, seeming to him like the docile little girl who went to school every morning with her head down and came back at noon looking sad.

Emboldened by this success, I decided to extend my explorations as far as the horseracing track outside of town. Soon, I found myself on a wide road lined with trees, leaving behind the last houses at the edge of town. Then I was in the woods, which seemed filled with mysterious murmurings. This time I would just keep going and never come back. Who knew what there would be on the other side of the woods? Maybe I would find a new country where all the people were *métisse* like me. I would have a *métis* father, a *métisse* mother, a *métis* uncle, and even my school teacher would be *métisse*. No one would notice me because I would look like everyone else.[9]

I walked for a long time. I told myself that it was past noon and that my uncle would have noticed my absence by now. Some kind of severe punishment would await me for sure. I smiled at the thought that I wouldn't be there to receive it. So, the die was cast; the only thing left to do was to continue on my way. I reproached myself for not

9. See Notes on Translation.

bringing along any food. A bit anxiously, I wondered if the racetrack was much further. What would I do if night fell while I was out here in the woods?

I ran straight ahead until I was out of breath. Then I heard the sound of whinnying; I had made it to the racetrack. I laughed out loud from relief.

A few colts were running across an open field. Some men were talking beside the fence. I walked up to the horses, filled with wonder at finding them so beautiful and especially so big. The only ones I had seen up to then were in engravings. I admired their coats and the trembling muscles underneath. From time to time a surge would run along their backs like a series of small waves. Lost in thought, I wasn't aware of how a child with a school bag might look shocking in a place like that. A few people glanced at me with puzzled expressions; so, I moved along, continuing to walk next to the fence. Further on, a group of men were quarreling violently. I tried to figure out the reason for their argument when a resounding slap made me stagger.

"What are you doing here?"

It was Uncle Tri. My surprise was indescribable. And what was he doing here himself? I stood there, open-mouthed, staring at him, dumbfounded. He hailed a rickshaw, paid the fare, ordered the driver to take me home, and commanded me to wait for him there so that I could get the punishment I deserved.

"What a deceitful race! I knew we couldn't trust you."

My grandmother, surprised to see me come home at an unusual hour, started fretting because of my disheveled look. And when I told her about my misadventure, she looked at me with a sigh. I knew that she disapproved of my behavior, but instead of reprimanding me, she said, "Look, if you want to run away, wait until you're older. You're still a little girl and can't manage on your own. Who will want to take care of you?"

I swore to her that this would be the last time. I held onto the panel of her *áo dài*, begging her not to turn me over to my uncle. I promised to do whatever she wanted, as long as she would defend me. She gently pulled herself away. My mistake deserved punishment and she could not intervene on my behalf. She then left to spare herself seeing me suffer. Before going out, she pushed a few coins into my hand.

"Go buy yourself something to eat this evening if you are hungry."

I looked at her in a daze, with the money in the palm of my hand. When I raised my eyes, she had disappeared.

In terror, I awaited the return of my uncle. The anguish of waiting became unbearable, so much so that I actually wanted him to get back so that we could be done with it. I stared at the door as if the power of my desire alone could make him materialize before me. I thus believed that a miracle had happened when his dark and massive shape stood in the door frame, between me and the light coming from outside. His black eyes cast threatening looks at me. I didn't lower mine from his. He moved toward me, a whip in his hand, like a lion tamer. I had never dared look my uncle right in the eye. Seeing his own eyes riveted to my own disturbed me. I actually found him very handsome, like one of the noble warriors from the *Romance of the Three Kingdoms* whose illustrations I had seen in the book my grandmother had. After all, I guessed I could consider it an honor to be whipped by such a hero. I closed my eyes, my whole body in anticipation. When the whip struck my flesh, the pain had a kind of exalting voluptuousness. But, in fact, all the whipping did was reinforce the idea he already had of me: I was a monster.

The next day he wrote to my mother, who was living in Saigon, demanding that she get rid of me. There were plenty of orphanages around. After all, it was up to the French to take responsibility for the bad seeds its army had sown all over the country. The independent Viet Nam of the future would not need its bastard children.

I spent the days that followed deeply despondent. My dream of staying with my grandmother had vanished. "It's my own fault," I kept repeating to myself. "I'll never get anyone to love me." And besides, I didn't even love myself.

My mother arrived on a stormy afternoon. The sky was so dark that one would have thought it was dusk. Inside the house I had a hard time making out the features of her face. She held a little girl by the hand. Behind her was a gathering of curious onlookers.

Crossing the threshold, she looked at me, made a vague move toward me, then, as if discouraged by the distance between us, turned toward her half-brother. My uncle invited his sister to sit on the teak platform daybed.

My grandmother said to me weakly, "Say hello to your mother."

I moved toward her hesitantly, spouting the usual formalities.

"I bow down before my mother."

My mother cried.

My uncle said, "My poor sister!"

My mother dabbed at her eyes with the panel of her *áo dài*. Tea was served. Everyone took their places on the daybed around the tray with cups and a plate of candied fruit.

My grandmother put me next to the little girl and said, "Take care of your sister."

She had deep, black eyes, a completely Asiatic face, and sparse, shiny hair. She didn't look like me at all. When I touched her, she scratched me. Our first contact went no further.

My mother explained, "She was still in my tummy when you left me to come here."

The tea was served. My grandmother sent my sister and me outside to play while the adults had a meeting. I knew they were discussing my fate.

On the doorstep, many children had gathered, eager to know what was happening at our house. I looked them up and down with an air of superiority. "My mother's come to take me back," I declared. I couldn't yet be an orphan because I had a mother. I took my revenge. Pointing at the little girl, I said with self-importance, "And this is my sister."

I was very proud, but then a voice replied, "Liar. She's not your sister; she's not a *métisse* like you."

The accusation struck me right in the heart, so I shot back an insult at her: "You're as dumb as an ostrich with its head in the sand."

The girl jumped on me, and we punched each other. I savagely pulled her hair, and she shrieked. My mother came running, alarmed by the sobs.

An instant later, my uncle appeared, slapped me, and dragged me back in the house. He looked at my mother, nodding his head meaningfully. "Now you can see it for yourself."

I stayed on the floor, my eyes dry and my face hidden in my arms.

I bitterly regretted my behavior. I would have wanted to present a different picture of the person I was to my mother, especially on the day of her arrival. I was furious with myself. "I am bad," I thought to myself. "My mother won't love me, not her either. No one could love me." I was deeply unhappy. I didn't dare raise my head or look at anyone.

My uncle then added, "As you see, there's no time to lose. The sooner, the better."

My mother answered "yes" in a weak voice.

She left the next day for Hanoi, doubtless with the intention of putting together the necessary paperwork for the administrators at the orphanage.

It wasn't such an easy matter. She had to prove that my father was French, and of course, I had no birth certificate. She remembered another officer whom she had seen often in the past and whose account could perhaps help us out.

She took me to Hanoi on a bright, sunny day. I was dressed up for the occasion: polished shoes, and a pretty dress made of a thin batiste or organdy, I don't remember which. What I do remember is the unpleasant feeling of the stiff material, which made me walk stiffly, too, as if I had a hoop around my waist. I walked between my mother and another young woman, probably one of her friends. My mother had her hair up in a chignon at the base of her neck, like Vietnamese women in the South. Her friend, who was younger, had her hair gathered halfway down her back with a barrette. Both were elegantly dressed in white silk.

We crossed a garden striped with flowerbeds. On the right, a pergola displayed purple bougainvillea. We entered a large, well-lit room with windows open onto the garden. In one corner, a man with a book in his hand moved almost imperceptibly in a rocking chair. He got up when he saw us. I registered in my mind his pink skin dotted with freckles as well as his light-colored eyelashes. My mother ordered me to go play in the garden.

I walked here and there, between the pathways, taking great care not to get my new dress dirty. I was bored. At the far end of the garden was a pomegranate tree covered with bright red flowers. I stayed there, squatting down, for a long time, watching the lines of ants crawling up and down its branches.

Finally, my mother reappeared, waving with triumph a paper she had in her hand.

"We're saved," she announced.

The paper attested to the fact that my father was indeed French and that he was forced to remain with his regiment, leaving my mother behind with a child she was unable to raise properly on her own. The document also stated that my mother wanted to give her daughter to the French government, which would be much better than she at preparing her for the future.

In return, she took an oath to renounce all her rights as a mother, and she swore never to see me or to try to take me back again.

The tone of the letter was convincing, and they agreed to take me.

My mother had left my younger sister in the care of her friend. She wanted to spend what little time we had left alone with me. I guess I'd become more precious to her, because she was on the verge of losing me. So, we found ourselves there together, a little uncomfortable to be alone so suddenly, just the two of us. I didn't know how to behave in this situation; it was something new to me. As for my mother, she was watching me surreptitiously, opening her mouth as if to say something, then closing it as if she had suddenly forgotten what it was she wanted to pass along to me. During all of this time, I pretended not to see her vague attempt to talk, losing myself in the contemplation of the painted patterns on the mat on the floor. We were going through a moment of mutual shyness, completely on edge, ill at ease because of the heavy atmosphere that reigned over us, filled with unspoken cries of agony.

Luckily, she was summoned a few times to take care of another administrative detail. Alone, I could finally let my fear surface without restraint. I rolled on the floor, my mouth open in a silent scream, ridding myself of the lump of anguish stuck in my throat. I was in agony until her return.

Finally, everything was ready. My mother checked the contents of my suitcase one last time. I watched her with indifference. I had a hard time believing this was all about me.

Once the suitcase was closed, my mother took my hand and we went outside. An animal moan seemed to shake my insides but no sound left my lips. Suddenly, as if struck by some inspiration, my mother stopped in front of a candy seller and bought me a cake.

"Eat it right away," she said, "because you might not have the chance from now on."

I did as she said. The bite I took seemed like it was made of plaster, and it swelled up so much in my mouth that I had a hard time breathing. I chewed and chewed but couldn't manage to swallow. My throat was completely dry, and there was no way I could get the mouthful down. As I was trying to swallow the tasteless mass that was slowly taking control of me, my eyes filled with tears. I threw up. I was six years old and about to be abandoned for good.

✎ 2 ✎

At the Orphanage

The orphanage was a large building surrounded by high gray walls like a prison. My mother rang the bell in front of the black gate. A nun appeared and led us along a gravel path to the parlor. There, another nun picked up my suitcase and took it away. I never saw that suitcase again, even though it was theoretically mine. I hadn't even touched it yet. We waited in the deserted parlor, each of us seated on a chair. The minutes passed. In the silence, the ticking of the clock on the wall took on outsized proportions. I could feel my heart beating in my temples. I tried to distract myself by looking at the tile floor, where mauve vines intertwined to infinity. I picked a stem at my feet and traced its twists and turns until my eyes reached the far end of the room. Seated upright in her chair, my mother was nervously twisting the panel of her *áo dài* with her eyes riveted on the door. A nun appeared announcing to us that all my personal effects would from now on carry the number 238. That said, she led us into another room where my name was written into the orphanage's registry, Eliane Tiffon, number 238. So, there was no longer any doubt possible. I would never see my mother again, nor my grandmother, nor the town of Tuyen Quang.

Meanwhile, my mother was chatting with a young girl about twenty whose name was Germaine. Ten years earlier, her own mother had brought her here, just like mine. My mother slipped a bill into her hand, asking her to be good to me. The young girl promised she would be, then quickly put the money in the pocket of her skirt.

We went into another office where the Mother Superior was waiting. After offering us chairs, she came over to me and put her hand on my head, saying, "You will have a new family here." Then, turning toward my mother, she said, "We will give her an education and a better life than the one she would have had. Don't be sad."

And she left the room, leaving us alone. My mother took me in her arms, crying.

"There's nothing else I can do," she said to me, her face buried in my hair. "Don't hold it against me. May Buddha protect you!"

I didn't hold it against her. I was completely overwhelmed by what was happening.

The Mother Superior returned a few moments later, accompanied by a girl my own age.

"This is Marie," she said. "She will show you the dormitory and the refectory, and will introduce you to her friends. Say goodbye to your mother."

Marie took my hand and led me out of the room. I heard my mother break down in uncontrollable sobs. Tears clouded my vision. On the threshold, I turned around. She was wearing a dark *áo dài*. I looked at her intensely, then left.

To begin with, Marie showed me the dormitory. It was an immense, high-ceilinged room with whitewashed walls. At the far end hung an extraordinarily large crucifix. I had never seen anything like it. The appearance of the man affixed to it, his head bristling with thorns and leaning down on his chest as if he were dead, was frightening to me. I wondered what crime he had committed to be punished in that way. To my surprise, Marie explained that the crucified man was God. I preferred Buddha, who seemed much more soothing, but my intuition told me not to say anything, so I kept my mouth shut.

Narrow high beds were aligned in three rows. I was afraid that I wouldn't be able to sleep in mine without falling out. Marie assured me that it was easy; even so, this fear stayed with me all day. Pointing to one of the chests of drawers that separated the beds from each other, my guide said that these were for our personal things. I didn't really have any personal things except for the clothes I was wearing. The rest were still in the suitcase that the nun had taken away from me so quickly. And besides, I had never had the chance to wear them and so didn't really consider them mine. We had left my real clothes, two pairs of black trousers and two cotton blouses, at my grandmother's.

Then we went out to the pavilion where a circle of little girls were

holding each other's hands while dancing and singing in a language I
didn't understand. Another child was lying on the floor with her eyes
closed and her arms crossed on her chest. She was Sleeping Beauty, and
the mission of the choir was to wake her up with their singing. I found
them very gay, and so my future seemed less gloomy. It was at that moment that I realized that not one of them was Vietnamese: they were all
métisses, like me. Most of them were brunette, but some of them had
light hair and transparent eyes like cats. I didn't dare look at their pupils, which seemed expressionless, almost dull, so much so that I couldn't
help starting when one of them spoke to me. For a long time, I was dis-
oriented by the enigma of their look, as I was by their halting, unmusi-
cal language. Marie advised me to learn to speak French very quickly if
I didn't want to be severely punished. I had no trouble believing her, for
you could see signs on all the walls forbidding the use of Vietnamese.

"Except for the first few weeks," she added, "because you are new."

She had been there only a year and seemed to take pleasure in
chatting with me in a language that was still familiar to her. As for me,
I didn't know how long it would take me to learn a language that difficult. I thought about my grandmother's words: "You are an alloy, neither gold nor silver." So, now finding myself among my own kind, "al-
loys," I still felt strange, alone in my corner listening to people like me
chirp away in a language that I didn't understand at all.

At mealtime about a hundred children crowded into a vast room.
I had lost Marie and didn't know where to sit nor what to do. I was
panic-stricken and stayed off to the side. The other girls, who kept
moving forward, stared at me curiously, whispering things that I
thought were offensive. I was ashamed. A young woman cut through
the group, took my hand, and led me to my place. Indeed, it would have
been impossible to make a mistake. Everything was marked with my
number, 238: my place at the table, my dish, my napkin.

"And it's the same for your bed, your sheets, your missal . . . ," explained the young girl.

Her name was Eugénie. I didn't know that it was customary in the
orphanage for some of the older girls to take younger ones of their
choosing under their wing. Eugénie had taken a liking to me.

She went back to her own table, which was far away from my
own, because we were seated according to age group. The older girls

had the right to refuse the dishes they didn't like. They served themselves, often getting an additional appetizer or dessert. This favor allowed them to keep a piece of fruit or cake that they could give to their protégées later on.

The refectory, now completely full, stood in stillness, waiting for the blessing, offered aloud by one of the sisters from a pulpit. I felt lost. When a signal was given, everyone sat down at once and ate in silence as another sister read passages from the Gospel in a contemplative voice. Not understanding a word she was saying, I was bored. But I wasn't angry at having to remain silent; I didn't know French, and my neighbors were not permitted to express themselves in Vietnamese. So, everything was fine as it was.

Soon, when a second signal was given, the refectory was filled with a loud clamor. Everyone was talking at the same time, really loudly. It was as if someone had freed a torrent of water which suddenly began to rumble. I said nothing; the food seemed tasteless, and I missed my rice. With my eyes lowered to my plate, I used my fork to poke distractedly at my food. I wasn't hungry. I looked at the severe shape of the sister towering over me without actually seeing her. Here no one could get up from the table without finishing her plate. I saw her lips move but no comprehensible sound reached my ears. As soon as she had turned her back, my neighbors hurriedly finished the food I had left on my plate, more to calm their own hunger than to help me out.

After dinner we had time for a quiet gathering in another room where decks of cards and other games I didn't know were put out on small square tables. On the far wall I could see shelves tightly packed with books. My companions seemed so comfortable, chatting and laughing. How I envied the ease with which they moved, took down a book, or leaned toward their neighbor to tell a joke! I didn't know what I was doing here in this strange world.

Marie came toward me, accompanied by a few other girls. Some of them spoke to me in Vietnamese, but the rest remembered only a few words. They brought me up to date with the secrets of the orphanage, pointing out the older girls who were harsh and those who were less so.

Then it was time for bed. We went toward the dormitory, the one I had seen earlier. I was struck by the heavy atmosphere that reigned there. Marie's face was impenetrable, and she seemed distrustful, as if she were in danger. At the entrance, a young girl who was very thin and seemed peeved if not harsh, was watching us. Her name was Andrée Corneveau, as I soon found out at my expense. She showed me my bed with a rapid gesture of her hand. I barely had time to register it. Again, I was panic-stricken. You could have heard a pin drop, so I didn't dare ask her to tell me again nor to ask my neighbor.

I stopped in the middle of the dormitory, arms hanging, my ears burning, my head buzzing. The others had to walk around me to reach their beds. Someone whispered something in my ear that I didn't understand. Andrée Corneveau yelled something in my direction. Only one bed remained unoccupied in the whole dormitory. It was obviously mine, so I walked toward it. On the bed was a pair of pajamas with my number on them; I gazed at them a long time, trying to engrave that number in my memory. Little by little I learned to react to 238 as if it were my own name. Throughout my life, I've occasionally forgotten important numbers like my social security number, the one for my bank account, even my phone number. But 238 is embedded in my memory indelibly, to the extent that I can still be startled when, by chance, I hear it.

I changed and then we went to the wash basins in groups of five. The first to return knelt for evening prayer, waiting in that position for the last to come back. Suddenly, Andrée Corneveau let out a cry of anger: "Who wrote this on my chest of drawers?"

No one answered. I looked at the chest of drawers. I hadn't noticed it during my first visit. It was a rather nice piece of furniture, made of wood with three drawers that were locked. She repeated her question in a very high-pitched voice. More silence. Her thin lips took on a cruel pout. She brandished a paper over her head, like a small flag, all the while continuing to scream.

Then she walked down between the rows of beds, shoving in our faces the piece of paper on which was written her own name in pencil. She asked each one of us the same question: "Was it you?" One by one, we shook our heads. We were still on our knees. No one dared move as we waited for the storm to hit. Andrée Corneveau then said, "OK, then! Since you don't have the courage to admit your mistake, each one of you will write a capital 'A' on this sheet of paper. I'll find out for sure who the guilty one is!"

In turn, we put all our effort into writing a capital "A" on the sheet of paper; then we awaited the verdict.

She took a long time to examine the results. I was perfectly calm; I knew I was innocent. But I didn't know that injustice was commonplace in the orphanage. Above all, I didn't know how much Andrée Corneveau was to be feared. She finally raised her head from the paper, stared right at me, and then pointed at me abruptly with her thin finger.

"You're the one who wrote it!"

I didn't understand what she was saying to me in French. (Marie translated the whole scene for me later on.) But from her tone of voice, I knew that I was the one being accused. The surprise left me stunned. Only Marie could clear me, but Marie lowered her eyes and didn't say a word.

Andrée Corneveau pulled me brutally from my place. "Dirty hypocrite!" she roared.

She dragged me to the bathroom and there, closing me up in a cramped shower stall, she took a long broom—the one used to remove cobwebs from the ceiling—and hit me with it. She didn't tolerate hypocrites. Her fury lasted a long time. I had no voice left to cry out in pain. Finally, she left me. I heard her steps growing fainter. I ended up falling asleep on the tile floor.

The next evening, in the dormitory, the punishment was repeated in a different form. Andrée Corneveau made me get down on my knees at the foot of her bed while she and the other children slept. It must have been winter. My feet were ice-cold, my knees swollen. I was falling down from exhaustion. But each time I thought she was in a deep sleep and stretched out on the tile floor, her voice ordered me to get back up on my knees. She frightened me.

That went on for a week. Sometimes the coldness of the early morning woke me up. The dormitory was completely dark. I could hear Andrée Corneveau's regular breathing; a few girls talked in their sleep. I thought about ghosts and imagined their shadows bent over behind me. I was seized with an unbearable dread.

After that, Andrée Corneveau never stopped persecuting me. As for me, I couldn't look at her without feeling possessed by a murderous anger. The violence of my hate was literally suffocating.

In truth, I wasn't the only one who detested Andrée Corneveau. I learned that she had had numerous "victims." The nuns who ran the orphanage were completely ignorant of her physical cruelty. We lived in a climate of repression, vengeance, and terror, and the nuns were far from having any suspicions about it. In their peaceful building, in prayer and meditation, they saw us as sweet lambs and were happy to nourish us with the charity that God and the colonial administration doled out to us.

It was, in fact, a nest of misfortune and nastiness. During the day, the oldest girls, from fourteen on, would do professional apprenticeships outside the orphanage. In the evening, they were supposed to return to spend the night and to take care of the younger girls. Unloved and mistreated by the older girls when they themselves had been little, most of them naturally took it out on the younger ones now. Regardless of whether they had relationships of love or hate with the others, it always involved, for them, a way to make the younger ones pay for the rebuffs and humiliations they had undergone themselves. Some of them had lived there from the age of five or six. Ten years in the orphanage would make you into a bitter and vicious person. I don't know what would have happened to me had I stayed there longer.

Each day we went to the public school a fifteen-minute walk away. We went out into the morning mist, two by two, bundled up in our navy-blue capes. These outings gave us a taste of freedom; they opened up doors to the outside for us, a world still sleepy and deserted in which our eyes, darting hungrily here and there, would register only the glimmering red glow of the lantern of an itinerant soup merchant or the fleeting outline of a passerby.

At school they put me automatically into an intensive course of study. My teacher was an old lady whose face expressed goodness. I was happy to be in her class. I studied easily and made rapid progress. I finally got to know the joy of having access to knowledge. My French improved day by day. Now I was the one called upon to correct the syntax errors made by the other students. So swift was my progress that at the end of three months, they moved me to the advanced class. This unexpected promotion gave me faith in myself. It seemed like a long time ago that my Vietnamese teacher had thought I was a complete idiot. Here I knew what needed to be done and I did it well. My success at school had practical consequences. The nuns congratulated me in public; my comrades treated me with more consideration. Even Andrée Corneveau, while still detesting me, stopped persecuting me. Mademoiselle Eugénie, who had taken me under her wing at the beginning, was doubly attentive. She encouraged me, holding me up as an example to the students who were less gifted, and promised me rewards if I worked as hard at my new level. Although flattering, her renewed attention made me sad at heart. I would have preferred that she love me for myself rather than because I had earned it.

After my promotion, Eugénie came every evening to see me in the dormitory, her hands full of candy that she made me eat in her presence. I couldn't share it, and that bothered me a great deal. We only rarely received candy, and it was almost painful for the others to see me eat it in front of them. If it happened that we got a banana or a cake for dessert on holidays, we would keep them safely in our pockets, munching on them all day to make the pleasure last. A mango or a custard apple was something coveted hopelessly. And I would have both. In front of Eugénie I would have to eat them so quickly that I had the feeling I was wasting them. I would have liked to savor them slowly in order to remember the exquisite taste of those precious fruits. My mind tried to find some clever excuse that would have allowed me to keep part of them to eat in peace when I was alone or even offer to my neighbors. But Eugénie made sure that everything was eaten before leaving. I would go back to my bed, a bit mortified that she wouldn't let me use the gifts that she gave me as I wanted.

Then summer came. In joy and excitement, the orphanage prepared to go on vacation to Sam Son, a charming resort town on the coast. It had white sand beaches, and to get there, you had to cross wide expanses of *filao* trees, a kind of spindly, quivering pine that the slightest breeze would turn into song. We spent long, peaceful days divided between swimming in the sea, playing games, and reviewing the things we had learned during the school year.

However, I never managed to forget my life from before. Often the face of my grandmother haunted my dreams. I would think of my mother's sobs at the moment of our separation. I was filled with a kind of desperation. I wanted to die. One day I ventured beyond the safety zone marked by a rope stretched on the surface of the water. They had to pull me out, and I was sick for a whole week.

꧁꧂

When September came, we didn't go back to Hanoi. Ho Chi Minh had
taken over there. It was 1945. The nuns didn't hide their anxiety. In
anguish, we awaited who knew what catastrophe. The nuns told us that
God had abandoned the city to the forces of evil. So, our daily life took
on a new rite; each evening we would gather in the chapel, reciting long
prayers in order to rid Hanoi of the communists.

In order not to stay idle, we went to the school in Sam Son. But
nothing was the same any longer. Imperceptibly, our standard of living declined. The amount of food diminished. In the end, we only had
a small plate of rice at meals. We were constantly hungry. At the table
each one of us struggled bitterly to protect our portion of the food.
We ate with only one hand, the other forming a kind of rampart
around the plate to shield it from any covetous looks. Eating absorbed
us completely. There were no longer jokes and gossip in the refectory
like before.

We were told that a famine was ravaging Tonkin, because the Japanese had thrown the rice that was available into the sea in order to
starve the population. Many had died, and we were lucky we still had
anything to eat at all. In the street people talked, not without some
admiration, about the surprising way that the Japanese had seized Hanoi and how they had killed all the French they had found there without pity. They had retreated leaving behind piles of corpses, and now
you would see Chiang Kai-shek's starving hordes walking along the
roads.[1]

A long time after, I had the chance to see the photographs taken
during that famine, which killed two million people. You could see
lines of carts piled high with corpses being taken to the mass graves.
Mothers were throwing their infants into lakes in order not to see them
die of starvation. At that time my mother was in the countryside,

---

1. This section references the Japanese Interregnum in Indochina during World
War II, the Japanese *coup de force* in 1945, the Famine of 1944–1945, and the Chinese civil
war between Mao Zedong's communists and Chiang Kai-shek's nationalists. For more
information, see, for example, Geoffrey Gunn, "The Great Vietnamese Famine 1944–45
Revisited," in *The Asia-Pacific Journal*, 2011: www.japanfocus.org/-Geoffrey-Gunn/3483
/article.html.

where people suffered less than in the cities. She and her relatives owed their survival to her father's full granaries; he was rich back then.

Food returned little by little to the orphanage. We had more rice, then meat, and finally copious meals like before. At that time I was plagued by great fear during the night. I dreamed every night about a big black bear that was always chasing me. I would wake up with a start, panting and covered with sweat. So, I would stay awake on purpose until morning, afraid that sleep would plunge me back into the same nightmare. I would calm down only at daybreak.

But as the sun would slowly set, the same anguish would take hold of me again. I would lose interest in everything at about five in the afternoon. From then on, my anxiety would only continue to grow. I would cry out of weakness, knowing that with nightfall the same dream and the same fear would take possession of me. These nightmares affected my physical health; I was frequently sick to my stomach and dizzy. I was working less well at school, and Eugénie was paying less attention to me. But that didn't make me sad; I had always been a little ashamed of my status as her favorite. Her neglect gave me back my freedom. Now I could be just like my friends.

We stayed in Sam Son until Christmas, which we celebrated lavishly as if we wanted to forget the war all around us. In Hanoi, the French and Viet Minh were fiercely fighting each other. According to rumors we would soon be forced to evacuate Sam Son, for the armed combat was getting closer. But we turned a deaf ear to the outside world, getting completely involved in putting up the crèche and preparing for the *réveillon*, the feast after midnight mass on Christmas Eve.

On December 25th, the older girls got new dresses while we put on our Sunday dresses made of écru linen, the bodice embroidered with a red tennis racket and ball. Andrée Corneveau had her own dress, a magnificent white one dotted with roses, laid out on her bed. She was radiant.

In the courtyard the girls were chattering in small groups while waiting for midnight mass. We talked about Andrée Corneveau and her harshness. We recalled the injustices she had inflicted on all of us. An impulsive desire took hold of me to do something mean to her. I left the group and returned to the dormitory alone. All clear. There was a pair of scissors on the chest of drawers. I grabbed them and cut a series of slits in Andrée Corneveau's pretty new dress. After putting the scissors back where they belonged, I rejoined the others. No one noticed my absence, brief as it was.

For the first time in a long while, I forgot about my nocturnal anguish.

At about eleven o'clock, at the sound of the bell, we returned to the dormitory. Andrée Corneveau announced to us right away that she would not hesitate to confiscate our gifts if we dared to be late. We dressed in silence. Suddenly, there was an exclamation followed by a sharp sob; our young lady had just discovered the disaster. We exchanged flabbergasted looks; we had never seen her suffer before and thoroughly enjoyed the spectacle. Looking upset, the nun who was told of what had happened gave us a long sermon. She couldn't believe that one of us was capable of such an act of vandalism, especially on the night of Christ's birth. She ran out of words trying to express her indignation. She hoped that the guilty party would come to her without delay to confess her mistake and regret. Otherwise, the whole dormitory would be punished. She stared at us severely, then left.

We headed to the chapel. Mass seemed longer to me than usual, but this time I didn't faint from exhaustion as I so often did, to the point that they would have to make me leave before the service had ended. Of course, I implored God to forgive me for my bad deed. I knew that vengeance was wicked, that you needed to turn the other cheek to the person who had just slapped you. That's what my mouth was saying at least. But deep inside, my vengeful hand seemed to me like that of the Exterminating Angel's. I had no remorse. The only thing that weighed on my conscience was the promise that the punishment would be inflicted on the whole dormitory if the guilty one didn't give herself up. I finally told Blanche, who had the bed next to mine, everything, leaving her the choice to denounce me to the nuns if she thought it the best thing to do.

The next day Blanche talked about my audacity with some of the other girls. The dormitory had a meeting and decided to do nothing, because my act had washed away everyone's humiliation. Andrée Corneveau was truly hated.

After mass we received our gifts according to our scholastic achievements. My grades being really mediocre, I didn't get much that year. But I paid it little mind. I was still in shock from the feat I had just carried out. My heart was jubilant. That night I slept like a log, without fear or nightmares. Thus ended my frightful dreams.

As expected, the whole dorm was punished. No strolls outside, no desserts. We didn't care about taking walks; on the contrary, being together in the dormitory tightened our bonds. But not getting dessert—the Christmas log cake, a real treat in these hard times—took true courage on our part. Some of the girls wondered if they had done the right thing by not denouncing me. But it was too late to turn back.

On the other hand, Andrée Corneveau had lost her arrogance. We weren't afraid of her anymore. We still remembered the twisted, pained expression that deformed her face at the sight of her ruined dress. So, she had flaws, just like us. Her prestige had been tarnished. Did she know it? Whatever the answer, she left us alone. Besides, we had something else on our minds; we were feverishly awaiting the Christmas tree celebration that the rich bourgeois of Sam Son had planned to give for the orphans. For a long time, we thought that all our wishes would then be fulfilled: each one of us carried deep inside a desire for things that would seem laughable to anyone who did not know total deprivation. For some it was a pencil or a bag of candy; for others it was a doll or a book. As for me, nothing would have given me more pleasure than to have a needle and a spool of thread. I can still remember my powerless rages against the rebellious thorns that would refuse to become needles when I wanted to make clothes for my rag dolls. I would always end up crying out of frustration. So, I ardently prayed that God would fulfill my wish.

On the long-awaited day, at about five o'clock in the afternoon, we set out, hearts beating with excitement. The Christmas tree had been put up in the ballroom of the Grand Hotel of Sam Son. Before leaving, we had been assembled on the front steps for a reminder about how little we deserved and for the advice to receive our gifts with humility. For more than a month, in fact, we had been preparing our thank-you speeches, songs, and skits in order to express our gratitude to our benefactors. Having a nice voice, I was entrusted with the final song.

Our mission was to present a pleasant, harmonious, if not happy image of the orphanage. In the crowd were all the French colonists from Sam Son, people who were highly placed and influential for whom we were to present the spectacle of poor, but touching, little girls. We especially had to make an appeal to their emotions, for the orphanage had great need of their donations. There were also "Frenchified" Vietnamese in the crowd. All these beautiful people treated us with a kindness that was condescending. They absentmindedly asked us questions about our life in the orphanage and then put on a smile when we affirmed that we were happy there. Some pursued their self-satisfaction to the point of making us believe they were sorry not to be orphans themselves, for wasn't it after all a great character-building experience?

Once the presentation was over, we were invited to a have a snack. Then came the long-awaited moment when the gifts were handed out. Hundreds of multicolored packages were attached to a big *filao* tree that had been used in place of a pine for the occasion. Right away I noticed a small wicker basket containing tiny spools of thread, scissors, needles, and even a gold thimble. Mine for sure. We moved forward in single file, filled with emotion, drawing with a trembling hand a number that was supposed to match one of the packages on the tree. Then it was my turn. I held out my piece of paper with a confident hand. What I got left me dumbstruck: it was a doll that was completely black. My mind a blank, I stammered a confused "thank you," then ran away.

I threw down the awful doll and stomped on it with all my might. I was still lost in my fit of pique when Andrée Corneveau appeared. She looked at the disfigured doll, told me how ungrateful I was, then slapped me hard.

A few months later, with the war threatening to reach Sam Son, we withdrew to Thanh Hoa. The situation there was so up in the air that we stopped going to school. A rich landowner temporarily put his residence at our disposal. It consisted of a three-story central building and two others, small outbuildings located at the far end of the garden. However, we were cramped in that space and had to divide up into two groups. At that moment, I was separated from Andrée Corneveau. For me, that was the first time I could relax.

In general, life in the orphanage had also loosened up simply because of the war. Aside from the three hours of class taught by the nuns, our time was taken up with singing, dancing, and maintaining the buildings. I really liked to sing, and it was a distinct joy to learn Gregorian chants or old French songs. Despite these different activities, we still had enough free time to play alone. As we didn't have any toys, we had to make them ourselves. We spent hours filing a broken piece of earthenware in order to make a round plate or flattening out a nail picked up in the courtyard to make a knife that, once sharpened, would cut properly. Without tools, we did all this work with what we could find: a slightly rough stone would serve as a file, and a pebble would stand in for a hammer, and we would get great satisfaction from it. I ended up fostering a great passion for handicrafts. From the morning on, I was in a hurry to take up my tools and my task once again. I felt a stimulating excitement working with raw material to make it into a useful object. I sought to refine my technique and thought up new ways of doing things. I was so absorbed that I had no sense of the time passing. Often I was punished for being late.

I also took pleasure from walking alone in the garden, listening to the rustling of the leaves, endlessly watching a spider spinning her web around a fly, and especially picking tiny flowers, invisible to the distracted passerby, small but perfectly shaped, so varied in color that they were pure wonders. I would make them into bouquets that I held in the hollow of my hand and never tired of contemplating.

A great silence and a constant, full buzzing sound reigned in the garden at the same time. I could take advantage of my solitude, all the while knowing that I was not alone, that life was teeming all around me, under the blades of grass crushed beneath my feet, behind the bark of the trees, up in the highest branches. Often, I would sit at the bottom of a tree, listening to the humming life of nature. These solitary walks dampened the fire of my rebellious soul.

At that time, our life in Thanh Hoa was dominated by a single feeling: that of precariousness. We didn't know if we could stay much longer in this town or if we would be forced to flee further away as the war spread toward us. What resulted was a kind of relaxing of our daily discipline. We were less formal, and life in the orphanage took a turn toward the more casual. This was one of the happiest times for us. We had only an abstract idea of what the war was. No reverberations had reached us in our protected world. We only knew that France was in danger, which was why we prayed every day for its victory. They had explained to us well that France was both our foster mother and our fatherland. It was toward her that our hearts were to be directed.

And so our days were filled with anxious waiting. We were on alert, with our bags always ready for a possible departure. In the beginning the whole situation seemed amusing to us, like a game that broke the monotony of the lives we were leading. But little by little our ties to the "mother" orphanage in Hanoi were cut. We had the feeling of being surrounded by invisible danger. As a last resort, the nuns decided to take us to France. Our lives were meant to be lived there and would continue there, they told us.

The news distressed us. What was France like? We had no idea. We were incapable of imagining it. Did it have the same blue sky, the same green trees as here? It was only a word in our minds, a word that referred to no reality whatsoever. It made us afraid. As French as we were, we had known only the country where we had always lived: Indochina, as it was called at the time. We loved rice and tropical fruit; we didn't know milk or cheese. As far back as we could remember, we couldn't find a single familiar face that was French. The songs that cradled our childhoods were melancholy Vietnamese laments.

How were we going to live there? How could we imagine not seeing Annamites in the streets? How strange a country it would be to have only French people there! We would ask these worrisome questions late into the night in the dormitory, vowing never to leave each other and to help each other in that unknown country. And no one took the trouble to enlighten our ignorance; the grown-ups had other problems.

The first was the impossibility of taking everyone to France. We numbered about two hundred in all. Whom should they take? And who could be left behind? Upon what criteria were they going to rely in order to choose in a fair way? Would they need to base their decision on physical appearance, choosing only the children with blond hair and blue eyes, the ones who looked most European? These children especially had no hope of making a normal life for themselves in Viet Nam, among Asians. Their faces would betray their origins, and they would always be considered foreigners whom no sensible Vietnamese man would want to marry. On the contrary, would they need to choose the most intelligent children, the ones who had already correctly acquired

French manners and language? Wouldn't they be able to adapt more easily to their new country and succeed in making a place for themselves in society?

These hypotheses would come to us and inspire either joy or anguish depending on the category we fell into. The orphanage was in the feverish grip of these questions for several weeks. We would get completely caught up in conjecture.

By dint of looking for an outcome, the nuns ended up finding a solution to this thorny issue. They would make an appeal to the families, nullifying the acts of abandonment they had signed. Considering the exceptional situation the war had put us in, they could take back their children if they wanted to. So, the choice would be simple: the nuns would keep all the ones whose families didn't want them.

One day when I was in dance class, I was summoned to the parlor. My mother was there and wanted to take me with her. The news left me with no immediate reaction. I felt as though I had been hit with a club. It was something I had never thought about. In crossing the room, I registered, with an almost painful clarity, the image of Marie holding a wreath of flowers above her head, her body bending gracefully to the left, then to the right in time with the piano.

I hadn't yet seen the parlor, which wasn't surprising since no one ever came to visit any of us. At the end of the long hallway, I came into a lounge. At first, I saw, from the back, the long black robe of the Mother Superior. She turned around, revealing a young woman also dressed in black, sitting on a rattan armchair. Our Superior asked me if I recognized my mother.

"I don't know," I answered.

In fact, I couldn't tell if the lady seated in front of me was indeed my mother. In my memory, my mother was a supple white silhouette that walked in front of me on a bright, sunny day.

An awkward silence followed my declaration. My testimony was of capital importance, for all the administrative documents were still in Hanoi and had doubtless been destroyed by the war; so we had no proof at all that the woman who had come to claim me was really my mother. The Mother Superior explained to her the delicate situation we were in. The lady began to cry, saying that she had come from afar to get me, and that she had risked danger in combat zones before managing to get here. No, it would be impossible for her to leave without me.

Her tears triggered something deep inside me: I had already seen her cry like that. Her face suddenly became familiar to me. I cried out that she was without any doubt my mother, that I had finally recognized her. I was sorry I hadn't recognized her the first moment I saw her. But it was too late: only the first spontaneous reaction counted.

All three of us remained powerless: my mother who wanted to take me back, I who wanted to follow her, and the Superior who wouldn't have asked for anything better than to let me leave if only she could be assured that this woman was telling the truth.

We looked at each other without saying anything. Suddenly, in a rush of words, my mother began talking about Germaine, the young girl whom she had confided me to when I was admitted. Surely, Germaine would recognize her and confirm what she was saying.

And thus the miracle occurred. Germaine recognized her without hesitation, immediately. And I was given back to her.

❦ 3 ❦

Family Ties

I left with my mother after taking some of my things and saying good-bye to the girls I had shared so much with over the past several years. I was the first one to leave. We hugged each other, me crying with joy at having found my family again, they shedding tears of pity for themselves, for who could say what the future held for them? For the first time, I felt there was a kind of sibling rapport between us that had replaced what had been rather arid relationships. We felt a new tenderness for one another and finally understood that we had shared the same destiny, that of the disinherited.

Thus ended my life in the orphanage. With nostalgia in my heart, I left, knowing I would never see this place again nor the people who had been my source of joy and sorrow for so long.

I was afraid of finding myself face to face with my mother. How should I behave in her presence? I had never experienced a mutual affective relationship. Tenderness is something you learn. I was uncomfortable with hers because I didn't know how to respond to it. The orphanage had made recluses of us, unable to express our feelings. I remained silent during the whole trip.

In town, she got a hotel room while we waited for the first morning train. I still have a very precise recollection of that cramped room, the big bed, the open window onto the street. I was about ten, but the fact of having a mother for the first time, and so suddenly, made me regress to my early childhood. I was unable to talk and could only cry during the entire night. Panic-stricken, my mother took me in her arms and rocked me until daybreak. Afterwards she told me how my pained

44

looks and crying like a baby had frightened her. As for me, I remember from that night only an unbearable suffering.

That night of closeness with my mother was my only physical experience of maternal love. Afterwards, life always constrained her to feign indifference toward me. I knew she loved me; even so, I never received any sign of her love. Many times, I had my doubts, but I had become so attached to her that I always ended up overcoming them. It was only much later, when she had gained the freedom that comes with age in relation to her husband, that her letters finally expressed the tender words that she had left unsaid during this time.

My loving mother, why did those words come so late? I listen to them—now that we can do no more for one another—like a shell you hold up to your ear, like the echo of a missed moment of happiness.

The next day, we took the train for Nam Dinh, the city where my mother's uncle lived. He had a brick-making operation that he managed on his own. About ten kilns were scattered in the enclosure at the rear of the house. Between the kilns grew cucumber, tomato, and squash plants.

Soon after our arrival, my mother wanted to go to Huong Tich, a famous religious site. She had always dreamed of making that pilgrimage. This time the occasion for the trip was easily justified: she could do nothing less than pay homage to Buddha for having looked favorably on our finding each other again. What's more, there were temples there where all you needed to do was pray ardently for your every wish to be fulfilled.

Her absence gave me some beneficial solitude. I learned to adapt to the kind of family life that the orphanage had made unfamiliar to me. Here there were no more schedules to give rhythm to my days; I was free. My great-uncle was a busy old man who asked nothing of me except to be on time for meals.

I followed the servants to the marketplace, a little lost at hearing only Vietnamese spoken around me. I had to relearn a language that I was supposed to have forgotten. I listened without understanding the

cries of the merchants hawking their wares, the murmurs of hard bargaining, the sounds whose music awakened memories of long ago inside me.

Sometimes I got permission to accompany the men who went fishing for cockles. We would bring back baskets laden with shellfish that
the women would fry with onion and kohlrabi. Other times I would
wander alone in the back enclosure, waiting for the moment when the
bricks would be taken out of the kilns to cool. I discovered the wonderful surprise of seeing the metamorphosis of cubes of gray, ugly clay into
beautiful, salmon-colored bricks. Sitting on a stack that was still warm,
I would savor my new freedom. For a moment I would forget the orphanage, its artificial atmosphere, devoid of happiness.

My mother returned from her pilgrimage, as overexcited as a
young girl who had been on some escapade. With her eyes shining, she
told of her trip by boat that had lasted for a day and a night. There was
a statue of Buddha that was so big it filled an entire cave. Innumerable
altars loaded down with offerings lined the paths leading from one
cave to another; there were so many caves that it was difficult to count
them all. Digging in her pockets, she held out to me a handful of wild
apricots that she had picked on the way down the path. I listened raptly
to her, my throat tight with emotion. I really had a mother. Finally.
Near her I had a feeling of complete well-being, as if I had always lived
at her side.

Soon we went to rejoin her husband and my young sister who were
waiting for us in the village of Van Xa, at her father's house. The train
dropped us off several kilometers from our destination. We finished
the rest of the trip on foot.

My mother held me by the hand. I closed my eyes, preserving inside me the happiness of this connection. But thinking that I was tired,
she tenderly suggested a bit of rest. Just in front of us was a shelter
made of mud and straw with a thatched roof and boards to sit on where
you could have something to drink or try a millet pancake. As is often
the case, it was leaning against a banyan tree, in its welcoming shade.
There were travelers deep in conversation over steaming cups of green
tea. Again, my mother told the story of her pilgrimage. Those assembled listened, nodding their heads, surprised that such marvels even
existed.

We continued walking on the narrow, slippery dikes. They weren't much wider than the ball of the foot and served to separate the rice paddies one from another. We walked with care, she in front, me following, single-mindedly occupied with placing one foot correctly in front of the other. We moved ahead for a long time like that. In the end, we got lost in the maze of dikes that all seemed alike. My mother had wanted to take a shortcut, and there we were, wading about in the middle of the rice fields, feet in the sludge. We sank down into the mud up to our calves; our feet were stuck there and pulling them out took considerable effort. I walked as if I were drunk, my sight blurred by the reflection of the noonday sun on the muddy water, like explosions of fireworks under my eyelids. We finally made it to the dirt path, our legs bloody from the bites of leeches. I looked with horror at my lower legs, where some were still attached, and cried out in terror as my mother tried to pull them off one by one. I've never been able to overcome my repulsion for these slimy bugs that expand right before your eyes, engorged with blood to the point that they drop to the ground from their own weight.

While we walked, my mother showed me the immense expanse of the fields that belonged to her father, as well as the piece of land that constituted her part of the inheritance. So, she had a father, a history. And that history was also mine, because I belonged to her. She showed me the grave of her mother, a simple earthen mound among the rice shoots. I discovered then with great surprise that she, too, had been a child, like me. She had lost her mother when she was about twelve. There were four children from the first marriage, three girls and a boy. But when her mother was still alive, her father had already taken a second wife who had given him two children, including Uncle Tri, the one who had frightened me so much. Disappointed by his elder son having become addicted to opium, my grandfather transferred his hopes to the younger son of his second wife. But, becoming aware of the yoke of colonialism early on, Uncle Tri left for Tuyen Quang, where he joined the resistance led by the Vietnamese People's Party, the VNQDD.[1] After this second disappointment, my grandfather became totally unin-

---

1. The Viet Nam Quoc Dan Dang, or VNQDD, was a moderate nationalist political party.

terested in any of his children. He took a third wife who was much younger than he.

Telling this story made my mother sad. In front of the grave she lit sticks of incense that she had made sure to bring along in her bags and recited prayers as she cried. She was sobbing, her shoulders bent. It was the second time I had seen her in tears. Her sadness moved me, and I wanted to console her, so I took her hand. She stood up and we continued on our way, hand in hand, until a bamboo hedge appeared in front of us. We had arrived.

As in all villages, the life of the community was organized inside this curtain of bamboo trees. For the most part, the straw huts were grouped together around the ponds where adults and children would bathe. The women would come there to wash clothes as well as vegetables, meat, and rice to cook. We drank the water as well. We lived off these ponds, and we would die from them, from the germs that they held, the source of infectious diseases.

My grandfather had the most beautiful pond where he raised all kinds of fish. We didn't fish there, but for special occasions, men with scoops would empty all the water from the pond and catch the fish stranded on the muddy bottom. My grandfather would choose the best ones for himself and eat them raw with their flesh cut into thin strips accompanied by fragrant herbs. He would give the rest to the peasants who worked his land, and so it would turn out to be a feast for everyone.

Once through the gate, we found ourselves in a courtyard paved in stone that was used to husk the rice during harvest season. I had never seen such a large courtyard. A hundred boarding schoolgirls— *pensionnaires*—could jump rope there and never so much as brush against each other. A few steps led up to the front of the house, a long building divided into three parts. The two wings that served as living space were hidden behind curtains. You could see only the central part, meant for visitors. In it was a large platform daybed covered with a mat with flower patterns; it was used to receive distinguished guests. Those of lesser importance would remain standing.

My grandfather was highly respected. For a long time, he had been head of the village and for a number of years was seated in the place of honor during festivals. When we ended up at his house, he no longer took part in communal affairs but still enjoyed great moral authority. We bowed down, my mother and I, to greet a man who was old and thin with a bald head and a white goatee. He welcomed us, did not look at my mother, shot me a furtive smile, then looked off into the distance as if he had forgotten about us. Then we went to pay our respects to his third wife whom everyone called "Dame Troisième," "Third Lady."

My mother harbored a persistent feeling of disdain toward Dame Troisième because of her former status as domestic servant. In my eyes, she was a young woman scarcely older than my mother, simple and kind, whom we had taken by surprise in the midst of raising her brood of children, one barely a toddler and the other still nursing. At the time, my grandfather was approaching sixty and each new birth aroused feelings of admiration mixed with spite in his peers.

The encounter between my mother and Dame Troisième was courteous but brief, the kindness of the latter being unsuccessful at thawing her stepdaughter's iciness.

Afterwards we made ourselves at home, settling into one of the outbuildings far from my grandfather's house. My mother found no consolation in being exiled like that while a concubine of lower social status became the mistress of the household. Upon her injunctions, we ostensibly avoided Dame Troisième.

In my grandfather's house, we were housed and fed. Twice a day, a servant brought us our meals on a tray steaming with succulent dishes. My mother still thought that she was getting the short end of the deal. As for her husband, he would patiently grin and bear it. Of Chinese ancestry, he had a southern accent and was considered a foreigner in this village in Tonkin. He learned in his turn about the solitude that my mother had endured during the years they had lived in Saigon.

I took care of my five-year-old half-sister. We would go out into the rice fields, where I would teach her to catch grasshoppers. Sometimes we would go fishing for tadpoles in order to raise them in small jars, but they never became frogs. In the morning, at breakfast time, we would venture into my grandfather's immense henhouse. It was a kind of small, rickety bamboo house, with a raised platform covered with a thick layer of straw. There, his hundred or so chickens would lay their eggs. Our intrusion caused a general panic, the frightened hens cackling at the top of their lungs, feathers flying everywhere. Even so, we took our chances climbing up the fragile bamboo ladder, and there in front of us was displayed the white row of freshly laid eggs. I had a thorn with me in one hand and a pinch of salt in the other. Comfortably settled in the straw, we delightedly gobbled down the still-warm eggs, punctured at each end thanks to the thorn, not forgetting to put a bit of salt on our tongues beforehand. Our gluttony pushed us to eat three or four in a row.

But what we liked more than anything were the festival days when the beating of the drum woke us from our sleep before dawn. In the Đình, a type of communal house, the men would kill a pig while the women took charge of cooking the meat. We children would try to help out in small ways in exchange for a leg to gnaw on or a ball of rice to savor. Very often, hampered by carrying my sister on my hip, I would miss out on the good morsels that a nimbler hand would snatch right from under my nose. At about noon, with all the food ready, we would put the dishes on the altar to the tutelary spirit of the village. There were hundreds of plates with flies buzzing over them. We would whisk them away while awaiting the arrival of the village notables.

They would arrive in single file, in brocade tunics with black turbans on their heads. Dressed in that way, they became the symbols of tradition. They bowed as one in front of the altar, droning on with endless prayers. Hunger was gnawing at us by then. When they had at last finished, bare-chested men beat the drum, thus announcing that the feast would soon begin. The whole village was invited to the festive meal. The kids jostled each other, trying to get to the serving platters. The women, waists tied with vermillion and violet silk sashes, pushed each other with their elbows, intimidated, each refusing to be the first to step forward. My mother wore a silver sash from which hung the precious tools that were indispensable in the preparation of betel. She was unquestionably the most beautiful. A few young men, fired up with alcohol, teased her with their joking. She blushed while the other women hid their laughter behind their hands.

These kinds of amusements distracted us from the growing tension between my mother and my grandfather. She complained to him about being relegated to the status of subaltern, housed at the edge of the property. But my grandfather held his ground. He preferred to favor a devoted concubine than to yield to the pleadings of his children, none of whom gave him any joy in his old age. In the end, my mother broke with her father. We moved away to a thatched cottage situated south of the village.

The life we led at my grandfather's had erected a barrier of wealth between us and the other villagers. I had no playmates, except for my sister. As for my mother, she never left her father's property. Our move cast us among the poor. Most of the time I played with kids who were naked, since they had no clothes to wear, their skin baked by the sun. The oldest children, the ones whom decency forced to cover themselves, wore patched-up undershorts as their only pieces of clothing. They never seemed to tire of looking at me, not hiding their curiosity at seeing my face which was different from theirs. And when I had told them about my years in the orphanage, the French nuns I had rubbed shoulders with, and the French language I knew how to speak, they looked at me open-mouthed, eyes wide with amazement. They had never seen a French person and had imagined them tall and very strong with booming voices like rolling thunder. I made fun of their ignorance. I described to them the blondness of some French people's hair, similar to rice straw after the harvest. I painted for them the blue and green eyes of my companions in the orphanage. Everything seemed to belong to some fantastic tale. They wondered how anyone could see with eyes that were blue or green, and on top of that, so transparent. Was I sure they could see everything? They would drink in my words. I felt very knowledgeable. Then I sang for them the *Dies Irae* of the funeral mass as well as the old French songs I had learned. They found them pretty, and at the same time, the French ceased being ogres and gradually became more human.

For days on end they harassed me with questions. I became the heroine of the group. The children talked about me with their parents, who also encouraged me to recount my little slice of life with the French. I told them about the meals, the games, the dormitory, and the discipline. My songs especially made them laugh till they cried. They found the French language halting and hushed, as if you were chewing a ball of rice while you were talking. Each one tried to pronounce a word while blushing, then burst out laughing faced with the impossibility of pronouncing the "je" or the "che."

Soon my mother didn't need to feed me anymore; I would eat at one house, then another, at the whim of invitations. My hosts showed me the same interest they would have given to a duck found in the midst of a brood of baby chicks.

Much later, in the '60s, I had a parallel experience in Dordogne. I was spending my vacation with a group of students from about ten other countries. International Encounters was a program sponsored by Maurice Schumann with the goal of fostering understanding between peoples. Participants would stay for a short time with French families. My hosts had chosen me because they had lived in the colonies and had retained a touching memory of Indochina. They received me as if I were a precious object—there weren't many Vietnamese in France at the time. And so it was that between duck *confit* and porcini mushrooms, I told them bits and pieces about my life in Viet Nam. I described the landscapes of my childhood, and to finish up, sang them the planting and harvesting songs of my Vietnamese village. They listened to me with a good deal of sympathy, without comment, despite the strangeness of the language. I felt both foreign and pampered.

In the village, my mother worried about my social success. Taking into account my stain of original sin, she would have preferred that my existence be more discreet. Everyone knew now that I was *métisse* and that I had lived in a French orphanage, a dangerous thing to shout from the rooftops in this time of great tension. After independence was declared by Ho Chi Minh in 1945 in Hanoi, an intense resentment emerged, born of past humiliations, repressed up to then by the French. People talked in public about the situation of the poor, weak men who pulled their rickshaws until they were exhausted from hauling the colonists three times fatter than they and getting kicked as a form of payment once they had arrived at their destination. And then there were the movie houses with their three entrances: one for the colonists, one for the opportunistic Annamites, and finally one for the colonized people where you were shoved and mistreated. People remembered with anger the obligatory reverence in front of the tricolor flag, to the sound of *La Marseillaise,* that you had to listen to at attention at the beginning of each film. My mother remembered it, too. She told me once about the fear that seized her when she found herself for the first time in the presence of a French officer at her aunt's in Hanoi.

A little while after this, upset and trembling with emotion, she confessed that she had given birth to a second child a year after my own birth. She had had a son she never saw again; his father took him with him back to his faraway country.

After my father had abandoned my mother, another officer had taken her in, touched by her beauty and her misfortune. The goodness of that man and the tenderness he showed her consoled her for having been abandoned by my father, whom she never talked to me about. I conceived even more hatred for the one who had fathered me. As for my mother, because of the way that she didn't look at me while speaking, I guessed that the wound was still fresh.

She and the officer had lived happily despite the language barrier that prevented her from expressing her full gratitude. I really believe that she was in love with him, even though she never once pronounced the word "love." Her happiness was short lived. One day in August, her officer was recalled to France. She couldn't follow him, because they weren't married. And besides, what would he have done with an ignorant Annamite woman? So, they agreed to separate. But the man wanted to take his child.

The day of his departure, she went to the barracks. The trucks there were loaded with military men, some of whom carried children in their arms, children who had just been torn from their mothers who, mad with grief, tried to throw themselves under the wheels of the GMCs. The children were crying as the mothers were tearing their hair out and scratching themselves in desperation. In the end, a reinforcement of armed soldiers arrived, making the crowd back off. The trucks pulled out onto the road in the midst of cries, tears, and insults. Lying in the dust, crushed, my mother remained a long time, listening to the sound of the trucks as they moved further and further away. With this memory, her voice changed and she sobbed sharply. I began to cry, too. At that moment, I felt an infinite love for her that would never leave me.

She couldn't stop talking about her son, Jean-Marcel Guillaume, my half-brother. With great care, she unfolded in front of me the birth certificate she had kept, sewn into the lining of her cotton jacket. The wrinkled paper, which she smoothed tenderly with the flat of her hand, bore witness to her tragedy, but at the same time it was witness to her only happiness. During her life, in the course of successive exoduses, she had had to abandon many things, but never this birth certificate, which she kept intact until 1960 when she gave it to me, without her husband's knowledge, before my departure for Paris. I often wondered how many times, out of everyone's sight, it happened that she would pull out the stitches of the lining of her jacket to gaze upon that paper while dreaming of her lost happiness.

My secretive mother, my taciturn mother. How many interior obstacles did you have to overcome in order to surrender, finally, the hidden part of your life? From that day on, I could no longer contemplate your face, calm as a quiet lake, without thinking of the interior storms that troubled you. My resigned mother. What was there to do in order to erase what had been? I would have liked to invent a world of goodness and offer you the throne of the queen. Instead, I continue to carry the wound of your withered life.

⁓ 4 ⁓

The Child in the Jar

The abrupt move from an animated residence to the gloomy straw hut where we were living was extremely difficult for me to get over. I spent many days getting used to it. My mother harbored a secret feeling of bitterness about it. She suffered from seeing me so quick to leave her behind and so happy away from her company. And even more so because my absence deprived her of the chores I did that made up my share of the daily work.

Like all the village's children, in my family I took on tasks suited to my age such as caring for my young sister, doing the dishes, cooking the rice and gathering water spinach. More than anything, I was afraid of that task, which was done in muddy canals infested with leeches. My fear of leeches was such that I would become paralyzed on the river-bank, crying all alone for a long time. Once I had cried all my tears, I would remain stunned, looking at the cloudy water while trying to overcome my panic. I knew I couldn't return empty-handed. So, with my teeth clenched and my eyes closed, holding my breath, I would jump into the water, blindly cutting the greens by the armload. I tried not to feel the sliminess brushing against my calves. Once the harvest was done, I got out as fast as I could, arms full, content with my victory. My mother, of course, took what I had gathered, never suspecting anything about the great difficulties I had to overcome to accomplish a task that seemed so simple.

The dishes were also a trial for me, especially in the winter when the grease was congealed on the sides of the bowls. I had only cold water and a little ash to get it off. When mixed with the grease, the ash made a kind of thick soot; it took five or six repeated rinsings to get a dish clean. There, too, I would often cry with rage, impatient to rejoin my comrades who were waiting for me under the tall banyan tree.

Not being able to find me when she needed me would drive my mother to despair. She would call out my name in a long incantation. Then, as if she had given some sort of signal, other women would begin calling their children in a worried clamor. At key moments of the day, mealtimes or before nightfall, the whole countryside would reverberate with the counterpoint of the mothers' calls. Flattened behind the bamboo hedge, we would hold our breath, curious to witness our own disappearance. We would have liked to see them cry over their loss in order to take credit for making them happy upon our return. But we knew that this was only a daily ritual, similar to the moment before sunset when the chickens are called home to roost. As part of the game, we would remain silent as long as possible. But hunger and fear would always bring us back earlier than we wanted to the fold where we would receive our punishment. Then you would hear the parents' cries of reproach, the sounds of the blows, and the wails of the children coming from all the huts. It was a scene repeated every evening with the same enthusiasm. It gave rhythm to our lives. I think that both we and our parents would have missed it if by some chance things had happened otherwise.

In the course of these escapades we would often wander around in search of something to eat. We knew by heart all the places where there was fruit to steal. We never made a mistake in distinguishing the orchards that were being watched from those that were accessible to us. We were capable of climbing to the highest branch of a thorny jackfruit tree in order to pick a piece of fruit that we would then share among eight or ten of us in a veritable feast. The fruit is as big as a rugby ball and its disappearance would cause a huge fuss in the village. The neighbors were all suspicious of each other. No one had any idea that we could possibly be behind such an important theft.

The wronged woman who owned the property would stand guard at the end of the hedge that enclosed her garden, invoking aloud the worst of curses that she wanted to fall down upon the head of the thief as well as on his third-generation offspring. These actions made her stand out. Members of the neighboring families, as connoisseurs of such invective, would lend an ear and praise her talents. That's why only the most gifted would risk such vocal maledictions. The others preferred to remain silent rather than bring ridicule upon themselves. Some women, known for the ferocity of their remarks, enjoyed a reputation well beyond the limits of the hamlet. In their case, you stopped what you were doing and went to listen, sitting on your doorstep as if you were at a performance.

Their only rivals were among the professional mourners, the best-known of whom were in great demand. Composing the texts of their lamentations themselves, they combined poetic talent with a gift for theatrical interpretation. Each set of circumstances required specific tones of voice they had to discover themselves. And some lamentations were so poignant and proclaimed with such authentic sadness that even those who did not know the family were moved to tears.

The most significant event in the village was the approach of Tết, the lunar new year; the orphanage had made me forget about this festival, right down to its name. Each family killed its pig which was shared with three or four others, sometimes more. As we were poor, my mother sent me to get our portion at her sister's.

I arrived at the end of the afternoon, in an atmosphere of extreme activity and overexcitement. The pigs that were going to be slaughtered, sensing their end was near, were screeching unbearably. I didn't know animals could protest to that extent. Four men were all that were needed to hold each animal down while a fifth cut its throat in one stroke, causing a red stream to shoot up. The adults shouted hurrahs of triumph. At the meal, the coagulated blood, which we ate uncooked, seasoned with lemon juice, fragrant herbs, and crushed peanuts, was the workers' first reward.

Dazed, I contemplated the bodies, suddenly shaken by a long shudder. I had never seen death up close; so, that's what it was, the lack of movement, the stiffness.

A white steam rose from the pots of boiling water. It was sprinkled on the beasts before they were cut up. The best pieces were reserved for my aunt, everyone's benefactor. My mother got her share, which I took home in baskets attached to the ends of a stick that had been covered with banana leaves to keep the flies away. They were entrusting me with an adult's responsibility. The baskets were heavy. Many times on the way, I had to stop, out of breath. A black sun danced before my eyes. Finally, I arrived at the house, on the brink of collapse. My mother ran up, humiliated to see me in such a state.

"My poor child!" she murmured. "A girl of your race is not a peasant!" And she began to cry. "If you were being raised in France, you would receive an education instead of living like the people here!"

She cried a long time, and I can't say if it was out of pity for me or for her own life.

In my family, we always lived on the lookout. The suffering brought on by colonization, constantly invoked in public, aroused an anger that risked being harmful for me, as a *métisse,* as well as for my mother, guilty of having had a physical relationship with the enemy. She would hide me as soon as any outsider set foot in the village.

One day, a Viet Minh cadre from the city proclaimed his indignation at the massacres perpetrated by the French in Hanoi. He had brought a witness with him, a young woman who poignantly recounted the loss of her family members, killed by enemy artillery. A muted sense of revolt ran through those who had gathered; I had joined them out of curiosity. Above my head, voices swore to wipe out all the French people who still remained on Vietnamese soil.

My mother took me back home and put me inside the large jar used to collect rainwater. It was the dry season, and the jar was empty. Huddled at the bottom, with my arms and legs in pain, I was numb with fear. I didn't know whose enemy I was. I didn't understand why I had to hide: I hadn't done anything to anybody. Images of French people with their throats cut at the time of the Japanese attack came to mind. Could it be that they would cut my throat, too? How could I explain to them that I was first of all Vietnamese and that it was only Vietnamese people who had shown me rare moments of affection up to now? To tell the truth, the only French people I had encountered were the nuns who ran the orphanage, and even they seemed really distant to me. I had not had any taste of the easy life of the colonists nor of their privileges. The injustice directed at me was intolerable as was the certainty that arose within me—and is still present, it's true—that Viet Nam wanted nothing to do with me. I cried quietly at the feeling that no one would come to help me. I fell asleep from fatigue, my head between my knees.

When I awoke, it was dark in the jar. Through the opening, I saw an oval of mauve sky. So, night would fall soon. I listened for the footsteps of my mother, who didn't come. Had she, too, abandoned me? Night surrounded me with its menacing shadows. I thought myself hopelessly lost. I cried some more, for a long time, and fell asleep again. The glow of a torch shone inside the depths of my hiding place. I opened my eyes. My mother whispered, "Come out, my child; they have left."

That night, I had difficulty sleeping. Old fears took possession of me. I had the feeling that a curse hung over my head. I wondered if I would be able to re-enter the huts that had welcomed me so warmly, if I would still be able to be a part of the gang of kids I had played with. I no longer trusted anyone. I knew that my life had no protective spirit. My mother, who could have protected me, was herself so destitute and so distraught that it was impossible for me to count on her. Something hard was taking shape in my heart. I curled up around this hard core that I guarded jealously, like a weapon against adversity. From then on I had two lives: one that was calm and that conformed to what was expected of me, and another heavy with a contained violence, like a volcano that threatens to erupt at any time.

Outside myself, the skein of time continued to unwind. Fear was followed by a period of calm during which I took my place again among the children of the hamlet. We didn't talk anymore about the French people whom I had rubbed shoulders with in the past. I understood that I had to disown that period of my life and conform to my current life here in order to be accepted. I made every effort to behave exactly like everyone else, to bend with the wind, to melt into the crowd. I became the most enthusiastic of anyone when it came to running half-naked in the rice fields in order to catch giant grasshoppers that we ate grilled, sitting next to the water buffalo herder. Or when we had to walk perilously along the bamboo hedges looking for eggs laid by some stray duck. In no time, my skin became as tanned as that of the others. I was as thin as they were; my face seemed to have been eaten up by my huge eyes, as one commonly sees with starving children. At first glance, no one could tell the difference between me and the others anymore, nor could anyone tell immediately that I was *métisse*.

Aside from these unusual moments, I liked to hang around with the gang of girls when the boys were working hard at school, where knowledge was reserved for them alone. We were bored without them. Sometimes we would venture to the forbidden place, spying on the studious life of our playmates through a crack in the wall.

Sitting cross-legged on mats, their heads bowed, they were trying to reproduce the calligraphy of the great masters. They looked pitiful. For those who were not completely attentive, the school master would let loose a rain of blows on their naked backs or their shaved heads.

When class let out, they would show us the swollen marks left by the whip on their naked skin. We would examine them and lightly touch them with our fingertips with utmost care. They would barely make a sound when we increased the pressure of our fingers. Then we would feel a kind of maternal pity for these budding men, already full of a kind of admiration at their courage. We found school constraining and were happy to be girls who were forbidden from such initiations.

For the wild children that we were, this was a moment of great sweetness. We felt good when we were together. We wished never to return to our homes, just run down the roads, go far away . . .

"Too bad that you're *métisse!*" one of them said with regret. "We can't take you with us; we'd have to hide you all the time!"

"And how would we know if you were going to betray us?" added another.

I protested, "Have I ever betrayed you?"

I was hurt. I knew that this was only idle talk, but I was sad all the same.

Time passed peacefully. Little by little the memories of my previous life faded. I had the feeling of always having been in this village. I ended up believing that I had been born here, among the ponds and the bamboo, the huts grouped in twos and threes, the children I felt deeply close to. By dint of seeing them without seeing myself, I had come to believe that I was just like them; I forgot my difference.

It was probably from this soil that my young personality was nourished and took shape. From this short period—a year, maybe a year and a half—I drew the essential images of my emotions and my nostalgia. I wasn't yet eleven. The more time passes, the more my thoughts turn toward those days of my childhood. I know that there will be no return for me. That's why I carry the emptiness, the loss of my native rice fields, which, on certain days, feels like the shooting pain of a badly healed scar.

Those long days, one similar to another, repetitious and monotonous, had the benefit of bringing me a stability and a security unknown to me up to then. I identified with the joys, the sorrows, and the dramas of the hamlet.

It was then that an event occurred that risked compromising my fragile anchoring point once again.

Because our village was in the zone occupied by the Viet Minh, cadres had undertaken a collection of funds destined to acquire arms that were indispensable to the struggle against colonialism. All the villagers were invited to present themselves at the communal house. They noted those who were absent with an air of disapproval. Behind the table that served as a rostrum hung an immense national flag. There were two men: a young man and an older one. Despite their appearance, it was the young man who took the floor:

"Comrades, our country is fighting to shake off the yoke of the colonizer. We know that liberty is won through suffering and blood. However, courage, though necessary, is not enough: we need arms. We can buy them from the Americans, but we lack the gold to do that. So, all patriots are invited to donate their gold for the homeland."

The man did not lack eloquence, and there was a ripple of applause. The entire room buzzed with a common feeling of patriotic emotion.

Once again my mother hid me in the jar.

"Don't move!" she advised. "I'll come back and get you out of there when they have left the village."

I was in despair.

"But why?" I cried out. "I have done nothing wrong. Leave me at home; I promise that I will stay inside."

She remained unmovable. I hated that jar; it gave me the feeling of being buried alive.

"Don't move!" she said.

As if I could have gotten out. Stuck like a mayfly in a bottle, what would I have held onto in order to climb up the smooth inside wall of the jar?

Outside, all was in turmoil. People were consulting each other in small groups. The richest ones were discussing, brother with brother or husband with wife, the sum they should offer. They wondered if anyone was aware of how much they really had since it was true that many sought to minimize the extent of their fortunes, out of superstition, to avoid bad luck or the envious with their bad intentions. To this end they sought to give an impression of themselves as relatively poor, if not indigent, which was far from the truth. They went out of their way to dress modestly and ate good things only in secret, one well-kept by their families. The surprising thing is that everything came out in the end, and the nasty gossips were capable of evaluating a fortune down to the last detail.

The tray, set out for everyone to see, was waiting. In single file the villagers came up to leave their donations. They were tossing earrings, bracelets, and engagement and wedding gifts on the pile. The richest ones, on edge, put down a few gold bars and wads of piasters, for, aside from not knowing if they had given enough in the eyes of the cadres, they feared the envy of those watching. A kind of insidious rivalry set those giving the most against each other, and the winner would be the one who showed the most generosity toward the homeland.

Near the end of the day, the tray was still half empty. The young officer was disappointed. He was sorry that the richest were not the most generous. In a threatening tone, he carefully made a vow that he would soon see the tray filled with the gold that, and of this he was certain, was sleeping uselessly in well-buried strongboxes.

My grandfather and some of the notables who had been absent the evening before brought their gold bars, "a humble contribution of their modest being to the national cause." They accused their old age of having prevented them from being as conscientious as they would have wished. They hoped that doubt had not been cast on their commitment. No one said a word, but everyone knew that they had acted only because they were constrained or forced to, for the cadres had more than one way to put pressure on the "greedy capitalists."

The poor peasants, open-mouthed, looked at the incredible quantity of gold that had come from some families. With some rancor, they played over in their minds the hypocritical tears of certain landowners who would make a case for their own destitution in order not to pay more. As a result, the peasants assumed that they had colossal fortunes, the fruit of their overheated imaginations.

As for my mother, she hatched the idea of robbing her own father. She took me out of the jar, sent me quickly to bed, and disappeared into the night, doubtless with the intention of turning over every square inch of her father's property. Ever since she had seen the considerable sum thrown by his own hands onto the "tray of the homeland," the idea that Dame Troisième and her descendants might profit from the fortune that really should have been hers tortured her.

In the early morning, she returned, empty-handed. I heard her sigh but pretended to be asleep to avoid her complaints and abuse.

The next day we had to put up with her bad mood. The climate in the house was continually deteriorating anyway. My parents quarreled frequently, saying harsh and hurtful words to each other that I didn't understand but whose effect I could see on their faces. My stepfather displayed the snarl he wore on his contemptuous days, while my mother would by turns fly into rages and break down in tears. I pitied her while at the same time feeling embarrassed to witness the spectacle of her powerlessness. In the war that pitted them against each other, I knew immediately that she was not the strongest opponent. This man—whom I never caught expressing the slightest gesture of tenderness toward her—was the stroke of luck that had allowed her to gain a certain social respectability. And I believe that he was fully conscious of that, especially now that he saw her living like a foreigner in her own village.

Even though she came from this hamlet, she had left at too young an age to feel at ease with her old friends, who, moreover, discreetly despised her. The women her age, the ones who had shared childhood games with her, had become stupidly calm, like the water buffaloes you see bathing in the muddy water of the ponds. They were simple women who saw my mother, with her beauty and nonconformist life, as the incarnation of evil. The old women with their venomous tongues said that she resembled her own mother, who had been a bad wife. In short, she remained for them a fallen woman, guilty of having had shameful relations with a Frenchman. Wasn't I proof of that? My very existence was the sign of her transgression and her exclusion. Thinking like everyone else, her husband silently bore a grudge against her.

It is true that life wasn't easy for him either. Without friends, he moped around doing nothing. The villagers, while not showing any hostility toward him, either paid no attention to him or kept him at a polite distance. He ended up taking refuge behind a wall of silence, where his homesickness only got worse. He missed the spontaneity of the people from the South, the easy cheerfulness of their character. He missed Cho-Lon,[1] where he had spent his youth and early adulthood. In this village in the North, everything seemed tense and arid to him. Even the food displeased him. For hours on end he would describe the feasts in his father's house, when he was still alive, how, with Tết coming, he would make the pork *confit* himself, a delicate operation that took five to six hours of preparation. We would listen to him absent-mindedly. My mother, working nearby, would gesture impatiently as if she were tired of hearing his stories. He wasn't looking at us anyway. With a faraway look, he was talking to someone who was invisible. More and more often it would happen that he would mutter to himself, just like a cracked and slowly dripping jar.

Finally, having had enough, he decided to return to Tuy Hoa, a small town in the central part of the country where his father was buried. For my mother, too, it was time to leave. She had finally understood that she could not live here in peace. For me, the departure was wrenching. I had become attached to the people and landscapes of this village. I was beginning to put down roots, and I was in the process of accumulating memories and writing my own story. I was experiencing a kind of continuity.

Up to then, my life had been nothing but a series of abrupt changes. I had never again seen those who had witnessed my past. I knew next to nothing about myself, and I had no one to tell me about my childhood. I would have liked to know if I had been a happy or morose baby. Did people find me nice? Did I resemble the wailing infants I saw around me? Even my mother couldn't answer these questions, for she had been far away from me at that time. The only thing she remembered was that a fortune teller had predicted to her that I would be the bane of her existence. What she told me made my blood run cold with

---

1. Cho-Lon, meaning "big market" in Vietnamese, was a separate city at the time and primarily populated by Chinese. Today it is a district of Ho Chi Minh City.

fear. I felt like a monster. I loved my mother and was thus in despair, knowing that I was inevitably going to do her harm! I would have preferred not to be her daughter. I imagined myself the child of another woman, already dead in childbirth, for that way I couldn't spoil anyone's life. She would no longer be concerned about the prediction, and as for me, I could then offer her tenderness and consolation.

I found my mother so beautiful that it seemed fair to me that she should have the best things in the world. Her face was a perfect oval shape, her hair jet black. Her heavily lidded eyes—which I recognized later as those of Marlene Dietrich—were surprising for an Asian woman. Her ebony pupils made her gaze look like two brilliant dots of infinite sweetness. Her mouth, even in repose, relaxed, always seemed to be on the verge of saying something tender and serious. A distinction, a grace that set her apart from those around her, radiated from her body. By comparison, even her elder sister, my aunt, seemed insignificant. And yet, I had never seen her happy. She seemed to want nothing more than a roof over our heads and rice in the cooking pot each day. She tolerated her frustrations as one manages to live with an incurable disease. The older I got, the more I became aware of the failure of her life. This discovery released contradictory feelings in me; I was anxious to stay near her to ease her sorrow, and at the same time pushed by some overwhelming need to flee far away. To draw a line through the moral and material misery that formed the web of her life, to find a new image elsewhere. To break the cycle of misfortune. To escape the chains.

❦ 5 ❦

The Stepfather's Fiefdom

I still have the feeling that the trip that took us to Tuy Hoa was interminable. We had watched the sun rise and set several times. We lay down like livestock on the floorboards of the packed train cars. We felt gaunt and dirty with our hair tangled by the wind and singed by the sparks that flew back at us from the locomotive. As one might expect, there was no water in the third-class washbasins. But we hoped to be able to give our faces a quick wash when the train stopped.

When it did, a dense crowd pushed in front of the sole water fountain. No one even dreamed of washing themselves. Instead, we grabbed everything we could get our hands on that might serve as a container to fill with water to quench our thirst during the rest of the trip. These ran from lavish empty soybean oil cans to small bottles that could hold little more than a few ounces. Those who could find nothing used dried coconut shells in which they had cut a round hole in the top beforehand. The drawback was that these didn't have lids. What's more, the train was stopped for only a short time. People pushed and shoved and got into arguments. Men insulted each other and got into fistfights. Women shouted abuse at each other and came to blows. The children clung to the legs of their mothers, screaming. The noise was dreadful. It was then that I realized just how degrading poverty is. During the terribly long days of the trip, I saw people who were very polite at the moment of departure argue later on over an inch of floor space where they might stretch out. We all hid our drinking water as if expecting the worst of droughts. Generosity dried up as the time passed. No one offered anything to anyone; we ate furtively.

No one could possibly know how long the voyage would last. The

train lines were hardly safe. It was not uncommon that the Viet Minh
would cause a train to derail. Beyond the physical danger, the train
could also undergo considerable delays or be prevented from moving.
Everyone was afraid. In the train cars, we put up improvised altars in
every possible spot: a corner of a mat where someone had put a bowl of
rice, a piece of fruit, or a few sticks of burning incense. The old women
would mumble prayers, invoking the spirits of the forest or the spirit of
the railroad to protect us. Panic seized everyone whenever the train
seemed to slow down for no reason. We lived in fear of the Viet Minh as
we had feared the tigers in the forest long ago. Outside of my family
and a very few others who came from villages in the North and had
seen the fighters of the People's Army, no one seemed to think that the
Viet Minh were our compatriots. These uninformed people were
equally afraid of French colonists and Vietnamese fighters.

On the third evening, the train had to stop all night for fear of a
communist attack. Everyone had to climb down to the platform. Some
tried to buy fish caught that very morning or dried shrimp from the
locals. You would have thought it was peacetime were it not for the
presence of the soldiers who stood guard across the tracks, peering into
the thick shadows of the forest.

The town of Tuy Hoa gave me the impression of a major city. The
shops were numerous, and people were always coming and going. I had
already lived in cities like Hanoi and Tuyen Quang, but I was too young
to really appreciate them. Tuy Hoa charmed me at once. I would take
off at the slightest pretext to the despair of my mother, who was afraid
I might get lost in this place that was still unfamiliar to me. But I was
impatient to mix in with the crowd. The only place I was comfortable
was in the street, in the middle of people I didn't know, enchanted by
feeling completely alone and at the same time surrounded. I spent my
time observing the children, whom I found very animated, very smart,
very naughty—in short, very different from those in the countryside.
Flattened against a wall or crouching behind the shop displays, I would
study their games, their arguments, their petty thievery.

The children would gather in small groups in front of the shops
whose abundance astounded me. They had everything: rice in hun-
dred-kilo bags, dried fish, bowls, cups, vegetables, woven mats ... I
didn't know there were so many good things to buy. I wanted every-

thing. All of a sudden, I was struck by the full measure of the rural peasant poverty I had lived in: the scarcity of objects, the daily parsimony that forced us to count even the stems of vegetables at meals. The city seemed like a place of riches par excellence, a font of well-being and pleasure. It suited me.

We moved in temporarily with one of my stepfather's aunts. She lived in the only brick house in the neighborhood. All around, the only things visible were straw huts tightly packed one next to another, housing water carriers for the most part. They were sickly men, their skin blackened by the sun. The only things memorable about their faces were the brilliant holes of their eyes and their prominent, toothy lower jaws, just like those of skeletons. You would never see them without their bamboo sticks across their shoulders, bent like a bow by the two cans hanging at the ends. They moved with quick, regular steps, their feet barely touching the ground, their shoulders burning from the rubbing of the stick. For a few cents they would provide us with the water we needed.

They would go get it at the public fountain a half-hour's walk away, where a dense, noisy crowd waited day and night. Fights were frequent. Women and children were eliminated automatically. Only a few well-muscled, loudmouthed men succeeded in getting to the water, so much so that the fountain became quite naturally the property of the carriers. All day you could see them running from the fountain to the various houses that they supplied, in silence, with vacant stares, their cans swaying in rhythm, phantom dancers, attentive to keeping the pace.

They worked from dawn into the dark of night, without stopping, without rest. They spent time with no one. Even among themselves they spoke little, exchanging just a few words during the time it took to fill their cans. Their comings and goings, like a loom's shuttle, wove the material of each day. I was obsessed by them. Sometimes they would be running in my dreams, sad and silent. I would see the leaves they put into each can—to keep them from splashing on the bumpy road—become huge. The leaves would grow big enough to become large blankets that would suffocate me. I would struggle as their skulls stared at me with vacant eyes.

I nurtured a combination of pity and hate toward them. Seeing their shoulders black and blue to the point of bleeding made me ill. I hated their wild expressions and their resignation. Wasting water became a crime; I would use it only for drinking. I stopped bathing despite my mother's invectives. I had a dirty face and my feet were black, because I went around barefoot like everyone else. My mother treated me like a tramp. She predicted that if I went on like that, I would end up looking like the children of the water carriers we saw hanging around in bunches in the dust of the unpaved streets, amidst the garbage, chased by swarms of green flies. The vision of such a future filled me with horror. In fact, all I had to do was open my eyes to see those children around me. They were skinny and listless with feverish eyes. Often the oldest ones would carry their little brothers, who were crying from hunger, on their hips, their tears leaving white rivulets on their dust-blackened faces.

As for the mothers, they were wet nurses for well-off families. They earned more than their husbands, and it was their pay that allowed the hordes of kids to survive, not counting the leftovers that they stole each day from their employers. Their lives would have been less difficult if not for the continual increase in the number of mouths to feed. To have milk, they had to keep having children. It was a vicious cycle from which they couldn't escape. Often they would cry at the sight of the plump babies sucking gluttonously at their breasts, drinking the milk robbed from their own starving kids. So, taking advantage of an inattentive moment on the part of their mistresses, they would return home to offer their breasts furtively to their own little ones, especially when they were sick. When I went to visit one of my aunt's acquaintances, I encountered one of these women, all skin and bones, so skinny as to make you afraid. Her body was a dried-out tree from which hung breasts like enormous fruits. As such, she seemed monstrous to me. Had anyone ever seen a dead tree produce such large fruit? That vision filled me with disgust. It seemed to me that the life that circulated in her body was completely contained in those breasts, which the babies sucked obstinately, blindly, day and night. I didn't like the babies. I imagined that in the end there would be only a large transparent envelope left over, similar to the molted skin left behind by cicadas on the branches of trees.

Later on, in the 1950s, when American movies inundated Saigon with images of the more than ample chest of Jayne Mansfield, I thought again about those wet nurses with their taut dark breasts, as a wave of nausea rose once again in my throat.[1]

Tuy Hoa was my stepfather's fiefdom. We discovered his numerous connections with surprise. This man whom we had seen only as isolated and alone was greeted by everyone in the neighborhood. He would smile at one, give a friendly tap on the shoulder to another, stop to say a few words to yet another. People took his signs of friendship as favors. He had a public life and, what's more, he was liked, something that filled me with amazement. I knew him only as sullen and severe, with a cold gaze and a cruel expression. Thinking that he could smile seemed incongruous to me. How could anyone like him?

In fact, his success came from his late father, a rich businessman to whom each one of these poor folks who greeted him with great respect owed something. Certain ones had not yet finished paying off their debts, contracted long ago to build their houses or to start a business. The word "business" actually gives the wrong impression of those sorts of open shelters with thatched roofs. On a low bamboo platform, a kettle would be on the fire; nearby there might be a dozen or so cakes and, for the richest customers, American cigarettes sold one at a time. In this almost indigent world, my stepfather cut the figure of an heir apparent to the throne. We lived off the interest he collected each month from those who were in debt to his father, now his debtors as heir.

My mother realized that she knew next to nothing about her husband. She learned—at the same time as I did—that he was a widower. His late wife was the eldest of a family whose fortune equaled his own. People said that their wedding had lasted a whole week. In everyone's eyes they seemed to be under Buddha's protection: young, carefree, and rich, their lives had only to follow a path that was already mapped out, the path of the privileged of this world.

Soon they had a daughter, followed by two other girls and finally a son. The male heir arrived in time to clear away the clouds that had gathered over the life of the couple since the birth of the second daughter and especially since the third. My stepfather, whose mood

---

1. During the First Indochina War and into the Diem presidency, the United States led a propaganda campaign to introduce American culture to the South Vietnamese.

had darkened, had even thought of taking a second wife who might be capable of giving him a son. The couple rediscovered joy in a house full of the laughter and tears of children, pampered by their respective families. The years thus passed by when suddenly, out of who knows where, the rumor spread that the young woman had contracted leprosy. People looked at her with fright and avoided her. The fear of contagion seized people the instant she approached. Her family denied the news, which reassured my stepfather's. But soon, the young woman's skin became spotted and swollen. With heavy hearts, her parents abandoned her in a leper colony, cut off from the world of the living for good. No one saw her again. Her mother, who went to visit her each month, listened—from behind a curtain, without seeing her—to the terrifying recitation of the physical and moral suffering that would precede the loss of a limb. She abandoned them like dead wood, on her bed, early in the morning.

After this ordeal my stepfather fled back to Saigon, where he was hired as a salesman for the Bastos Cigarette Company. His return surprised everyone. He reconnected with his wife's family and with his children, the youngest of whom didn't remember what he looked like. He suddenly recalled that he had a son and did so with the pleasure of knowing that my mother had only been able to give him a daughter. He was jubilant.

We would no longer see him during the day; he was either at his former in-laws' house or at the homes of former friends. He lived with my mother as a stranger, hardly speaking to her. Often she didn't know whether to wait for him for dinner. The dishes of food she had prepared would slowly get cold. My sister and I would fall asleep out of fatigue or boredom. Later, my mother would reheat the food and wake us up. We would eat without interest, in silence. During the night I would hear her crying softly.

In spite of that I have to say that I was not unhappy. I had managed to join the gang of street kids who were thought of as brats. I made an effort to adopt their crude and colorful language, and I imitated their behavior as children who weren't afraid of anything. They introduced me to their games, and they taught me the art of stealing fruit from street displays and candy from large glass jars. Being a girl, I felt obligated to be doubly bold in order to gain their admiration. My mother no longer recognized her dear child in the insolent and hard little bitch I had become. When she sent me to the marketplace in the morning with the list of groceries to buy, I would take off running and not return until noon. And so, every day, the same scene played out. She reproached me for my lateness, let out cries of desperation, beat me, and ended up lamenting her misfortune for having given birth to a child who was so ungrateful. My stepfather, who sometimes witnessed these scenes, would roll his eyes, let out the sigh of a man who was exasperated but who could control his emotions, shoot me a sidelong glance, and leave. Each time, I would ask my mother to forgive me, promising her to change my ways. But I couldn't keep my promise. The city was too enticing to me. The noisy and colorful marketplace was like being at a celebration. The street was my life. My new friends kept me close in the warmth of their friendship. I never tired of wandering with them from street to street. They taught me to steal from my mother. For that, I had only to overprice the food I had bought. It wasn't hard when bargaining was the common practice. The ones who were good at it could get the price announced by the vendors down by a third. If I had spent a piaster for fish, all I had to do was tell my mother that I had paid a little more. So, I was able to earn, on all the purchases, almost a piaster, which I would hand over in full to the group.

As one might expect, my stepfather brought his children from his first marriage back home. My mother suddenly found herself the stepmother of three grown-up, adolescent girls and a boy who was a few years older than I. Their number scared us. From the first instant, we were face to face in a pitched battle: two enemy camps. My stepfather's children felt an immediate and irreversible hostility toward us. As for my mother, she could not hide her own hostility from the intruders. Such was the rule. My sister and I got ourselves pinched as soon as my mother turned her back. I was more at risk, because I wasn't even the daughter of their father. The girls had fun making me fall down by tripping me and then laughing at my pain. Their cruelty took me back to the ambiance of the orphanage. I got back at them as best I could. If they happened to forget a comb or a mirror on the mat, I would grab it right away and throw it down the well. We spent our days spying on each other or hatching plans to do harm to one another. I was only happy when I saw them in distress; I was becoming mean. What hurt me the most was their malicious whispering about the way my mother and "her Frenchman" had conceived me. I would foam with rage and would hurl myself at them, hitting and kicking them. But there were three of them, much older than I, and I would always end up losing. I would go and hide to cry, not because of the blows but because I couldn't tolerate their scorn for my mother. I would have preferred to cease to exist. To compensate, I invented a story in which I was the child of two parents of Vietnamese origin.

For a long time, I held on to that dream that negated my birth. I avoided all mirrors, and I passed over puddles of water without looking at my reflection. I fiercely wanted to forget that I was *métisse*. Above all, I wanted to make others forget it. I only realized the inanity of my efforts with the passage of time.

In the earliest stages of my adolescence, when I was being wooed by schoolmates, I had discovered that the flame that lit up their eyes was destined for the *métisse*. This discovery left me completely stunned. How could anyone desire what was scorned? Far from flattering me, their attentions left me cold. I had the feeling that they were lusting after me like some forbidden fruit, like some strange object that they would like to possess once, just to see. It would never enter their minds to put me on the same level as their mothers or sisters. That feeling was confirmed for me over and over the entire time I lived in Viet Nam. The men might change, but their deep-seated attitude toward me was always the same. That's why, even though I was born in Viet Nam and my being was shaped by its culture, I never once had sexual relations with a Vietnamese man. Except for the fact that every false step on my part would have been considered a vice rather than a mistake, their desire cheapened me. In order to make myself respected, I had to feign total indifference. But I suffered from this artificial behavior, for I, too, dreamed of love.

The little domestic war wore out my mother's nerves. She had dizzy spells and moments of exhaustion; she could do nothing in the house. The family circle took advantage of this to convince my stepfather that he was mistaken in bringing home a woman from the North, "cold and calculating like they all are," and who, on top of everything, was dragging around a past that was fraught. The past was, of course, me. He suddenly seemed to see the evidence for himself. He began treating her with disdain and manifested toward me the cruelest form of contempt: total repudiation. He drew a line through my life; I no longer existed. He never said my name, never spoke to me, and didn't look at me. When I happened to be opposite him, he looked right through me as if I were nothing but a veil of smoke. His little game impressed me enormously. I wondered if I hadn't become invisible without my knowing it. I had nightmares in which my body dissolved into thin air, light as a cotton flower.

The less he looked at me, the more I needed to attract his attention. I watched out for his slightest wish, eager to satisfy it. Was he uncomfortable because of the heat? I was there, fan in hand, ready to soothe him. But with a frown of refusal, he would change places. I would have preferred being struck to this kind of insult. His indifference made me weak inside. I resorted to the worst; I stole money from his wallet. I assumed he would know immediately that it was me and would scold me, maybe even beat me. I would then give it back to him, proving by this gesture that I was worth more than the idea he had invented of me. But when he discovered the disappearance of his roll of money, he let out a cold laugh, gave me a look that expressed all the disgust he felt for my bastard race, pitied my poor mother, ordered his daughters to avoid all dealings with a thief, and then left the room. His children followed him out. My mother left behind him. I stayed right there, crushed. I heard my stepfather's daughters poking fun and my mother's voice ordering my sister to wash her feet before going to bed. What happened to me was of no importance to them.

My stepfather harbored a cold hatred toward me, and my mother, in his presence, behaved with me as if I were a stranger in order to win him back. I fervently wished to see her, if only once, stand up to him. But she never did.

❦ 6 ❦

Now That You Are a Woman

I made it to eleven. One day when I was returning from the market, streaks of blood began to run down my legs. I shut myself up in the shed in the courtyard, the place where brooms and useless things were stored. I undressed in haste, noticing the bloody space between my legs with horror. "It's probably an internal wound," I thought. Had I inadvertently swallowed a piece of glass that might have torn my insides? I didn't know what to do to stop all that blood from flowing. I thought I was going to die if the hemorrhage didn't stop, and that idea seemed terribly unjust to me. Our lives were so happy now that my stepfather was almost never there during the day. Our house resounded with our laughter, and often neighbors would come by to share in our gaiety. We only resumed our hypocritical act in the evening when my stepfather returned home. My mother wouldn't talk to me anymore, my sister would play silently in the corner, and me, I would be absorbed in some complicated embroidery.

Happy with this joyless atmosphere, he would toss out a question to my mother: "Is the meal ready, mother of Dzung[1]?"

Dzung is my sister's given name. Back then, married couples would usually address each other through the given name of their first child.

---

1. There are two ways to pronounce the consonant "d" in Vietnamese. The crossed "đ" is pronounced as it is in English. The uncrossed "D" in words such as Đung, the name of Kim's sister, or in Điem, the President of South Viet Nam from 1955 to 1963, is pronounced as a "z" in the North, sometimes rendered in English as "dz," for example *Dzung*. I have opted for this spelling of the name of Kim's sister.

75

My mother would answer, "Dzung's father will be served when he wishes."

That was all they said. But we knew that it was only an awkward moment to get through, and we played our roles conscientiously, just waiting for him to leave the house the next morning.

I thought of all those things while looking at my bloody thighs. I didn't want to die.

"Stop whining," scolded my mother. "You're having your period; you have become a woman!"

And she handed me some rags. I was feeling dirty. I walked clumsily, hindered by the wad of cloth between my thighs. I had the feeling that I had regressed to my childhood. I began to cry again. On the contrary, my mother seemed delighted. She ran out to buy me a few yards of white cotton material. Seeing her, you would have thought she was preparing my trousseau. We spent the whole day making my sanitary napkins. While sewing, she explained to me that I was no longer a child and that I was not to run around in the streets and play like a little kid any longer. From now on I had to change my behavior, speaking with a soft voice, making slower gestures, and lowering my eyes with modesty, especially in front of men; in a word, constructing my femininity. She told me that a woman's life is full of pitfalls, which was why her foremost quality must be suspicion.

"Believe me, my daughter, I know what I'm talking about. Don't make the same mistakes as your mother."

I was listening to her, dumbfounded. She advised me to avoid all familiarity with men, including those who were as old as my father.

"A woman has only one treasure, her virginity."

As proof, she told me the awful stories of those girls repudiated by their husbands, because they were no longer virgins. The only thing left for them was prostitution or a life of misery, for men always know when a girl has lost her virginity.

"But how?" I asked.

Her revelations crushed me; I didn't want to become a woman. I wasn't any different than I had been the day before. I didn't understand why this blood could upset my life so much.

"And if they are wrong? If the woman is still a virgin?" I asked.

"They are never wrong!" And then after a short silence, she added,

"In any case, no one will believe a woman who proclaims her innocence."

I was appalled. The fear of losing my virginity was making me ill. I was having nightmares in which a tall, old man, armed with a sword, was chasing and kicking me, shouting, "She has lost her virginity!" The crowd gathered around me would cover me with spit. I would try to defend myself, but no sound at all would come out of my mouth.

After the day of my first period, my mother treated me with more deference. She insisted that my sister show me a politeness that I found exaggerated. She seized upon every opportunity to announce my new condition to the gossips of the neighborhood, who would stare at me in a way that was very embarrassing. They would say "my older sister" when talking about me, as if I had suddenly become an adult. They seemed to find a new interest in life and made plans to make me a new pink blouse, the color traditionally reserved for young girls. They took on these new expenses without batting an eye.

"It's time to think about your future," my mother said to me. "You are far from being ugly, and if you know how to play your part well, you can hope to make a good marriage and, with a bit of luck, get us all out of this mediocrity."

But the war opposing the French and the Viet Minh that year, 1946, put an end to her illusions. The aerial bombing intensified; there were up to five or six air raids per day. At the sound of the sirens, we would leave whatever we were doing and everyone would run to where they thought they might find shelter. At our place, my stepfather had dug a trench close to the house. We were so tightly packed in there that I had to put my sister on my lap. We lacked air because of the piece of sheet metal that covered the entire length of the trench. It was as hot as an oven inside. My mother would pray that the air raid not last too long. We would wonder if it would be better to perish from the bombs or to die of suffocation in the trench. Sometimes, not being able to take it anymore, my mother would push back the sheet metal a few inches, leaving our heads uncovered. Explosions were making the ground shake.

At the end of the bombings, we would emerge from the hole, in a daze. Outside, volunteers were carrying the wounded on improvised stretchers. We could hear their cries and groans.

Then fear set in. We would only go out if absolutely necessary, to get supplies. The streets were deserted, and the shutters were kept closed on all the houses. Dead silence reigned in the town, a silence interrupted every now and again by the voice coming from the loudspeakers, exhorting the population to remain calm.

"Don't panic, compatriots! At the first sound of the sirens, the enemy planes are still far away, and you will have time to get to your shelters."

Despite these reassuring words, we were sick with fear. As the alerts came, people ran in every direction, losing precious time, like a woman I once saw zigzagging and shouting, with her infant in her arms, as if she were stricken with madness.

Little by little, meetings were organized in the neighborhoods to inform the population of the gravity of what was going on.

"The French seem determined to take Tuy Hoa, and we think they will land on the coast. The intense bombings are meant to intimidate us. We must act with calm and discipline, compatriots! For the moment, we don't have the forces to endure a siege. That's why, if they land here, we will burn the town before retreating. In the meantime, we will evacuate the old people and the wounded."

These words had a double effect: on the one hand, people were reassured to see that the revolutionary army was taking charge of their fate; on the other, they were perfectly aware of the precariousness of their situation. The merchants and those who had a little extra money made bets on the arrival of the French. People sought to get rid of their paper money in order to buy gold, a sure thing. In spite of the more and more frequent bombings, now even at night, people went out to stand in line at the jewelers'. My mother, doing what everyone else was doing, left us alone at home, in an indescribable anguish.

It was past noon, and we were waiting for her when the air raid siren broke the silence. I led my sister to the trench. The planes made such a deafening racket that it sounded like they were right over our heads. Suddenly, the explosion of a bomb nearby blew away the piece of sheet metal that covered our trench. I had the impression that the whole town was going to be destroyed. I flattened myself against the ground with my sister underneath me, closing my eyes and plugging my ears. I didn't even have any strength left to cry. I stayed in that position a long while after things calmed down. It was my mother who took us out of there. In the house, the chickens were pecking peacefully at our plates. I broke down in tears at the sight of the lost meal.

"Calm down," my mother consoled me. "We are going to prepare another."

But I didn't succeed in stopping my sobs, nor in repressing the spasms that were shaking me.

Since that experience I have hated war. Sirens that wail at noon awaken bad memories within me. I know what people say, that war pushes people beyond themselves. Taking aim at an enemy probably gives you the feeling that you are the master of your destiny. Chasing the invader, with a firearm in hand—what could be nobler? But above all, those are men's concerns. I only knew war from the civilian perspective, in the company of invalid men, old men, women, and children. We only had one feeling: fear. Blind and impotent fear. War means life interrupted. It means losing in an instant what it took a whole life to build. It means leaving your home, your town.

It means setting out on the road, slow and endless convoys of carts on which you pile up the little you can save. It means walking toward the unknown; it means fatigue, thirst, and hunger. And fear, always fear. The fear of losing those you love; the fear of airplanes, of tanks; the fear of stray bullets. In that confrontation, we are always the hunted, never the hunters. And when, after a long and exhausting march, you arrive somewhere, you have to settle down in places no one wants. You become refugees. With only some vague instinct to endure.

The fall of Tuy Hoa seemed imminent. Many times, we were jolted awake in the middle of the night by shouts that the French had landed. People emerged from their homes, sleepy, frantic, and questioning each other only to find out that it was a false alarm. But every family had its belongings ready to go. The cadres were encouraging people to leave in order to avoid a last-minute crush. We witnessed the first departures with sadness. The rich loaded up their possessions onto big trucks while the poor used carts or bicycles. The ones who stayed behind watched the others leave with tears in their eyes. They bid each other farewell, some for the last time.

At our house everything was ready, at least as far as my mother was concerned. She had done an inventory of her possessions: about ten pieces of gold leaf, two pairs of earrings, two solid gold bracelets, a few rings. She had sewn everything into a silk belt that she wore around her waist, under her trousers.

"In time of need, I can always sell them. Above all, don't tell anybody about this. Even your father doesn't know what I have."

Her secret confidence didn't surprise me; all women had possessions they hid from their husbands.

As for my stepfather, he was procrastinating. He didn't want to leave. He was waiting for the French to arrive, without daring, however, to admit it to us. After all, he wasn't Vietnamese. He thought that his being Chinese would shield him from the suspicion of the French police. He hoped to put himself under the protection of his new masters. But events overtook him.

One morning soldiers were crisscrossing the town, entreating the population to leave. This time we were up against the wall. We piled everything we could into carts. Everyone was in the street, trying to use ropes to steady the heaps of furniture, cooking pots, mats, and suitcases while the army was placing explosives in each house. No one could go back home. People were watching the soldiers in amazement. How could this be? The houses built by their grandfathers, where their fathers had lived, wiped out forever. It was intolerable. Someone rushed up to the soldier setting the explosives, begging him to stop his work of destruction.

"Would you prefer to leave your house to the enemy?"

The man hung his head.

The convoy set out as if full of regret. My stepfather decided that we would go to Quan Cau, a village not too far from Tuy Hoa where he had married off one of his daughters. She was the kindest of the three, the one who showed the least hostility toward my mother. For us kids, still unaware of the seriousness of the situation, this departure seemed like a festival. The bombings were over. We were running around the carts like wild little puppies. We were hoping for adventures, new landscapes, another life. Unlike us, the adults were leaving their town, heartbroken. Old women gathered handfuls of earth that they wrapped in handkerchiefs so that it could be thrown later into their graves. Their biggest regret was having to die far from the place where they were born.

When we got to the edge of town, groups separated from each other, going in the direction that seemed the most favorable to their destinies. Once again, the wrenching farewells. In the dying light of the day, we shared one last meal, a silent meal during which each person made it a duty to show the others a model of dignity. Suddenly, we heard violent explosions, as if the earth itself had just burst open like a ripe fruit, spitting out its seeds. Everyone lay face down on the ground. Someone shouted, "Look!"

We got up. Before us, the town was catching fire.

Then, losing their composure, people howled in despair. Women swayed forward and backward with their arms raised, with heaven as witness to their misfortune. Lamentations and sobs arose from all around. Then there was an incredible ceremony. Facing Tuy Hoa in flames, punctuated every now and again by the sounds of explosions, the women, sitting in groups scattered in the night, were hitting their heads on the ground and mourning the death of the town. In half incantatory, half sung tones, broken by sobs, they recalled its past, the heroism of its great men, the beauty of its streets, the sweetness of the evening sitting on the thresholds of its doorsteps, in the peace of days gone by. They lamented for some time, inconsolable. In front of us, the fire rumbled, terrible. Flames were moving in our direction, licking at houses closer and closer. The wind was blowing its hot breath at us; it was getting hotter from one moment to the next. Indifferent to the progress of the fire, the women's poignant threnody continued. No one moved; no one could look away from the sea of fire whose flames were devouring the fruits of the work of many generations. Finally, a few people, breaking away from the spell, shouted that we had to leave before it was too late.

Like a ghostly convoy, the carts moved out, each in its chosen direction. Soon, ours, too, plunged into the darkness. That was my first feeling of reaching a point of no return. The profound grief of this wake for Tuy Hoa, delivered to its destruction by fire, will never be erased from my memory. Later, when I discovered *The Trojan Women* by

Euripides, reading it troubled me. I could hear Queen Hecuba's lamentations, and it seemed that I was hearing those of the Vietnamese women weeping over their city reduced to ashes.

> Rise, stricken head, from the dust;
> lift up the throat. This is Troy, but Troy
> and we, Troy's kings, are perished.
> Stoop to the changing fortune,
> Steer for the crossing and the death-god,
> hold not life's prow on the course against
> wave beat and accident.[2]

Sadly, we made our way forward, under the light of the pale crescent moon. A long and monotonous march. My young sister had been put on the cart that my stepfather and a neighbor were pulling. Two men pushed it from behind. The women and children advanced while holding on to the sides of the vehicle in order to keep up the pace. I collapsed regularly from lack of sleep and fatigue. Each time I fell, my mother would pull me up and drag me like a sack of bran flour without ever slowing down. In the end, she succeeded in attaching my hand to a side rail, getting me back into the general rhythm. I followed the convoy with my eyes closed, my hand holding on firmly to the rail, putting one foot in front of the other.

A change in the terrain woke me up. We were almost imperceptibly sinking into sand. I could hear the labored breathing of the men and their grunting. The cart was sinking and we were far from any place where people lived, an area well-known for its tigers. So, we lit a large fire as a deterrent. We waited for dawn, packed tightly together while the men stood guard. In the morning, the long march resumed.

At the end of the afternoon, we emerged onto the marketplace of Quan Cau. The square was deserted. Not a living soul, not even a stray dog. We had scarcely put down our bags when my stepfather took off to visit his daughter's in-laws. While waiting, we sat down in the covered part of the market, attempting to divide the twenty-foot-long

---

2. Euripides, *The Trojan Women*, in *Euripides III*, translated by Richmond Lattimore (Chicago and London: The University of Chicago Press, 1958), 131.

space into five equal parts by hanging up sleeping mats. Each family settled into one of the tiny, improvised bedrooms. As if to emphasize our misfortune, it began to rain, a tropical rain with heavy drops. The mats, which were only attached at the top, waved in the wind like banners. The rain drenched us with its powerful downpour, creating little streams on the ground. We danced, we jumped, we ran after each other, and we laughed with joy. Only upon returning to our shelter did I begin to feel cold and hungry. We had a half-ball of cooked rice left, but my mother didn't dare touch it in the absence of my stepfather. It had been a long time since he had left to scout around. The village was tiny, so he must have already gotten to his daughter's house. Right then, they must have been in the process of exchanging the usual courtesies, for it would not have been proper for him to announce from the start that his family and close friends were waiting at the marketplace like beggars. Soon he would have tea while recounting the misfortunes that had befallen our city . . . That was how we imagined the different stages of his visit. We could hear the snoring of the neighboring families. My mother finally made up her mind to cut us a few slices of rice, which we devoured greedily. I fell asleep immediately after.

My stepfather returned the next day, accompanied by a few village notables. He had been kept for the night by his family of in-laws. The villagers then proceeded to the lodging of the refugees. Some of the landowners offered the outbuildings of their large residences, while others, less well-to-do, offered a room in their houses. We naturally went to move into the home of my stepfather's daughter; their house was large enough to put all of us up.

We walked through a large gate topped by a kind of balcony. In raising my eyes, I was, at that very instant, enchanted by the handsomeness of a young man leaning over a book with a writing brush in his hand. Our eyes met. I was ashamed of the slovenly way I looked. We crossed an immaculate courtyard before arriving at the main room. "Our sister's" stepmother received us courteously, but not without coldness, it seemed to me. Tea was offered to us. Through the window I looked for the man with the brush. I only saw a vague shadow, but it seemed to have a great presence. I felt like I wanted to cry without really knowing why. "My mother was right. I'm no longer the same," I thought.

At that moment, a man came in. He bowed in front of my parents, calling them "my father" and "my mother." I thus found out that he was the husband of "our sister." He seemed kind but completely ordinary, with nothing in common with my hero on the balcony. We hadn't yet seen our sister. Even my stepfather was unable to see her despite the night he had spent in their house. Such was the custom: our sister did not have the right to show herself to her parents before her mother-in-law had ordered her to do so. And customary practice forbade my stepfather from asking for her. Besides, from the time he had agreed to marry her off, she no longer belonged to him. Parents know that they work toward their own downfall in raising a daughter destined by fate for her future mother-in-law.

They moved us into the east wing of the building, with our sister and her husband occupying the west wing, while the mother-in-law and her young son—my young man on the balcony—lived in the central building.

On the morning of the fourth day, while I was going to draw water to wash up, chance put me in the presence of our sister. She was thin and pale, her look dull. She followed me to where we lived. Crying, she confessed to my parents that she was unhappy. Despite being a widow, her mother-in-law ran the household with a masculine authority. She treated her like a domestic servant, forcing her to work from the crack of dawn and not letting her stop until late into the night. She never saw her husband during the day, and in the evening she didn't dare complain to him about her mistreatment at the hands of her mother-in-law. She knew that her husband was an obedient son, and besides, she would not have wanted him to brave his mother in her defense. She suffered in silence, for such was her role in life. But life had become intolerable from the day when her mother-in-law's hostility was nurtured by a new grievance: for more than a year since her marriage, she had been taking her time giving her a grandson. She had consulted with the most renowned healers, in vain. She continually wondered about the mistakes she had committed in a previous life. In an attempt to redeem herself, she strictly observed Buddhist fasting, not only the first and fifteenth day of the month according to precepts, but every single day. She would eat only vegetables now, and she was at the end of her strength.

Believing she was playacting, the mother-in-law had even considered taking a second wife for her son, one that we call by the name "vợ bé," or "little wife." It was common practice. However, if the "little wife" enjoyed the favors of her husband, the first wife was often supported by the mother-in-law and custom allowed her to exercise the same tyranny over the newcomer as had been used on her. What was unusual in the case of our sister was that she had no children, which meant that she would have to confront both the mother-in-law and her husband's new wife. She begged her parents to come to her aid. But what could they do? She was no longer a part of our family. It was as if her father had sold her. She sobbed, then left.

My parents remained silent after her departure. With terror, I thought that I, too, was a woman. Was I going to have to suffer the same fate? Not that, no, never. If need be, I would disguise myself as a man, like the heroines of my books. They were women whom pride or an exceptional destiny had taken off the beaten path. They were as learned as mandarins, were perfectly familiar with the martial arts, and scorned men who wanted to treat them like exquisite flowers.

From that moment on, I took control of the wild beating of my heart upon seeing the young man with the brush. I avoided looking at him with my young girl's eyes. I wanted to seek out his masculine friendship, taking pleasure in imagining the two of us bent over the same books, like simple friends. But, paradoxically, he looked at me as if I were a little girl, or more precisely, didn't look at me at all. His lack of interest confirmed the very paltry idea I had of myself. I had nothing of the beauty that poets sang of: I didn't have eyes like deep pools, a jasmine complexion, the grace of a weeping willow, the light step of the morning dew settling onto the grass! At that very instant I found myself too *métisse* even to hope to please a Vietnamese man, just like in the past in Hanoi when I found myself too Vietnamese in the Frenchified world of Ba Tu's daughters. And I had the same feeling each time: I didn't love myself because others didn't love me.

My parents, for their part, had to face up to a delicate situation. They could not live any longer with a family where their daughter was tormented without losing face. They had to find another home. A pharmacist agreed to put us up. He had a big house whose street-side façade served as a shop. In back, a series of outbuildings were lined up, their doors opening onto a vast, shared courtyard.

In spite of these promising negotiations, we stayed yet another month with our sister's in-laws, out of propriety. A precipitous departure would have raised curiosity and caused gossip in the neighborhood.

On moving day, my stepfather announced suddenly that my mother was about to give birth. I was flabbergasted. I hadn't even noticed her condition. She had such a slender figure that no one would have suspected that she was pregnant, let alone that she was close to delivering. Our sister received the news as a personal affront. It's true that the situation had something funny about it. People would criticize the indecency of a stepmother letting herself get pregnant at her age—thirty-five, an old lady for that time—with the same fierceness as the daughter-in-law's sterility. Our sister could not forgive my mother for this humiliation. She broke off with us. We lived in the same village like strangers, without ever saying a word to each other.

As for me, I never ceased to be surprised by my mother. I looked upon her as if I were seeing her for the first time. It suddenly seemed to me that I didn't know anything about her. I was completely ignorant about her life before, about her thoughts, about her emotions. So, she was already carrying a child during the exhausting march that had brought us to this place. She didn't complain about her fatigue or about her privations. Why hadn't her husband given her any special treatment? I thought back to that night when we had been waiting for my stepfather in the covered market. We were alone; she could have shared her secret with me. I held her silence against her. I had only her, and here she distanced me from her innermost secrets.

Our new accommodations were radically different from the previous ones. We lived, so to speak, with an open door onto the communal courtyard. Ten refugee families shared the single kitchen and the central well with each other. We had to organize ourselves to take turns getting water and especially scheduling meals, which was a constant source of conflict, for everyone was hungry at the same time. During the whole day, we were subjected to the noise of quarrels, arguments, and reproaches. We had peace only for a fleeting instant, in the evening, just after dinner, when everyone was using toothpicks, sitting quietly in front of their doors. At night, the cries of nursing children and the snoring of the adults kept us from sleeping.

That was also the time when I would have two malaria attacks

every day, one at about ten in the morning and the other at about five
in the afternoon. My complexion looked waxy; I was very thin. We
didn't have quinine, and so I wasn't taking any medicine. My attacks
became part of the routine. I awaited them out of habit, resigned to the
inevitable: an insidious coldness set in along my spine, then took over
my entire body. I was frozen to the bone and would roll up in a ball, my
teeth chattering furiously. I would turn one way, then the other, changing position, not knowing how to roll myself up a little bit more. Then,
without warning, my mother would pour a large basin of cold water
over me. I would gasp for breath; the surprise would cut the attack
short. It was an unquestionable remedy, and everyone used it.

The coldness was followed by a fever. A blazing fire took hold in
my guts. I was nothing but burning flesh. My breath was fiery hot. I
would be delirious, babbling incoherently, my eyes rolled back. That
would last an hour, sometimes an hour and a half. And then it was over.
I could live happily until the next attack.

When she reached term, my mother prepared her things and went
alone to the midwife's house. This was a matter exclusively for women,
something in which men and children were not to be involved.

My stepfather awaited the birth in a state of extreme feverishness.
He was hoping for a boy; they told him it was a girl. He was beside
himself. He had more girls than he knew what to do with: three from
his first marriage, and now two more. Five useless mouths to feed! And
how would he do that in these difficult times? The web of the life of a
refugee was temporary. No one could say how long the war would last.
There was no work; everyone gradually ate away at the meager savings
they had brought along. In my family, we had already sold off the few
pieces of furniture we had. I tried to make myself useful, but my stepfather was always in a temper. He didn't need me to sweep the house,
cook, do the laundry. The only thing I could do for him was to stop
eating. But that I could not do.

My mother returned. Far from rejoicing at the return of his wife,
my stepfather became morose. He would spend hours puffing on one
cigarette after another, taciturn and scowling. His silence was broken
only by long sighs to make us aware of how tired he was of our presence. I would run over to the newborn at the slightest sign of crying
and take her outside.

My mother let herself be overtaken little by little by her husband's despondency. She was stricken with languor; she was wasting away. Quite naturally, I served as a mother to my sister who had just been born. At eleven, I got up early and worked as much as an adult. My first task was preparing the rice gruel for the infant and the morning tea for my parents. Then, with my sister attached to my back by a wide swath of cloth, I would leave to do my marketing. I scarcely had time to dawdle, for my stepfather had the habit of eating lunch right at noon. So, I had to get organized quickly: decide on the menu depending on the money they had given me, bargain hard for each food item in order to get the lowest price possible, cook, wash the dishes, and not forget the porridge for my sister four times a day, her diapers, etc. Don't think for a moment that I was mistreated. Eldest daughters in every family had to do the same tasks as I did. My singularity was a result of my *métissage.* People considered me with more pity, as if the French part I carried inside myself—that is, the part from the colonizers, from the masters— made it improper to put me on the same level as little Vietnamese girls. It was all about setting me apart in order to better reject me. As for me, I accomplished these tasks with pride, considering them as the sign of my social integration.

I worked from morning till night, getting a break only at the time of my malaria attacks. I lost a lot of weight. But I didn't feel bullied or unhappy. Wasn't my situation normal? My only hardship was washing my sister's diapers. The pond I had to use was a half-hour walk from the house. I would carry a large basket filled with diapers on my head, and the strong smell made me sick to my stomach. I would do the laundry crying, so upset that I would almost faint.

Once out of her torpor, my mother began to worry about my poor health. She bought for herself and me a bottle of Dubonnet, a French liqueur considered to be a powerful tonic that was given generally to women in childbirth and to convalescents. Every day, we would generously pour ourselves two glasses, one in the morning before eating, the other at bedtime. The intoxication made my eyes shiny and my cheeks rosy. My mother found that I looked well, and her belief in this remedy only grew. Unfortunately, Dubonnet was almost impossible to find in time of war, and above all, very expensive. So, we had to give up this treatment.

I have to say that, in an undernourished society, putting on weight was a collective obsession, the dream of the poor and the poorly fed. A woman was not beautiful unless she was a little plump. What was a skinny *métisse* worth?

During that time, my stepfather would brood over the profound disappointment caused by the birth of my sister. Of course, he took out his rancor on his family. Understanding that he was unhappy, my mother suffered his bullying as her rightful punishment. But he didn't need her resignation; what he needed was for her to give him a son. The only thing she could do was hang her head. What to do in the face of this cruel destiny except remain silent and wait for the heavens to take pity on you?

It was at that time that an unexpected distraction interrupted the course of my stepfather's somber thoughts: mah-jongg. It's a Chinese game played by few Vietnamese. The pharmacist, a man of Chinese origin, had always played it. Once when he needed a partner, he asked my stepfather to sit in. That was the beginning of our ruin. Settled in for a trial game, my stepfather didn't leave his seat for fifteen straight days. Meals were served by the lady of the house right on the gaming table, expensive meals for which she made the players pay dearly. They would eat while continuing the game. Each one would get up for rare and brief absences, when nature called. Two times a night, precious dishes of food were brought to them as fortification. Here as elsewhere, the privations of war affected only the poorest.

My stepfather had to sell our porcelain dishes as well as two ancient vases in order to pay his expenses. As if that weren't enough, he was hardly lucky or talented, and so, powerless, we saw our embroidered woven silk wall hangings, then the batiste tablecloths with eyelets, and finally the copper pots fly out of the house. My stepfather continued to lose until we had nothing left to sell. My mother tightened up the silk belt around her waist even more fiercely, the belt with the gold leaves sleeping inside. She congratulated herself for keeping it all hidden from her husband. For her, that was the striking proof that a woman could count only on herself.

Then came the moment when my stepfather was no longer able to keep his place at the table. He was asked to yield his spot to another player. He felt humiliated but accepted and bowed out. However, he still had debts to take care of and didn't have a cent left. He was desperate, for it involved his honor. One characteristic of the Chinese diaspora was the complete respect for one's word. Dealings that put considerable sums in play were made without official documents, with only one's word as guarantee.

My stepfather was living like a zombie, obsessed by his debt. At night we could hear him pacing back and forth, sighing; during the day he remained prostrate like a man who had taken leave of his senses. My mother would explode at him in terrible scenes, crying and bemoaning the misery he had plunged the family into. But he would remain silent as if her cries didn't affect him.

Beside herself with anger, she shrieked, "You are so egotistical that you would sell your own children to settle your gambling debts!"

Usually, my mother was very calm and only rarely had I heard her raise her voice to her husband. Her audacity scared us. But you can only imagine my surprise when, instead of beating her as any self-respecting man would have done, he considered her with a strangely interested air. In reality, without wanting to, she had just saved his face. I was going on twelve. I wasn't stupid; I knew how to cook and to keep house. He accomplished her prophecy; he sold me.

My mother tied up my bundle of clothes and took me to my new masters, a young couple whose house was located a few steps away. I wasn't upset. On the contrary, I saw in this turn of events the beginning of a new adventure that would brighten up the monotony of my existence. As for my mother, she knew that with her hidden gold she could always buy me back when the time came. As a consequence, our goodbyes were lighthearted.

My mistress was about seventeen and her husband scarcely seemed older. Her father had decided to marry her to a man she didn't love. The story in and of itself was banal, even more so in that everything went back to normal with the passage of time. Daughters married off by force suffered enormously until the birth of the first child consoled them. Motherhood completely absorbed them, and they ended up accepting their fate. Once old, they applied the same rule to their children, thereby perpetuating tradition.

However, there were exceptions: young girls who didn't want to be ungrateful toward their parents or betray their love would throw themselves in a lake or hang themselves, thus ending their days. These beautiful feminine figures had made my mistress dream. She had wanted to marry the one she loved or die. But circumstances had saved her from the dilemma. With the great fire that devoured the town of Tuy Hoa, people had other things to do than to be caught up in the romantic life of a young girl. She had taken advantage of the crush of people and run off with her beloved.

They had chosen this village where no one knew them. Everyone suspected that they were just living together. In other times, they would have been subjected to widespread reprobation, but in this troubled period of war, everyone could close their eyes on this sort of bending of the social rules. Besides, they seemed rich, led an honorable life, and needed no one. Everyone left them in peace.

My work consisted of keeping the house clean and taking charge of the meals, exactly as I had done at my parents'. It was, however, less tiring because we were fewer. My mistress treated me with kindness, considering me a little like a younger sister. She would often keep me company in the kitchen while I prepared the meals, and it was in the course of these chats that I learned her story.

They owned a grocery store that she ran during the day, less as a going concern than as a pastime. In the evenings, when I had finished my work, they entrusted me to take care of the store before they joined each other in bed, separated from the place where I was by a thin partition of woven bamboo. I would overhear their whispering, their panting, then the soft moaning of my mistress. I felt the birth inside me of a kind of delightful agitation and at the same time a wave of warmth moved through my lower abdomen. I wanted to take her place, on the other side of the partition. I liked their love-making very much, their ardent whispering which I couldn't make out, the strange sound I had detected in their moaning which seemed to indicate a pain they wanted to feel with all their heart.

From then on, I observed them with increased interest. They paid thoughtful attention to each other, constantly concerned for the other. Sometimes they would look at each other for a long time, for no apparent reason, and it seemed to me that I would see something distressing in their eyes as if the mud at the bottom of a pond had been stirred up. I was passionately attentive to their slightest gestures. I had the feeling that they fulfilled each other's needs completely. If one was thirsty, the other would metamorphose into a spring to quench the thirst. They were not one person; no, they were two people, but their union created a fullness.

I lived in the happiness of my masters like a plant in the sun. When I visited my mother, she noticed, satisfied, that I had grown taller and put on weight, and so had taken on the appearance of a veritable young woman. But that observation in itself made her anxious. She tried at length to find out if my master had not been too kind toward me or if he had shown an interest in me that was too sustained. I swore to her that his behavior was irreproachable.

"And besides," I cried out, "he is very much in love with his wife!"

My mother was scandalized by the use of an expression as improper as "in love." She advised me to watch my language before adding, "Now that you have become a pretty girl, don't be gullible. Beware the lust of men."

As for the "lust of men," I already had a bit of experience. It was not unusual when I was alone in the shop at night for men to come in furtively on the pretext of buying a box of matches or some other trinket in order to pinch my nascent breasts. Each time I remained stunned for a long time by the pain. I hated them with all my might. To see them in the streets with their heads held high, who would believe that they had just cornered me in the shadows of the shop? I hated the greedy looks they cast on me, their sly smiles. Even more, I hated their hypocrisy, their respectable air, the lofty moral speeches they made in public. But I would brood over my hate in silence. I knew that, even if caught red-handed, if they could turn things around in accusing me, it would be they whom people believed.

It became more and more difficult for me to take care of the shop in the evening. Seeing my reticence, my mistress wanted to know the reason. But I lied, saying I was afraid of ghosts. After all, I wasn't yet twelve. She consented to keep me company some evenings and allowed my mother to help me the others. So, imagine my delight at seeing vexation set fire to the eyes of the men who would discover that I wasn't alone.

I really liked these nocturnal conversations alone with my mother. Since I had begun working as a servant in another household, her attitude toward me had changed a little: we chatted more willingly to-

gether. She dreaded the fact that the customers in the evening were almost all men. Had they sometimes bothered me? I answered no.

"My daughter," she said, "you should fear those men much more
than your ghosts!"

For while there was only one kind of man for my mother, there
were two in my view: those who were in the image of my master and
those who resembled those repulsive gentlemen who chased me into
the back of the shop. But it was impossible for me to explain this to her
without having to reveal, at the same time, the bad experiences I had
hidden from her.

I lived happily until the day when an unexpected tragedy occurred
that shattered my masters' happiness. The young woman was bitten by
a dog and contracted rabies. There was no serum, no vaccine. She died
after several days of suffering. Her lover sent me back to my parents
and left for who knows where. Their tragedy deeply affected me; I no
longer believed in a happiness that was lasting. I discovered the other
face of love, the one of precariousness and suffering.

❦ 7 ❦

The Viet Minh and the Colonists

Once back home, I was struck first of all by the decline in my parents' circumstances. I found my sisters really thin. At bottom, it had been a stroke of good luck for me to be sold; I had been the best fed. In other refugee families the situation was the same. People had exhausted what they had set aside. Many intended to leave, and even more so because the French had reached Tuy Hoa, about thirty kilometers from our village.

The situation was worrisome. Thus, there had been an appeal for the active participation of the population in the anticolonial struggle. To that end, a kind of dress rehearsal of the resistance had been organized once a month in case the French advanced their offensive lines as far as where we were. We had to stock up on food and water in advance, because for three days all the village's civil activity would cease. Only combat units would be moving in the streets.

The adults had been divided into two camps: the colonists' camp and the side of the Vietnamese resistors. The ones who played the role of the French had to take on their interests and psychological outlook in order to act, in this simulated warfare, like they would have acted in reality. As for us, the children, we had the privilege of all being on the side of the Viet Minh. Our mission consisted of keeping our eyes and ears open, of nosing around everywhere, and of bringing back the most information possible about the enemy. Some members of the group suggested that, given my *métissage*, I should be on the side of the French. But I didn't want to be on the side of the enemy. I started crying. Moved, the one responsible promised to keep me on the condition that I show that my patriotism was even more impassioned than that of the others. It was up to me to dispel the distrust the others had of me; that was normal when all was said and done. I promised to do my best. I was in a hurry to prove myself. I had no idea how difficult the game would be.

It was an imaginary confrontation, and at the same time you had to be in the moment as if it were real. So, I was disguised as a little fruit seller in front of the French soldiers' barracks when a nurse recognized me and accused me of being a member of the Viet Minh. I denied it. An officer nicely took my hand and promised to buy my whole basket of fruit if I told him where the others were hiding. I shook my head. He slapped me hard. It hurt me a lot, but I held my ground. He changed tactics. The nurse brought a large bowl of white liquid that she ordered me to drink immediately. I complied. The liquid was salty to the point of bitterness. I couldn't manage to swallow it, choked, and threw up. I had always had trouble swallowing something, even something as small as an aspirin tablet. They poured the contents forcibly down my throat. I choked and thought I was going to die. They gave me a moment's rest, then began again. I couldn't take it any longer. After all, it was only pretend, a game. There were no French people around. The nurse was our neighbor, and the officer a man I'd passed a hundred times in the street. They knew who I was. They, too, knew we were playacting. I told them where our hiding place was. They released me.

The punishment that awaited me was terrible. I hadn't understood. It wasn't a game; it was a very serious rehearsal for possible combat. I was stung by the shame of facing the scorn of all the others. They all had the right to hit me as they wanted. Then they brought me two bowls of the same liquid and made me drink it. Crying all the while, I begged them to grant me the favor of letting me drink it at my own speed. I don't remember how much time it took to finish the bowls. One thing is certain, however; I drank them. So, what I wasn't able to do out of courage, I had to do out of repentance. They concluded that they shouldn't trust me from then on.

The situation didn't get any better; my stepfather attempted to get us out of the village. We had fled the war in Tonkin to end up here; there was no question of returning there even if, logically, our only possible retreat in the face of the advance of the French consisted of moving back to the north. Thanks to the numerous relationships of his Chinese friends, he succeeded in getting his hands on a fisherman who was willing to take us to Nha Trang by sea along the coast. All that was left was discussing the cost of the trip. The fisherman demanded an exorbitant sum, which was understandable because the risks were serious for him, too. Who knows what would happen if we were intercepted by the Viet Minh? But my stepfather had nothing left at all. So, my mother took out the gold leaves from her belt, saving us yet again.

We spent the days prior to our departure in a kind of excitement that we tried to hide from the neighbors. We could take along only the bare minimum. My mother got rid of her useless or compromising mementos. Among other things, she threw an entire box of photographs, remembrances of her youth, into the fire. It was then that I saw a picture of me for the first time. It had been taken just before my admission to the orphanage. Thinking she was going to lose me forever, my mother had wanted to keep some proof of our kinship in case chance drew us back into each other's presence someday. Now that she had taken me back, she could burn it without regret.

It was an identity photo of a little girl with a round face and short hair with bangs. I couldn't believe that it was me. That image was of someone else, some stranger. She seemed so unusual, so different from the others! She had neither the same appearance nor the same expressions as those who were familiar to me. I examined her for a long time, with the feeling that her universe was not my own. I thought of myself as Vietnamese, and I saw myself, in every way, as intimately resembling my mother and my sisters. How could I be that one who seemed like she came from somewhere else? I was completely ignorant of what I looked like, for I had had few opportunities to see myself in a mirror. At home only my stepfather had a mirror, a rectangular one that he used only for shaving and put away right afterwards. My mother fixed her hair without being able to see herself. Only coquettish girls would gaze upon their reflections furtively in the deep, bottomless, silvered well of a mirror when they thought no one was looking.

Seeing the photograph upset me so much that my mother, out of worry, ran to get her husband's mirror which she handed to me. I looked in the mirror; my surprise was profound. I wasn't anything like I had imagined. I had to admit that I looked more like the photo than the idea I had of myself. That strange face, that questioning look of someone who didn't really know where she was . . . so, that was me. I became painfully aware of my otherness. But, as shocking as it was, that discovery at least had the advantage of curing me of my inner blindness. From then on, I knew that I was not like the others.

With the preparations done and our bags concealed, we awaited our departure. We had nothing left to do. One day stretched into another, long and boring. In order not to raise suspicion, my mother and her husband went about their business, without changing their routines. But in the house, out of sight, we remained still and silent, ready to respond to the first signal from the fisherman. For the hour of our departure depended both on omens and on meteorological conditions. A fortune teller had indicated two favorable dates for this trip of major importance. What remained was making these dates coincide with calm seas, something we had no control over. We had already had to let the first one go by because of bad weather. If the weather didn't change, we would have to postpone until the next month. With each passing day, the risk of exposure increased. Luckily, on the second date the sea was calm, and the weather was good.

Toward midnight, when no one else was around, we left the house, dragging our bags in the dark. In my arms I had my eight-month old sister whom my mother had put into a deep sleep with a little alcohol. We left Quan Cau like robbers, without saying goodbye to anyone.

A horse-drawn carriage was waiting for us and took us to the beach where we would board the boat. My parents were thinking about the reaction of the neighbors when they found out about our escape. How long would it take them to inform the local authorities? We were afraid, and getting on the boat took place in a panic. The boat was tiny, scarcely larger than a small craft. We were seated like a row of objects in a box, piled between suitcases and bundles of clothes, under orders not to move. Seasickness was torturing me. Leaning over the side, I found some relief.

In the paleness of dawn, the thin coastline of Nha Trang appeared; we were out of danger. My stepfather left us on the beach with our bags. In his pocket, he had the address of an old aunt with whom he hoped to put us up. The same old story was beginning once again. We were exhausted. Passersby looked at us with curiosity. To their questions my mother poured out the story of our trip, emphasizing the details likely to move her audience, giving the impression that we hadn't fled to live a better life, which was the truth, but out of opposition to the Viet Minh.

My stepfather returned three hours later, perched on a cart that was to take us to our new home. We left the center of town. Little by little, the pavement gave way to a dirt road lined with coconut trees. In the distance, a river flowed. I have always liked that unique moment of encountering a landscape for the first time.

The horses stopped in front of a vast estate. We had trouble believing that this would be our residence from then on. The old lady offered us the whole house, keeping only a small bedroom overlooking the garden for herself. I explored the numerous rooms of the house, my sister at my heels, impressed by the luxuriousness of the premises. We admired the ebony chests of drawers inlaid with mother-of-pearl, the openwork sandalwood screens, the Chinese vases, the ivory figurines ... The idea that we were going to live in the midst of these marvels filled me with enthusiasm. But my mother decreed that we use only the ground floor, the part of the house that was the emptiest and the least beautiful. We hung up a hammock. It was there that I was going to sleep each night with my sister Oanh, the last-born. Long months of malnutrition had damaged my mother's health. I was thus responsible for my little sister whom I watched over jealously, carrying her on my hips all day long, both at work and at play. In the evening, lying down in the hammock, I would put her on my chest like an egg that I would protect until morning.

Once the time for settling in had passed, my stepfather left to look for work in the center of town, about ten kilometers from the place we were living. As we no longer had any means of support, he had to walk the distance, taking along with him each day the container his wife had prepared for him. Each evening he came back, worn out and empty-handed.

Our meals were reduced to a bowl of rice that we ate with a brownish sauce prepared by my mother. The situation became critical the day when my stepfather brought home Tu, his only son who had been sent to him from Tuy Hoa. Now there were six of us to fight over the same amount of food. The family atmosphere soured. Meals became battlegrounds where each one accused the other of cheating, and where my mother was reproached for having favored one at the expense of another.

Up against the wall, my stepfather went to Saigon in the hope of getting back his job at the Bastos Cigarette Company. We stayed behind in Nha Trang without money, without support, and without any certainty as to when we might be able to join him. Tu, my elder, and I attempted to come to the aid of the family. We began by going to the forest to gather wood, which we made into bundles that we could sell to the neighbors. But these expeditions, very tiring given our young ages, didn't bring in much. So, we decided to pick wild fruit and vegetables that we would sell in the marketplace. We had to leave very early, well before dawn, if we wanted to be back in time for the opening of the market. These predawn forays into nature forged a new friendship between us. We were surprised by the feeling of being so close to each other. We remarked on how similar our destinies were. We were both orphans and were outside the group formed by his father, my mother, and their children.

This modest work permitted us to ensure that the family had its daily ration of rice. We were leaving earlier and earlier and bringing back more things to sell. Subsequently, we were able to treat ourselves to a little fish, which we ate sparingly.

It was then that another opportunity for me to earn money came up. An old lady whom I had helped out by writing down a prayer for her insisted on paying me. Wherever she went, she told people that I had the most beautiful handwriting she had ever seen. She called on me often; she could read, but her rheumatism prevented her from writing any longer. And she always paid me. Inquiries came pouring in thanks to her, from illiterates for whom I would write administrative requests or sentimental letters to the family or to the beloved. My mother excused me from doing housework, taking on the cooking and housekeeping herself. She also agreed to let me keep part of what I earned for personal use.

I immediately bought an oval mirror that I kept in my pocket all the time. I wanted to know what other people experienced when they saw me. I had great difficulty because the mirror was very small and I couldn't manage to see my whole face at the same time. That didn't prevent me from being constantly surprised by my own facial features. I couldn't succeed in superimposing the image in the mirror on the subjective representation I had of myself. I would tirelessly repeat to myself, "It's me. It's me," without managing to believe it, for all I saw in the mirror was someone I didn't know. A stranger to myself . . . I was also a stranger in the eyes of others.

I still have a bitter memory of an afternoon of swimming. At thirteen, I was much taller than Vietnamese girls my own age. With my growing breasts, my body hair had also begun to appear. So, when we entered the water of the river naked, the girl next to me, seeing the shadow in my armpits and pubic area, alerted the others whose sex organs were as smooth as children's. They formed a circle around me, dancing, laughing and making fun of me as if I were suffering from a shameful disease. Later, alluding to this darkness, they nicknamed me "baguette d'ébène," or ebony chopstick. That nickname pursued me until the end of my stay there, leaving its wound, while the taunting giggles flew from all sides behind my back.

We still had no news from my stepfather. We were wondering if he had found work or some help. He had been gone for over five months, taking very little money. What would become of us if something bad had happened to him? Despite all the ingenuity Tu and I deployed, our lives could not continue this way.

Our worries increased when, one night, a man's voice pulled us out of our sleep. A Viet Minh soldier issued his message, made all the more solemn by the nocturnal silence.

"Don't be afraid, compatriots! We are here for your liberation. Let's throw off the yoke of colonialism together!"

I stopped rocking the hammock.

"Did you hear that?" I whispered to my mother.

"Yes," she answered in a muffled voice. "Don't move. And above all, don't light the lamp."

Outside, the voice continued its exhortations. I went over to the window; the street was deserted, and all the houses seemed to be in a deep sleep. In the moonlight, you could clearly see the outline of a man, holding up a megaphone to his mouth. I wondered if the empty windows I saw were hiding shadows behind them, immobile, watching. I turned to my mother.

"What should we do?"

"Nothing. We are staying here unless others come out."

No one came out that night. I went back to my hammock, but we had a difficult time falling back to sleep. Should we go out? Should we stay inside? In the first case, we would run the risk of incurring the sanctions of the colonial administration. In the second we would inevitably attract the displeasure of the Viet Minh. We were caught between the devil and the deep blue sea.

The next night the same voice was raised in the silence:

"Compatriots! The days of colonialism are numbered. Join us before it's too late."

This time it was my mother who went to the window.

"If what he says is true, it's time to go outside," she murmured.

I joined her. In front of us, the doors of some houses were half-open. On the thresholds people were waiting expectantly.

"Don't hesitate, compatriots!" the voice continued. "The path of liberty is in front of you!"

A few moved forward timidly toward the marketplace; soon they were followed by others. We got ready to go outside as well.

"Hurry up," my mother urged. "Don't get us noticed by being the last ones."

When we arrived, there were already a lot of people. Some torches as well as a red flag adorned with a yellow star had been stuck into hollow bricks. People continued to pour in. Soon everyone we knew was there. The first to arrive were smiling, content to see that they weren't the only ones to take this risk.

From that moment, a strange kind of double life began for everyone. During the day we went about our business without the slightest allusion to what was happening at night. There was a kind of collective amnesia. But warned who knows how, French patrols began traveling around the outskirts of town, asking everyone what they knew. People shook their heads; no, they hadn't seen anything; they didn't know anything.

Soon a curfew was imposed, putting an end to our nocturnal harvests. Deprived of our principal means of subsistence, we didn't know what to do. My mother thought that it was her turn to go look for work.

The Oceanographic Institute of Nha Trang was looking for a cook. My mother was never a cordon bleu chef but necessity called. She treated herself to a horse-drawn carriage that took her to the Institute and applied for the job which, as modest as it was, was completely beyond her abilities. I don't know what they could have said to each other that day, the director who didn't speak Vietnamese and my mother who knew nothing about the French language. But he chose her over a few others. My mother couldn't hide her pleasure in announcing her victory. It had been a long time since I had seen her looking so lively, with a gleam in her eye. Up to now I had only seen her sad and re- signed. Tu refused to go with us. He preferred to stay with his grand- mother. Our separation caused me intense sorrow but it didn't last; I liked change and was already completely oriented toward the new life that awaited us.

My mother wondered how long it would be before her boss discov- ered her culinary incompetence. She thought he wouldn't keep her. But what did it matter as long as it ensured our survival until my stepfather came to take us away with him!

From the moment of our arrival the beauty of the landscape took our breath away. The director's house sat on a promontory, a solitary sentinel overlooking the ocean whose waters were as green as the pur- est jade. From the outbuildings where we were staying, bunches of viv- idly colored flowers ran along the cliff right down to the fine sand of the beach. We were filled with wonder.

The two rooms at our disposal were large, very light, with win- dows giving onto the open sea. In our eyes it was a dream house. But it was not furnished, and we had nothing. My mother laid out the only blanket we had on the floor, and we all lay down on it, packed together like a litter of puppies. Often she would move off the blanket to give us more room. For my part, I considered that period as the sweetest of my life; I worked little, we were well fed, and I was free of my stepfather's presence. My mother seemed happier herself, more cheerful, as if she had found a second youth for herself. All four of us were happy to be living together.

My mother did her job with zeal. She thought that it would be enough to add a lot of butter and potatoes to a Vietnamese dish to transform it into French food. She felt she had freer rein because her boss wasn't demanding. And what's more, he would allow her to keep her children with her while she served him at the table.

The dining room was immense, and the director, sitting at the other end of the room, looked like a giant. We sat quietly on the floor

against the wall facing him while my mother served, extremely intimidated. The man would usually cast an amused look her way before lift-
ing the lid that revealed the plat du jour. My mother would look down
at the floor and would only raise her head after he had tasted it and
given his approval. Sometimes, as if out of spite, he would look her directly in the eyes. I was still too young to realize that my mother was
beautiful and that she wasn't yet thirty-seven. What inner turmoil
might have troubled her soul in the face of that man's gaze? Did he recall past memories? In reality there was nothing between them except
that hint of emotion, vague and floating.

At other times he would signal me to come over and would examine me for a long time, saying things that I guessed were nice. I slowly
let myself be won over. He wanted to introduce me to the French language and, with this goal in mind, made me move around the large
room, touching and naming everyday things . . . *la soucoupe, la cuillère, le
couvercle,* saucer, spoon, lid . . . I moved about, going through the words
to the rapture of my mother and sisters. My teacher seemed satisfied
with my progress. One day, as I had picked things up better than usual,
he burst out laughing, then took my face in his hands with a gesture so
affectionate that I ran away, frightened. I wasn't used to people showing me so much affection, even less so in such a direct manner.

My lessons continued from dinnertime to dinnertime. We were
an unusual group: on the one hand, the Vietnamese women, my
mother and sisters, and on the other, the director, a flamboyant giant
with a milky complexion, translucent eyes like a piece of hard sugar
candy, a large mouth, a thunderous laugh. And me in the empty space
between the two, a little bee landing on one thing, then on another,
chanting my litany of nouns. But at the time, our little scene seemed
completely natural. This was our daily celebration, the magic ritual
that, for a moment, abolished our differences and permitted us to
draw our laughter from the same clear spring. It was only later in the
evening, when we were back in the two rooms reserved for the domestic help, that my mother expressed her amazement at the director's
unbelievable familiarity.

For the first time she complained about the austerity of her life,
about the coldness of her husband, and especially about the hostility he
harbored toward me. She tried to imagine what her destiny and mine

might have been if she had remade her life with a French man as kind as the director.

"You would have gone to school; you would have even had a servant. You would have pursued scholarly studies; you would have become a professor, maybe even a doctor. And seeing you happy, I myself would have found peace."

And so she dreamed, her face tilted upward, her arms around her knees. I listened to her, enchanted to hear her tell the story of my life, the one that wouldn't happen. For me it was a fairy tale. That I might be the heroine of such a tale satisfied me completely; but I could not create any link between that imaginary story and my real life.

The same was not true for my mother. Her reveries had allowed her buried hopes to spring to the surface. The idea kept running through her head that I needed an education. She talked about it at every opportunity, repeating without letting up that it was my only chance. It became a fixation. So, neglecting her work, she ran out to get information from the schools to which she might entrust me. I replaced her at the stove.

The results were catastrophic. My mother was far from being a good cook, but at least she had a touch and some experience. My inexperience threw me into a panic. I begged her to give up her plan. What would we do if the master booted us out? In any case we were too poor for her to be able to buy the notebooks and books that every schoolgirl needed. My mother paid no attention to my arguments. She threw herself into her investigations with a kind of frenzy. Sometimes it would even happen that she would be absent at mealtimes, so I would serve in her place. I knew enough French to be able to carry out the master's simple orders, but finding myself alone with that man intimidated me beyond all words. I was in agony.

I held it against my mother for having put me in this embarrassing situation. I had no idea how wonderful the crazy dream she had hatched for me was. She ended up talking about it to her boss, explaining in a pitiful pidgin the necessity of placing me in a school. After all, I was also of his race, wasn't I? All the Annamites considered me as such, in any case. Would he want this bit of intelligence from his people to disappear in the darkness of ignorance?

He listened to her without understanding very well, surprised at her volubility. My mother continued her halting speech. She was now expressing herself in Vietnamese. He didn't understand anything at all anymore. She talked about how worried she was about my destiny. She wanted to arm me against adversity and, in her eyes, that arm was education. She begged him to help her. She had run out of arguments. She sobbed and then we cried afterwards. Without a word, the director got up and left.

In the days afterwards our pleasant evenings ceased. We no longer had the right to enter the dining room where my mother was serving him all alone now. He had reinstated, between himself and his servants, the natural distance he should never have reduced. We conceived a regret about it but not a grudge, because for us, too, this distance was part of the order of things. I thus broke off my French lessons. Evidently, he did not consider me part of his race, and he had no interest in saving the "bit of intelligence from his people" within me, as my mother had wished. I wasn't hurt by it, for what I had always wished for was to belong to the Vietnamese people. I quickly forgot the few words I had learned, and my mother again took up her role as cook. She was very disappointed, but she promised me that one day, I, too, would be sitting on a bench at school.

We finally received news from my stepfather. After lengthy steps, he had been able to get back his old job as foreman at the Bastos Company. It was now time for us to rejoin him. We bid a moving farewell to the director. He had doubtless forgiven my mother for her unworthy behavior, for he slipped a fifty-piaster bill into her hand, a sum that was the equivalent of double her monthly salary.

With regret, we left behind that place and the pleasant life we had led there. I walked along the coast, melancholic, my bare feet wet with bubbles of white foam. I knew that I would never walk this length of sand again. I dreamed of all the places I'd lived and left behind, of all the people I'd known and who were now only memories. I was saddened by the thought that one day I would forget their faces, their voices. My life was like a blind rush forward, but to where?

~∞ 8 ∞~

Aunt Odile

Once again, we packed up our things for a long trip. That was the third time I had taken the train along the coast of South Viet Nam. Everything blended together in my memory: the jammed cars for poor Annamites where not once did we have a chance to sit down on the wooden benches, the arrival on the platform where, lost among the baggage, we wondered where we would spend the night.

My stepfather welcomed us without joy. He had not found a single good soul whose generosity went so far as to want to put up a family of five. We spent the first night together in the waiting room, sleeping as best as we could right on the floor, our heads propped up on our bundles. My stepfather went to work early, leaving my mother with a little money and the job of finding us a roof over our heads. She had only one address filed away in her memory, and even then, she wasn't sure that it would still be good after so many years. It was for one of Ba Pho's "boarders," the sweet young girl whose presence had brightened my days back when I was living under the tyranny of my cousin Monsieur Yves.

In order to have more freedom to get around, she left us in the waiting room with a few provisions, asked me to take good care of my sisters, and swore to me that she would be back before evening. Her leaving hollowed out a kind of huge emptiness inside me. I felt lost. What would become of us if she abandoned us? I thought once again about the stories that were told about families who, incapable of feeding their children, were forced, with broken hearts, to abandon them. In almost every case, the mothers did as mine had, promising to return. But however long the children waited, however much they cried to exhaustion, no one would come. Most often they would swell the ranks of the beggars or the kids who shined shoes. I recalled this prospect with terror, although I was surprised to note that there were never any girls in the groups of beggars or among the shoeshine boys. So, where did they go? And what were they doing? I would have sobbed in distress had I not had my sisters in my care.

My mother came back in the afternoon. Upon seeing her, my tears flowed irrepressibly. She was surprised by my sorrow right at the moment when she had finally found us a home. But I didn't know what to say and followed her, still choking on my suppressed sobs. We took a rickshaw, and all four of us piled in with our bundles stacked up on the running board.

The man who pulled the rickshaw was puny and had trouble dragging such a heavy load. Between the narrow slit formed by my sister's head and one of my mother's arms, I watched his thin back cave in under the strain. We brushed by backfiring motorbikes, impatient bicyclists, automobiles spewing out streams of black smoke. And so, distracted by the spectacle in the street, we arrived at our destination without realizing how long the ride had been.

Before us, a dead end. Two rivulets of dirty water outlined the narrowness of the street. In the middle, a few children played.

"It's the third house on the right," indicated my mother, her finger pointing.

The third house on the right had a façade about five feet wide and a second floor. After having passed through a narrow door, we crossed the ground floor, occupied by an old Chinese couple. My mother's friend, the young girl I had idealized in my childhood, lived up on the second floor. Climbing the stairs, I had an exact vision of a young woman with long hair, framed by the door like a marvelous painting from long ago, in Hanoi. I had the feeling of moving backward, toward my past.

A woman welcomed us with a great many smiles and exclamations of joy. She stared at me intensely before saying in a low voice, "Do you remember me?"

I lowered my eyes. I didn't remember her. In my mind I had the touching image of a beautiful young girl and not this woman already in ruins, whose forced laugh was somewhat unpleasant. I was disappointed. My disillusion grew when I saw the cramped room where we were going to live. The great city of Saigon, rich with shops and gardens and full of activities, the city I had seen from the rickshaw, seemed to me as promising something else besides this sordid place.

I stayed in a corner, looking sullen, while the young woman recounted the events of her turbulent life. She wanted to see in my mother the sister she hadn't had and required that we call her Aunt Tha.

The man she lived with, whom my mother was waiting for impatiently, returned home late in the evening. He was a man the likes of whom we hadn't yet known. He was dressed meticulously. Up to then I had seen only men who were properly or respectfully dressed. Their clothes served the purpose of indicating their fortune or their rank in society and never suggested their bodies underneath. This one was dressed as one might undress, in order to show what was hidden. He had a kind of rough beauty and the assurance of someone used to being appealing.

He greeted my mother, came over to me in an unaffected way, took my hand, which he held too long in his own, and exclaimed in a natural tone, "Well, now, you're a very pretty girl."

I was thirteen, so I was surely a girl. This man reminded me of that, less by his words than by the disturbing warmth that passed from his hand to mine. I blushed and cast an embarrassed look at my mother and Aunt Tha, but the two of them, absorbed in their conversation, didn't seem to notice anything.

At that moment my stepfather appeared, and the conversation among the adults broke the spell under which he held me. I was relieved. I thought that being a girl was not an enviable situation to be in.

After that, his eyes and his entire attitude didn't stop telling me how much I might please him. Often, seeing me alone, he would take advantage of that to come up behind my back and immobilize me with his two hands. I would feel his warm mouth against my ear, murmuring about his taste for *métisses* like me, "so much more desirable than Vietnamese women." The fact that I was *métisse* added some spice to the attraction he had for me. It was like a disability I was suffering from and which awakened in him some sort of perverse inclination. I would feel a murderous rage rise within me; but I would just stay there, incapable of uttering the slightest sound.

This situation continued until the day when my mother ended up seeing her Eurasian cousin again, Aunt Odile, one of Ba Tu's four daughters, the one who had tried desperately to make me into a French girl. Her name brought to mind the painful meals of the past, meals during which I had had to sit up straight with my mouth closed, chewing elegantly and discreetly.

She was married to a Eurasian and had two children. Put up in a "holding camp," they were awaiting their repatriation to France. When my mother had revealed to her the motive for her request, they both agreed that they could not leave me in ignorance like other Annamite children. It would be unworthy of the French blood circulating within me. As a consequence, Aunt Odile agreed to take care of me for a while in order to introduce me to a lifestyle more in line with my nature. But my mother, whose goal it was to send me to school, consented to leave me at my aunt's only on the condition that she give me an education. Giving in finally to her pleas, Aunt Odile promised that she would do everything possible to get me enrolled at the excellent institution of the Sisters of Innocence. My mother left this conversation completely satisfied.

Without delay she made me a dress of blue material with pink stripes that I can still see clearly. The tightness of the skirt hindered my every movement; I didn't know how to move or how to sit down, for the skirt would then ride up toward my thighs, making me feel as if I were stripping in front of everyone. Stiff and awkward, I walked forward toward the mirror; the image I saw filled me with shame. Astonished, I looked at my skinny, bare legs. I began to scream that I would prefer a thousand times over to remain Annamite and ignorant than to show myself in public in such a ridiculous get-up. Didn't my mother see that I was a disgrace to her dressed like that?

But my mother remained calm, faced with the intensity of my distress. She explained to me in a sweet voice that it was only a question of habit, that French women were all dressed like that, which didn't prevent them from thinking they were much more beautiful than we were. Her line of reasoning didn't succeed in convincing me; I knew perfectly well that I didn't look like a beautiful French woman. The memory of my reflection in the mirror still stung. I didn't dare go out any more, spending my days hidden up on the second floor.

Aunt Tha's live-in husband lost interest in me from that moment on. I didn't understand his turnaround and was deeply wounded by it. It was only later, with some experience, that I understood the subtle, emotional ambiguity that Vietnamese men had for me. They liked me as a "yellow" *métisse* and not as a "white" *métisse*. To sharpen their interest, I had to be Vietnamese first, with a certain French je-ne-sais-quoi, a certain something that made me exotic in their eyes. I was no longer attractive when I took on the appearance of a white woman.

I was awaiting my departure with apprehension and sadness. I didn't want to leave my mother. Since getting out of the orphanage, I had become accustomed to the sweetness of having a family. Taking up my bundle to go live with strangers tore me apart. I knew nothing about the behavior of the French, and what's more, I had become a *nhà-quê*[1] during all those years and wanted to stay one.

That morning, I woke up in tears. I put on my dress mechanically. My mother kept repeating that she was doing this for my own good, but I couldn't prevent myself from suffering. It seemed impossible to me that I had to leave my own family; I cried continuously until the moment of final goodbyes. I clung to my sisters as if they could change the course of events.

We set out. With clenched teeth, I listened to my mother describe the radiant future promised by my stay at Aunt Odile's.

"And so, who knows what destiny holds for you? Maybe a French man will notice you? He might even marry you."

In her ignorance, my mother didn't know that French men don't usually marry little girls of thirteen. In silence, I licked the salty tears that ran along my lips.

"In any case, you will go to school. I beg of you, don't cry, don't break my heart. I'm doing all this so that you can avoid having the same life as me."

But I was walled up in my sorrow. I wasn't willing to understand my mother or see her pain.

We finally found my aunt's house. The idea of seeing her again after all these years piqued my curiosity. I wondered if she had changed, for I hadn't forgotten the disappointment caused by the reunion with Aunt Tha. To my great relief, Aunt Odile was as beautiful as before,

---

1. Vietnamese for *peasant*; often pejorative when used in French.

doubtless a little older and assuredly less arrogant. In the blink of an eye I saw her again in her white dress on the veranda in Hanoi, arms arched above her head, suffering from the heat and crying out with impatience when the maid who was fanning her wasn't doing it fast enough. But the gentle smile she gave me instantly erased that former image.

The two women spoke of the past in emotional voices while drinking tea in little sips. Aunt Odile offered me a glass of lemon soda. I held the glass against my cheek with my eyes closed so that I could hear the murmur of the fizzy bubbles bursting with a fine mist on my skin. I wanted to believe that this visit would be short. Soon, we would say goodbye, my mother and I, and we would return home together. I was relaxed, calm. I was no longer thinking of the dress I was wearing.

Suddenly, my mother let out a cry, surprised at seeing that the time had passed so quickly. The road back was long; she couldn't linger any longer. She begged Aunt Odile to be good to me, thanked her effusively, then, crying, left me. I was stunned. So, we had to part. I would have liked to ask her when we were going to see each other again, but, confronted by her haggard expression, I understood that her pain was even greater than my own. I promised to be well-behaved and to take advantage of the instruction I would be given. I followed her with my eyes until the moment when the panel of her *áo dài* had completely disappeared from my field of vision. Then I cried.

To console me, my aunt held out a candy that I refused to take, not without regret, for it would have delighted my sisters. This thought moved me so much that I cried even harder. Aunt Odile's husband entered at that moment. He was unpleasantly surprised to see my sad, flushed face. I was standing there stupidly without saying anything, shifting from one foot to the other, while Aunt Odile gave him a long spiel. I was extremely uncomfortable to be in the same room with them. My mother saw no French people regularly, and when we found ourselves in their presence, it was always because we were working for them as servants. She did indeed have some friends who lived with colonists, but they would receive their compatriots in the kitchen, in the absence of their men. Being in the same place as they for no reason seemed improper to me, just as it would have been improper to stay in the same room as one's master without a valid motive.

I was relieved when Aunt Odile sent me to the bedroom where her two daughters, aged four and six, were playing. The company of these children, simple and direct, put me at ease. I looked at their beautiful clothes and the toys they had in abundance, thinking of my sisters who had nothing.

I contemplated the beautiful dolls lying side by side in the minuscule white bed with a feeling of envy, despite the fact that I was beyond the age of playing with them. For a long time I harbored this unfulfilled childhood desire. During the 1960s, when I arrived in Paris to study for a doctorate in literature, my first act was to go to Galeries Lafayette to buy the most beautiful and most expensive doll in the store. I sent it immediately to my sisters, who had remained in Viet Nam. I felt the satisfaction of knowing that I had provided a great deal of happiness for them on that day.

I felt ill at ease in my aunt's home where everything was well organized. There was a time to eat, another to work, yet another to sleep. You had to abide by this extremely constraining timetable without fail. I had a lot of trouble keeping to such a rigorous schedule. I longed for the time when I had lived with my parents, free as a river following its course.

Since Aunt Odile had no servants, I helped her every day to make the beds, do the housework, and prepare the meals. It was only after lunch, at naptime, that she would devote a few hours to my education. I memorized conjugations by heart that I would recite every evening to her husband, whom I had been asked to call Uncle Albert.

I was as sad as a bird in a cage. Aware of not being in my own home, I didn't dare to come and go in the house as I wished. Sometimes I would stay seated for hours in the same chair. However often I repeated to myself that I had been granted a great opportunity, I couldn't help feeling unhappy. At the end of a few weeks, my aunt enrolled me at the Sisters of Innocence School, as she had promised my mother. I don't remember the class they put me in any more. On the other hand, what I do remember is that I was the oldest of the girls, all of whom were about the age of my youngest sister. I tried to stoop over when I was standing so that I would look as short as the others. I thought about my mother and sisters all the time. My only consolation was that they lived in the same city; so I hadn't lost them completely.

Little by little I made friends with the pupils who lived in the same "transitional residence." We got into the habit of meeting at the home of one of them, a pretty girl of English extraction. She had a knight in shining armor whose first name was Guy; he was distinguished, romantic, and as reserved as an Asian. In my eyes he was a dreamboat. I was completely captivated by his transparent green eyes whose limpid depths left me helpless as if confronted by an enigma. I had no hope of appealing to him, but I liked contemplating him for my own pleasure. I was there each day, timid and silent, devoured by passion for this mysterious boy who hadn't noticed once that I even existed. Sometimes when no one was paying attention to me, I would steal a furtive glance at him, like the wing of a swallow grazing the surface of the water. Then I would experience indescribable turmoil. I would go on like that, plagued by romantic tumults, without anyone realizing it.

Finally, my aunt received orders to leave for France. She had waited so long for them that she ended up not believing that it would ever happen. So now, instead of being thrilled about it, she felt like she was in a huge predicament. She could see only the negative side of all of it: the forms to fill out, the trunks to pack, all of it a greatly complicated thing to organize. She was absolutely counting on me. I left school to devote myself to doing laundry and tidying up. When everything was ready, my aunt sent me back to my mother's, enriched with a bundle stuffed with summer clothes she would no longer need, for in France, it was already winter.

❧ 9 ❧

A Sweetheart

My family had moved during my absence. They now lived in a modest place in the suburbs of Saigon. There was no running water or electricity. Twice a day, I would go get water from the communal faucet at the end of the narrow street.

My stepfather was out of work, money was scarce, and we ate just enough not to go hungry. But I didn't stop growing despite this diet. I was becoming an adolescent, already catching the eye of the boys, while my heart hadn't yet left childhood behind. When I would go for a walk with my young sister on my hip, with her weight pulling on my white, short-sleeved blouse, thus accentuating the curve of my breasts, aimless boys would stare at me in an odd way and hound me with their jokes, which I didn't yet understand but suspected were indecent. I would quicken my pace as crude laughter accompanied my flight. If the narrow street was deserted, I panicked. Sometimes a boy who was bolder than the others would follow close behind me and bother me until a passerby came into view.

I was terrorized by these idle boys who were on the lookout every day for me to come by. Leaving the house became a real test; I seized upon every pretext to stay home. My mother took my reluctance as whimsy, but I was careful not to worry her with what was going on with me.

On the days when my stepfather stayed home, we were asked to clear out early. He didn't tolerate my sisters' chatter and my presence even less. As for my mother, she confined herself to the kitchen so as not to bother him. We would find ourselves in the street; the neighborhood was poor and sad. Two rivulets of dirty water ran along the sides of the unpaved, narrow street. During the rainy season, we would slog through the mud, garbage, and excrement. The houses were made of whitewashed adobe and had corrugated metal roofs. Toward noon you roasted as if you were in an oven. Outside it would be a hundred and four degrees in the shade. We didn't begin to come to life again until the sun was on the wane. I don't know why, but I was more bothered by the heat than most people. Frequently, I would get nauseous, dizzy. These feelings of being ill would terrify my mother, who feared who knows what catastrophe, and that would entitle me to my daily lesson on the bestiality of men and on virginity, that precious flower that had to be preserved at all costs. Her lecture was peppered with allusions that were totally obscure to me, for I had no idea how a man was made nor indeed what constituted the intimate parts of my own body.

But, being prudent, she cast a net of tight surveillance over me; my sister Dzung was in charge of following me everywhere I went. From then on, the three of us went out together: the little one whom I carried and my sister Dzung, who took her mission seriously and carefully noted everything I did. While putting a damper on the usual coarseness of my admirers, her presence was noticed by the whole neighborhood. Seeing us, people said, "Hey, look! There's the *métisse* and her escort going to get water!" They would stare at me without restraint, with cold curiosity. I didn't understand why they didn't see that I was Vietnamese, like them. Sometimes tears would spring from my eyes before I had a chance to hold them back.

One day when I couldn't hide my distress any longer, looking around to see if anyone had noticed my weakness, my gaze met that of a young man who was leaning against his door and who was smiling at me. Upset, I continued on my way, unaware of the sympathetic message he had intended for me.

In the days following, the young man was still there, looking at me, offering the same smile. His presence in this poor neighborhood intrigued me, for he didn't seem to belong to our world. He was well dressed. In the beginning, I wouldn't look at him, and he wouldn't say anything to me. I knew he was there, and he knew that I knew, and that was it. I would go down that street as if by chance, while in reality I was going to a silently planned rendezvous. This little game lasted until the day when he proposed pointblank to take care of my young sister.

"Younger sister, *em*, you're going to deform your hip if you carry her continually like that," he said.

"Younger sister, *em*" and "older brother, *anh*" were affectionate and intimate appellations used by lovers to address each other. I wondered how I should take such a suggestion. Should I admit that he had addressed me in such a tender way? I looked at his face; he looked like an honest man. I opted to trust him and accepted.

From then on, I confided my sister to him in order to run around in the streets in the company of a friend I had just made, a girl who was a little older whom I found beautiful and who taught me a thing or two and especially helped me give a name to the emotions of my young, inexperienced heart. I would go back to his house after a few hours of escape, more timid than beforehand and more reserved, for I was more conscious that I was a woman and he, a man.

Gradually we got to know each other. I learned that he was studying medicine. His parents, owners of all the houses in the neighborhood and thus ours, too, had set aside this place so that he could better devote himself to his studies. I would stay longer and longer in his company. We would spend wonderful days, him working on his anatomy plates, me looking at movie magazines, and my little sister playing on the floor. He lamented that I had to take care of the dishes and cleaning and offered me a pair of transparent gloves he had lifted from the hospital in order that I not ruin "my pretty hands." I put them on awkwardly, trying to pick up rebellious objects that all escaped my grasp as if they had minds of their own. He laughed at my difficulties.

"You see that your hands are not made for cleaning!"

He wanted to do the work in my place.

"I will transform myself into a household spirit, and I'll accomplish all the tasks you're in charge of, like in fairytales."

It was a joke, but one that moved me deeply. Up to then no one had expressed such great interest in me; I was overcome with gratitude. I would have liked to kiss his hand, but the voice of my mother resounded in my head, advising me to beware of men. I was thus torn between my surge of affection and my fear.

One day when his gaze was deeply riveted to my own with more insistence than usual, I fled, frightened. I said to myself, "That's it. I've lost my virginity!" I thought I would soon become pregnant. The idea made me tremble from head to toe. What was I going to do if my mother threw me out of her house? I was scarcely fourteen and what's more, I was *métisse*. I would probably end up in the gutter. I cried all the tears I had in me, and I didn't dare go to his house anymore. When, finally, he wanted to know the cause of my unhappiness, I shook my head, sobbing. Faced with his obstinacy, I confessed that I had lost my virginity in surrendering to his gaze. He took some time before understanding the meaning of my words, then broke into irrepressible laughter. When he had calmed down, he explained to me that I was only a child.

"Be reassured, little sister, nothing happened!"

I was saved.

That was a happy period in my life. I had emerged from the obscure time of childhood when I could do nothing but put up with life, without understanding what was happening to me. I was discovering the advantages of being considered a pretty girl, the happiness of being appealing. I knew now that being *métisse* didn't entail only disadvantages. My affective universe had also broadened: I had a girlfriend and an admirer, and I was no longer dependent solely on my family environment. I viewed my family with more distance. My stepfather's hostility affected me less than before; I thought that I would never have the same life as my mother, and I was firmly resolved never to suffer from it again.

Tired of being unemployed, my stepfather wanted to try his chances elsewhere. We would have to return to Nha Trang where he had negotiated a job as a sales representative for the Bastos Cigarette Company. The salary they had offered him was laughable, but he had jumped at the opportunity, for he had ambitious deals in mind. My stepfather consulted no one in making this decision, not even my mother. When he announced the news to us, at lunch, no one said a word. We continued to eat in silence. At the end of a few moments, my mother said that she was happy to leave this miserable neighborhood. My sister Dzung, who was nine, declared that staying or leaving was all the same to her, but her father pointed out to her that he had not asked for her opinion and that a child who was well brought up should not interfere in adult conversations. As for me, I said nothing.

I had only one pressing thing to do: to run and tell my student admirer of our imminent departure. I was busying myself in the kitchen, waiting for the moment when I could slip out without attracting attention, while my mother was making a mental list of the things she wanted to take along. Then naptime began to weigh heavily, the heat was unbearable, and the neighborhood seemed momentarily dead. In the sole room of the house, my stepfather snored, open-mouthed. My mother was still deep in her calculations, and no one was paying attention to me. I went out without a sound.

He was surprised to see me; I had never come during afternoon naptime. I announced the terrible news; he listened without saying anything. For a few moments, he remained as if dumbfounded before saying in an almost inaudible voice, "So, we won't see each other again, *em.*"

His words, definitive, resonated within me in a strange way. I had not thought of our relationship in terms of its duration. Up to that day, neither the word "always" nor the word "never" had crossed my mind. I felt comfortable in his company, and that was enough for me; I wasn't going to go any further. I would have liked to say something serious or moving to him, but my mind was as empty as an eggshell whose contents had just been gobbled up. Silent, I contemplated the wall in front of me. I must have looked really stupid.

Suddenly, he had an idea.

"I want to keep a photo of you; do you have one?"

What a question! No, I didn't have one. That was a question a rich person would ask! With what means would I have gone to get myself photographed? And first of all, what for? Did he think that a proper girl would spend her time looking at herself in a photograph? But, without considering my reaction in the least, he took me to the photographer's.

A mature, pudgy-looking man with a brocaded shirt greeted us. He took me right away into a brightly lit room, sat me down on a chair, and then left me alone, awash in the middle of that light. Sitting like a little girl, legs hanging, I had the feeling of being ugly enough to be frightening. How shameful to go along with such an indecent plan. I wanted to run away, but the two men were smiling in an encouraging way.

"Look at me. Tip your face slightly forward and smile."

The voice of the photographer reached me as if through several layers of cotton padding. He had his head engulfed in the black cloth that extended from the camera. I could have cried right then and there; instead, I had to smile. My mouth twisted up comically. The photographer could not hide his disappointment. In a brusque tone, he advised me to think of something happy. I was dying of shame at the thought of being so ridiculous in front of the man who was courting me.

The photographer yelled, "Smile! Smile!"

I didn't smile. Exasperated, he squeezed the rubber bulb at the end of a black tube. There was a flash; it was done.

I returned home without looking at anyone and didn't go out again until a few days later when time had softened the bad memory of that session. My student admirer welcomed me with his usual kindness, as if he had never seen me looking so stupid. He held out the photograph to me.

"Look at yourself, little sister. You're not very happy, but you are very pretty!"

I looked away; even so, I was not going to look at myself in his presence!

"Take it!" he insisted, his hand still out.

I grabbed the photo, but I didn't look at it. I was torn between curiosity and the fear of finding myself ugly on that glossy piece of paper.

"Look," he added in an encouraging tone.

I looked and saw a big girl with thick, pouty lips. I grimaced.

"How foolish my little sister is!" he said, smiling. "Keep it; I am giving it to you."

But I refused this burdensome gift. What would I do with it? I wouldn't know where to hide it and my mother would discover it. I gave it back to him.

We were on the eve of departure. The suitcases were closed, and the bundles carefully tied. My mother went from one thing to another, checking this, fixing that, with a knitted brow, anxious not to forget anything. I witnessed these preparations as if they didn't concern me. I just didn't believe it.

I was shocked when my stepfather showed us the tickets he had bought. Reality set in: I was not going to see my friend ever again. The words he had spoken—"So, we won't see each other again, *em*"—came back to me. I began to take the measure of their meaning. Losing him was like becoming an orphan all over again. I didn't know if I loved him, but I had never asked myself the question. A well-brought-up girl was not to be concerned with these kinds of feelings: love and pleasure were fine for girls with bad reputations. One thing I was sure of was that I needed his presence to feel happy and especially his admiring gaze upon my person to persuade myself that I was worth something. During all the time I spent in Viet Nam, I didn't stop feeling torn between the desire to be loved and the desire to be respected, incompatible wishes in a society where it was good to marry the woman you didn't love and to love the one you would never marry under any circumstances.

My sorrow worsened by the hour. The impending goodbyes made the situation intolerable. I wanted to see him one last time; I was ready to throw myself into the river after that. Casting all prudence to the winds, I ran toward his place. We stared at each other. He understood immediately and took me in his arms. I forgot everything; the only thing there was for me at that moment was the sweetness of his voice, murmuring, "My little sister . . ."

My mother burst into the room, surprising us in that position. At first, her surprise left her speechless. Then she slapped me.

"Your father will kill you," she screamed.

I ran out.

She returned home without looking at me, without saying a word. I waited for the dreaded scene until evening, but to my surprise, she had said nothing to her husband. I realized that she would say nothing to him about it. So, she loved me, then. I wanted to thank her, but her impenetrable expression dissuaded me.

During the trip my mother avoided talking to me. As for me, I remained imprisoned in my sorrow and regrets.

❧ 10 ❧

The Birth Certificate

When I emerged from my inner loneliness, we were living in a rather large house in a neighborhood near the center of the city.

In the courtyard there was a well that was used for washing food and dishes as well as for personal ablutions. On moonless nights we would take advantage of the darkness to rush to the edge of the well completely naked, splashing ourselves with big buckets of water. I loved these nocturnal showers when the very fact of seeing nothing made us appreciate even more the marvelous sensation of cool water on our sweaty skin.

We had left Saigon, taking along only our bundles of clothes. We had to buy everything: dishes, pots, mats . . . My mother, wanting to enter a lucky period, acquired two beautiful copper pots, one for rice, the other for soup. My stepfather brought back flowered mats that he must have paid dearly for. The family atmosphere had never been so happy. Our house was pleasant and the street wide, bordered by shady tamarind trees. My mother wondered how she had been able to bear the miserable life we had led in Saigon.

As soon as we were settled, my stepfather made contact with his compatriots who were established in Nha Trang. During the trip, he had conceived of a project for a shop for storing tobacco. He wanted to be both the broker for the Bastos Company and its supplier of raw material.

But such a project required a capital sum of which he didn't have the first cent. He needed some partners. During the day he went door-to-door to the rich Chinese merchants' shops, showing them that his idea could be a source of profit for them all. He even found some friends who were ready to stake what they had in the enterprise. He launched into a series of business dinners and went into debt to meet the expenses.

Every day was a celebration. The quality of the food and alcohol was worthy of a mandarin's table. My mother had to hire a Chinese cook for a month; this was indispensable to reassure the future partners about my stepfather, making them believe that we were rich.

The guests would arrive at about eight in the evening. They showed all the signs of their well-established prosperity: they were fat, potbellied, and big-bottomed, with resounding and self-assured laughs. In their midst, my father looked like a dried herring. He looked so thin that it seemed incongruous. But he would laugh heartily like the others.

Glued to the crack in the door that separated the kitchen from where the feast was taking place, we would contemplate the gathering of men with curiosity. They had removed their masks of concerned coldness, which was their usual expression. They drank abundantly, falling backward on their chairs, their faces glistening with greasy sweat. They told each other jokes, breaking out in thunderous laughter. My stepfather had bloodshot eyes, fixed and narrowed like a snake's. His high cheeks were flushed like two red spheres, which gave him a vaguely feminine air. When he laughed, with his head thrown back, I could see the pink plastic of his dental plate shining. I found him very indecent. I hadn't ever looked at him so attentively and especially for so long. I had the feeling of seeing him for the first time. How had my mother been able to put up with such a person?

We would carry in the dishes of food when the alcohol had made the men fairly limp, cautiously putting down on the table all those good things that weren't meant for us. Even so, we hoped to glean a few leftovers. Delegated to the observation post, I would keep my sisters informed about the fate of each plate.

I wasn't going to school; nor were my sisters. This didn't bother my stepfather. A girl's place was in the kitchen. But, an obstinate woman despite the submissive air which she almost never seemed to drop, my mother dreamed of providing me with a profession. She had tried many times to enroll me in school and had failed as many times, always for the same reasons: my stepfather's refusal or yet again the lack of money.

Taking advantage of our definitive settling down in Nha Trang, she risked trying again. In an uncertain voice, with the utmost precaution, she informed her husband of the "wish" she had to send me to school. Her appeal was instantly displeasing. He looked off into the distance with a somber air, without answering. When he finally did speak, his voice was harsh. He explained that it was out of the question that "girls" go to school. He said "girls" in order to show his impartiality clearly, since his, that is to say my half-sisters, would undergo the same fate. On the other hand, he intended to take back his son who was living at his grandmother's in order to "prepare a decent future" for him.

The allusion to this son from his first marriage wounded my mother, who had not succeeded in giving birth to a male heir. Without noticing how upset she was, her husband got up, indicating with this gesture that the conversation was over.

Later on, my mother cried silently, sitting on the edge of the well.

"Why weren't you a boy?" she said with regret.

I had no idea how to answer. But in my heart I swore to become more educated than the son who was not hers.

Standing up to the will of her husband, she took me to the only school in town, holding my hand as if I were a little girl. It was the month of April, and the flame trees were in bloom; summer vacation was near. The secretary opened her eyes wide when she understood what we wanted.

"But we are almost at the end of the school year, Madame. Come back in September."

But my mother didn't move.

"I want to meet with the principal," she said, obstinate.

The secretary opened her mouth, then gave up.

"As you wish," she said with an exasperated sigh. "The principal is teaching a class right now. Wait for him over there."

She pointed to a bench against the wall. We sat down. From time to time we could hear the voice of the teacher, full of authority. A long hour went by. Eventually, a little man with a tan complexion and a round face like people in the South came into the room. We knew immediately that it was the principal.

My mother laid out the goal of her move. He listened to her politely but confirmed that it was not possible to enroll a new student two months from the end of the school year. So, she begged for his pity.

She made me ashamed. I hated the pitiable depiction of what was supposed to be our life, which she tried to make touching. I didn't dare look at the principal, certain of meeting his disdainful smile. But I was wrong. My mother had succeeded in moving him. He accepted to take me on a trial basis in the class of those who were to take the examination for the completion-of-study certificate.

Clandestinely, I began school. My mother had succeeded in unearthing an old schoolbag that I carefully hid under a pile of firewood, behind the house. In that way I could take it and leave my house without attracting my stepfather's attention.

Despite the considerable academic delay accumulated by years of wandering from north to south, I had no trouble following the lessons that were given to me, with the exception of arithmetic, which, with its problems about purchase and cost prices or fields to divide up, remained incomprehensible to me. On the other hand, my being older than my classmates and my life experience brought some maturity to my thinking that allowed me to excel in what were called literary subjects. My years in the orphanage also gave me advantages, for French, learned not long ago and which I thought I had forgotten, gradually came back to me.

As for my teacher, the idea of leading an intelligent child to success, someone who, without him, would have been cut off forever from knowledge, stimulated him highly. His excessive faith in my abilities pushed him to treat me with consideration that, although a bit awkward, gave me a better opinion of myself.

I filled up my brain in the way geese are force fed, gulping down notions of history and geography at breakneck speed, trying to fill in several years' gap in two months. The most difficult thing was to do this without my stepfather knowing.

Everything was going well when the first obstacle sprang up: putting together a file whose principal component was the birth certificate that I didn't possess. I had never had one. In truth, many lived without papers, like me. There were very old people who had never existed legally.

My teacher opened his mouth wide in amazement.

"You have no paper of any kind concerning this child?"

"Unfortunately, no," whispered my mother.

He raised his arms in a gesture of helplessness while his face expressed complete discouragement. He looked at us in turn, shaking his
head as if to say how ignorant he found us. I wanted to leave, but my
mother, whom I looked at for advice, avoided my gaze. I knew then that
she would not budge before a solution to the problem was found.

Suddenly the teacher opened a drawer, took out a sheet of paper,
and wrote, without stopping, something that seemed to satisfy him, for
he looked at us, smiling.

"I think I've found the solution. Here is a note from me that you
will give to the secretary at the city hall. I have explained to him here
that all your papers were destroyed with the arrival of the Communists
in 1945. So, it will be enough for the child's father to go to the city hall,
accompanied by two witnesses, to re-register the birth. But do this
quickly; there's no time to lose."

He held out the envelope, which my mother took respectfully with
both hands. We then backed out.

Outside, the sun's rays of fire beat down. We lingered for a few
seconds on the shaded steps of the entrance, taking in a bit of the coolness before confronting the furnace. With her head high, my mother
gauged the position of the sun, squinting, then began walking resolutely. I followed her. We didn't speak. In my mind the same words kept
coming back: "It will be enough for the child's father . . ." That meant
that we would need my stepfather to take these steps, and it would be
necessary, as a consequence, to admit to him that I was going to school
without his consent. How could he help us when we had fooled him? I
imagined that he would not deprive himself of taking advantage of this
to show his hatred of me more openly. There would be no other possibility for me than to return to the stove. Near me my mother continued
to walk in silence, her conical hat tipped toward the sun like a parasol.
Her face betrayed no anxiety. I begrudged her serenity, for I was sure
that she was aware, as was I, of what little hope we had. I was going to
tell her that when she stopped moving.

"Go on home alone. I need to go to the pagoda to find out what's
appropriate to do. If the signs are auspicious, I will tell the truth to
Papa tomorrow and implore him to come to your aid."

She had the habit of using the general term "Papa" with me, unable to bring herself either to say "my husband," which would have

sounded like she were excluding me, or "our stepfather" in order not to remind me of my situation as an abandoned child. "Papa" implied that it could mean my sisters' father as well as mine.

My mother returned from the pagoda, serene once again. Briefly, she announced to me her intention to tell everything to her husband after naptime. It was without doubt the best-chosen moment, for she hoped he would be in a conciliatory mood after some refreshing sleep.

"Above all, go away during the conversation," she recommended.

She showed her husband the letter that the director had given her. He was impressed by it. Taking advantage of this opening, she insisted on what he could get out of my education. Wouldn't it be worth it to have a secretary available at home without having to spend a single piaster? He looked at her, surprised but not insensitive to her argument. After some reticence for form's sake, he agreed.

It was to this victory, won by my mother, that I owed my rebirth under the name Lam Kim Thu, legitimate daughter of the Chinese man Lam Khe and of the Vietnamese woman Tran Thi My. The stamp glued next to the official seal, added to the signatures of the two witnesses, attested to the veracity of my identity.

Of course, the precious birth certificate, which my mother put under lock and key, didn't convince anyone. More than once, I caught the ironic smile of administrative personnel when they happened to compare my face with the document I would hand them. What did it matter? I was fifteen, and I had just attained legal status. After all, my stepfather had given me an inestimable gift. I still carry the name he gave me.

Afterwards, everything fell into place with stunning ease. I received my certificate of study. I signed up right after that for the entrance examination for sixth grade.[1] There were 300 of us candidates for sixty places; I had only a little hope, but my recent success encouraged me to be optimistic. In fact, I was accepted, without fanfare, it's true, for the sixtieth spot. Even so, it was a sign: I had just put my foot up on the step that would lead me toward a new destiny.

---

1. "Sixième" in the original text, the first year of secondary school in the French system and here in the Franco-Vietnamese system, would be the equivalent of sixth grade chronologically in the United States.

Passing two examinations in two months conferred genuine prestige upon me. That summer I was not lacking for girlfriends. I had chosen two among them, Dô and Ghi, more or less the same age as I, that is to say, older than the others, and experienced an exclusive friendship. In the shade of the flame trees, we would spend day after day inventing the elements of a language that would remain impenetrable to the others so that our conversations would stay secret. We were seen everywhere together. As we were studying the work by Alexandre Dumas, the others nicknamed us "The Three Musketeers." This masculine designation for our trio delighted us, for it flattered our adolescent taste for originality at any price. The others seemed to forget my difference, for good. Finally, I was like everyone else. I was eternally grateful to this city that was going to become my first connection point: Nha Trang.

On the map, Nha Trang is only a black dot on the edge of the coast of South Viet Nam. It is almost unknown abroad. If by chance someone mentions its name, it's often in relation to Da Nang, a city nearby that the American war in Viet Nam made famous. Back then, in the 1950s, Nha Trang had three attractions: the big commercial street that traversed the entire length of the city; the beach, which was lined by the superb villas belonging to the French during the colonial period; and the famous Beau Rivage Hotel. At that time the villas were abandoned, all their shutters closed, their owners having packed up at the moment of independence.[2] The hotel, however, was still receiving guests, Europeans coming from who knew where.

Usually the beach was the preferred place where my girlfriends and I would go every day as soon as we got out of school. At that hour, it was still deserted and belonged entirely to us. In the distance, toward the Beau Rivage Hotel, the outlines of bathers, as minuscule as ants, didn't bother us at all. Lying next to each other on the fine sand, we would listen to the fury of the waves, all the while dreaming of our lives. We wanted them to be uncommon, rich with events. We imagined them as being heroic like those of the Trung Sisters, who had liberated the country from the Chinese yoke and whose reign seduced us

---

2. This is a reference to Ho Chi Minh's declaration of independence in Hanoi in 1945.

by its very brevity.[3] Making a mark on the history of the time, then fading like a shooting star—that's what was intoxicating in our eyes. We deplored only one thing: our femininity, a major disadvantage to our great aspirations.

Poetry especially occupied our time. We had assigned ourselves the arduous task of reading the great masterpieces, such as the very popular *Kim Vân Kiều,*[4] *The Song of the Soldier's Wife,*[5] or *The Double Flowering of the Cherry Tree.*[6] These readings were followed by exercises during which we would practice imitating classical versification.

These activities, which I considered to be of the utmost importance, were the cause of my more and more frequent absences. My mother observed my outings with a worried eye, imagining I don't know what kind of guilty rendezvous. She submitted me to long interrogations, seeking to get out of me the name of "the boy who had turned my head." Suspicions so far removed from reality made me smile with derision. She got angry. No more going out.

Deprived of my friends, with nothing to do from then on, I was consumed with boredom. It was then that my mother consented to sign me up for a mixed chorus. The first meeting took place in a classroom. I rejoined my two friends, whom I hadn't seen in several weeks. We slipped onto the same bench to be able to chat as we pleased.

Our schedule would be simple: one hour of musical theory and two hours of singing per day. Given my situation, this was a real godsend. I would have the right to spend three hours a day outside of the family fold; in cheating a bit, I could even be absent the whole afternoon.

The music teacher, silent up until then, took a violin out of its case and proposed that we audition. He would play the melody of a song we knew, and we would come up and sing it one after another. The chat-

---

3. The Trung Sisters resisted the Chinese in 39 CE and are considered heroines in Viet Nam. Temples are dedicated to their memory, and streets named Hai Ba Trung are common throughout the country.

4. See, for example, Huỳnh Sanh Thông's translation, *The Tale of Kiều: A Bilingual Edition of Nguyễn Du's Truyện Kiều* (New Haven: Yale University Press, 1987), with the original Vietnamese and English on facing pages.

5. See Chapter 1, Note 7, p. 11.

6. *Nhị Độ Mai* in Vietnamese. The original text is available at www.vietlex.vn/ebook/NhiDoMai/index.htm.

ting ceased immediately. We were all paralyzed with stage fright. A young girl passed between the rows, holding out a hat full of small, folded pieces of paper: we were to draw the numbers that determined the order in which we would take our turn.

The first victim climbed unsteadily onto the rostrum. The teacher gave her the first chord, then attacked the piece. Incapable of making the slightest sound, the candidate turned pale, her lips twisted in a grimace. When the music began again, the sharp, thin sound she emitted made us laugh until we cried. As a result, the atmosphere became more relaxed.

Number two, a boy, jumped onto the rostrum with ease, as if encouraged by the failure of the one who had preceded him. Unfortunately, his voice was right in the midst of changing, so we heard him switch octaves suddenly, singing with the high-pitched voice of a little girl. Once again, the room burst out laughing. We weren't afraid at all anymore. Number three sang correctly, nothing more. It was the same for the ones who followed. The room listened almost with boredom.

When my turn came, I walked up to the stage with a firm step. I was quite relaxed. I attacked the song. There was complete silence, a surprise that disturbed me to the point that I lost the rhythm, slowing down with each measure like a traveler tired of continuing on his way. I was vividly aware of this but incapable of retaking control of the situation. I continued, like a spinning wheel, without taking the accompaniment into consideration. I must have been really bad. It was then that I heard the music once again. The violin slowed down, as if it were wanting to wait for me, then gradually sped up. I followed it. Applause burst out.

I was getting ready to return to my place when the teacher touched my shoulder with his bow. Worried, I turned around.

"That was very good," he said to me.

We looked at each other; he smiled sweetly. I blushed. I was embarrassed by this unexpected aside.

I was placed in the soprano section while Dô was going to join the mezzo-sopranos. I was ashamed to observe that, plunged deeply into my thoughts, I hadn't noticed her audition or Ghi's.

⚮ 11 ⚮

The Chorus

From the first meeting of the Musical Youth Chorus, my feelings and dreams had crystalized around one image, that of the music teacher. I had gotten into the habit of devoting the muggy hours of afternoon naptime to conjuring up his face. I would then feel a sharp sensation, of pleasure or pain, I couldn't say. These reveries had the merit of filling my inner emptiness; I stopped fidgeting and stamping the ground like a horse without a master. My mother congratulated herself for it.

It was by hiding my feelings in this way that I had gotten permission to go to chorus. I lived these favored moments in a daze, even though the teacher had stopped being interested in me. But his presence, even indifferent, made each moment precious in my eyes. I had an extraordinarily intuitive perception of his physical presence; just trusting the burning sensation at the back of my neck, I would know, without fail, where in the room he was standing. Very often I would give in to this game; its accuracy was always confirmed by Dô and Ghi, to whom I had revealed my feelings. I gave in to these confidences with a pleasure made all the more intense by their allowing me to talk about him. My girlfriends didn't quite share my taste; they found the man "too old" for me.

"He's thirty-five; he could be your father," they pointed out to me. But they knew that my solitary, platonic love was of no consequence; the teacher was just a subject around which I could spin the threads of a novel's imaginary adventures; it added some dimension to my days, which lacked great diversions.

I almost never went to the movies, scarcely twice a year when the family would consent to going out for a comic or edifying film. I read little, for there were hardly any books that didn't contain passages that were considered immoral and which were for that reason forbidden to me. For each book I had to deploy a thousand tricks, first to get ahold of the work, then to read it on the sly. I would read in the street when my mother sent me to the market or on the way home from school. I would choose a secluded place, the low wall of an abandoned garden, for example. I wouldn't leave my lair until the last moment, just before the merchants put away their displays. I would buy merchandise no one wanted from unauthorized peddlers at high prices. My mother was left speechless when confronted with my ineptitude at practicing an art that all girls she knew exercised with virtuosity: the art of bargaining. To shame me she would cite the long list of young girls my age, "not more intelligent" but certainly "more gifted," who would bring home the best products for which they had paid ridiculously low sums. Often, her indignation made her forget all the time it had taken me to accomplish my task. I thanked the heavens for this distraction, without which she would have imagined who knows what shameful act and would have shut me up one more time.

It was a miracle that she consented to send me to the chorus rehearsals without supervision. For her, it was as if I were going to school, and it was her custom to respect the school as well as the teachers whose mission it was to educate us. Nevertheless, this confidence didn't come without friction. My mother rebelled against the growing frequency of the meetings. The crisis hit when we were asked to rehearse in the evening. She flatly refused; nighttime was the moment of temptation and weakness. She threatened to withdraw me from the group if I had the intention of carrying on regardless of her rules. I missed a session for the first time and cried from anger and sorrow. I refused to have dinner that evening, but my mother remained inflexible.

I learned later on that the other parents had reacted in the exact same manner as mine. Realizing that they were on the wrong track, the organizers went around to all the families, assuring them that evening rehearsals would take place only occasionally. My mother stated that in that case she would have my younger sister accompany me. During the discussion that took place between my mother and the teacher, I pretended to be concerned with something else. Such was the custom; this was a conversation between adults in which I was not to interfere. This pretense amused me, for in my eyes the teacher was not quite an adult. The proof lay in the cheerful look he favored me with as soon as he arrived and which clearly said that he did not consider himself to be like my father in any way.

The explanations of the organizers having calmed the worries, we joyously set out once again on the way to chorus. This form of collective leisure, valued by serious and respectable persons, delighted us. Ordinarily, we were scolded when we wanted to sing, read, or chat...but, nothing of the sort happened. I was congratulated for my pretty voice, the same one that had so irritated my stepfather. When I confessed timidly that I was learning to play the mandolin on my own, the music teacher kindly offered to give me private lessons. His proposal threw me into a panic. I blushed deeply. I was certain that I would seem stupid and uninteresting when he saw me up close. I broke out in sobs, to the amazement of everyone else. My comrades stared at me curiously. I imagined the cleverest among them confiding to each other that my reaction was clearly a confession. I was appalled. Ghi got me out of this fix by expressing the desire to join me, a request that the teacher gladly accepted.

That rehearsal held no charm for me. I didn't feel like singing, even less so with people around. I didn't dare look at the teacher anymore. The end of the rehearsal was a relief. I returned home alone. My girlfriends watched me leave without making a move. They, too, had abandoned me. I was disgusted by everything. I longed for the time when all the girls had been proud to count themselves among my close friends.

But I was unfair: Ghi came to see me that very evening. Sitting on the steps leading into the house, we talked about trivial things because my sister Dzung had been sent to supervise us discreetly. Of course, her presence prevented us from broaching the subject that was close to my heart. I tried to make a few allusions that Ghi refused to understand.

When it was time to go, taking advantage of my sister's inattention, she quickly slipped me a message. I had to wait several hours before finding a good time to read it. Ghi let me know that our first lesson would be that very day, at the teacher's house. "We will come by to get you," added the missive. I felt myself come back to life. So life would follow its course. No one had noticed my bizarre behavior; no one had pointed a finger at me.

As expected, my mother was annoyed by these new lessons. I had recently noticed the utter antipathy she felt for the chorus. In her eyes, it was a den of idleness. She didn't really understand why teachers could spend their time having young girls sing instead of introducing them to more useful work. I expected to hear a refusal, but to my surprise, she hesitated, unable to make up her mind to accept or refuse.

We waited, sullen. I knew that she would have kept me at home had it been up to her, but she had a Confucian notion of the teacher, whom you had to venerate. If he had said I should take mandolin lessons, it wasn't up to her, an uneducated, lower-class woman, to prove him wrong. I guessed what contradictory feelings were upsetting her, but I knew she was going to give in. And that's what she finally did, retorting in a surly tone, "Go out discreetly, so that your father doesn't notice you're not here!"

We slipped out without having to be urged to do so. On the way, Dô confirmed that the teacher was paying special attention to me. She added that she knew this attention had touched me. However, she insisted that I be on guard against him.

"The rumor is going around that he is a great 'consumer' of young adolescent girls. Watch out," she said.

And she cited for me, all jumbled together, the names of the pupils who had passed "through his hands." I knew these girls, at least by sight. Some were very pretty, but others had no merit other than being fourteen or fifteen years old. Her revelation disappointed me; I didn't know any more if I should chase that man out of my mind or continue to dream about him.

Then we walked on without saying anything. The echo of the unpleasant news I had just learned lingered inside me. "It's foolish to suffer," I told myself. I decided to exhibit total indifference. Neither hate nor love—now there's the wise course of action. But my wounded heart hardened with rancor as we neared his house.

A woman of indeterminate age opened the door for us. I assumed it was a relative or his servant. She seemed scarcely younger than my mother, with an ordinary-looking face, a lackluster gaze, dressed with no special care. The teacher came forward, his usual charming smile on his lips. He pointed his finger at the woman and introduced her as his wife. She didn't seem to hear him, paid no attention at all to us, and left calmly through the far door.

I was shattered. I hadn't imagined that he could be married, even less so to such an insignificant person. How could it be that no one had mentioned the existence of this woman? My inner turmoil was indescribable; I had a heavy heart out of commiseration for the wife as much as out of sadness for my futile dreaming.

With perfect naturalness, the teacher invited us to take our places and explained the values of the black and white notes, those of the eighth rest and of the eighth and sixteenth notes. I listened, inattentive, taking in the detail of each object in the room as if one of them could reveal its secret to me. But everything around me was banal: a table, two lopsided chairs, a cot where the three of us were seated while the teacher dispensed his knowledge, straddling a chair that was turned backward in front of us. This last detail was without doubt the only one that set him apart; in fact, no adults would have permitted themselves this posture, one gladly adopted by kids with nothing to do. He seemed terribly ordinary to me. In his house, in this decor without elegance and without originality, he had completely lost his aura. I stared at him coldly.

He looked over thirty; a vertical line creased his forehead down to the top of his nose. "He is indeed too old for me," I thought to myself, not without triumph. He had curly hair combed back and smoked a lot, lighting one cigarette after another, Bastos brand, my stepfather's. With a hint of malevolence, I observed his fingers, which were stained with nicotine, as well as his teeth, yellowed by the tobacco. I was desperately trying to find all the specific details about his person that would lead to his fall from grace in my eyes.

Upon our return, we gently made fun of the teacher as well as his morose wife. I admitted that I was wrong about my hero. My girlfriends were thrilled to see me finally being reasonable. We decided to put an end to these private lessons.

At home, my stepfather was busy cleaning the oil lamp, a ritual that he performed each night in a state of concentration. He shot me a look loaded with murderous intentions. I would have preferred straightforward anger or even insults, but he didn't deign to give me that satisfaction. "Spare the rod, spoil the child." He didn't love me. He would never condescend to scold me or punish me. He preferred to condemn me with his indifference.

In the kitchen my mother scolded me sharply for being late, put the musical group on trial, "a veritable depository of all kinds of vice," and to finish up, forbade me to return to the teacher's house. I knew that we didn't want to go there anymore. I promised her to obey. My unexpected docility made her raise her eyebrows; she searched my face for a long time as if seeking some sign of treachery.

Our great preoccupation in the days following was making uniforms: white *áo dài* for the girls, white suits for the boys, with a blue scarf to add a note of color to this immaculate ensemble. Everyone was delighted to have new outfits. Ordinarily, we got new clothes only at New Year's, for Tết. We would wear them all year until the following Tết. My wardrobe consisted of a pair of black trousers (soiled less easily) and two short-sleeved blouses. I had no *áo dài,* the privilege of girls to wear, for it was to the short-sleeved shirt what long trousers worn under the *áo dài* were to shorts.[1]

The certainty of finally having *áo dài* put us in a state of great excitement. The chattering was spinning out apace about the kind of cloth to choose and the cut that was appropriate. The afternoon went by to the detriment of the rehearsal.

But a uniform requires a large expense, and I knew that my mother didn't have any money. I was discouraged. I hated our poverty, and I hated my complicated family situation. I envied Ghi, who would have no trouble getting what she wanted from her parents, and I envied Dỗ, whose mother would readily offer her the uniform, despite a large family to take care of.

The atmosphere of Dỗ's family was exceptionally harmonious. Each month her mother left her salary in a drawer accessible to everyone. Each one knew about the amounts necessary for food, clothes, and school supplies. The children could use what was left of the total without having to ask for permission. When a problem came up, they would all discuss it together. I had never yet seen that in any family.

At my house, on the contrary, it was constant dissimulation. My stepfather never admitted to his wife exactly what he earned. For her part, she fiercely hid the slightest piaster saved from the monthly budget allocated by her husband.

---

1. A reference to a girl's school clothes, short-sleeved shirts and short pants for elementary school, *áo dài* tunics with long trousers underneath for secondary school.

Following their example, I chose craftiness, waiting for the right moment and carefully choosing the right words to present my request so as not to meet inevitably with a refusal. The stakes were important. I couldn't give up the chorus for lack of a uniform, nor could I tolerate that my parents could be seen as poor or miserly.

I waited for the moment during the preparation of the meal when I would find myself alone with my mother. I particularly loved these moments of the day that shielded us from the presence of my stepfather. In the closed and strictly feminine space of the kitchen, my mother would finally drop the mask of coldness she showed toward me in order to satisfy her husband. There, I would rediscover her affection and her intimacy. Sometimes we even joked and laughed. These happy moments, when she gave me proof of her affection, had often helped me endure the indifferent face she would confront me with in front of him.

My stepfather had not forgiven her for my existence. He suspected her of transferring to me the feelings she had nurtured long ago for my other parent. He watched intently for each look and each gesture that was even vaguely directed at me as if, finally, he was going to catch her in the very act of adultery. My mother was aware of everything about this game and made it a point of honor to frustrate such hopes. Of course, I bore the brunt of this underground war. At home I found myself as if in a hostile country, caught between the genuine hatred of my stepfather and the pretended coldness of my mother. Naturally, this situation made me suffer. But what wounded me the most was my mother's attitude, which I considered as a betrayal. Often, I would go cry at the far end of the garden. Then she would say that "tears came easily to me," which would infuriate me. My violence at these moments was such that it made me afraid. I wanted to murder someone. I hated my mother, I wanted to kill my stepfather, and I wished to die to be done with it.

But these crises were of short duration. Very quickly, life's events would seize my attention and distract me from my pain. I would thus move, without transition, from tears to laughter. My mother didn't like this trait of my character, which she judged incompatible with the image of the ideal young girl whose mood was always supposed to be even. Violent feelings in a woman were the worst fault ever. She would be considered indecent, indeed obscene.

My mother was very worried about me. She wanted to cure me of this violence. At first she resorted to simple remedies, carefully choosing herbs that were likely to soften me. Every day, I was treated to a bowlful of a bitter, brownish mixture that she forced me to swallow. This concoction made me want to heave. My disgust with this brew was equaled only by my aversion to the cod liver oil that she had administered to me when I was little.

I, too, aspired to have a peaceful and calm character. But how to succeed? I knew the cause of my difficulty: it was seeing my mother disown me all day long in front of the man who despised me and for whom she felt no love. She alone would be able to heal me.

Finally, on the appointed day, I found my mother in the kitchen and announced in a detached tone that the chorus required wearing a uniform.

"A uniform? Like soldiers?" she exclaimed, stunned.

I burst out laughing in spite of my intention to remain impassive. I explained that I needed a new *áo dài* and a pair of trousers—expensive things, I admitted. She was in complete agreement with me; it was, in fact, too much money. She couldn't dream of taking it out of the meager monthly budget her husband gave her. She sighed.

"Well, then, you won't go to chorus anymore!"

I didn't answer. I had expected that reaction; however, tears stung my eyes. I avoided imagining my life inside four walls in the company of my stepfather's eternally scowling face and the mournful resignation of my mother.

I abandoned the chorus the very next day. I deliberately put on a sad face. I did it in the hope of moving my mother but also from genuine discouragement. Sometimes I would understand her reasons, and sometimes I would be in a rage to be a prisoner there, stupidly, like a pebble in a riverbed while the sparkling water flowed off into the distance. My mother looked distressed to see me so sad, yet could not bring herself to satisfy me. Sometimes she looked at me, sighing, as if to tell me about her inability to make me happy despite her affection.

My prolonged absence raised disagreeable comments in the chorus. It was assumed that I had committed a rather serious infraction for my parents to have considered it a good thing to keep me at home. Of course, each one had her idea about the nature of the mistake. When she heard about this gossip, my mother got angry.

"Since it's the only way to put an end to these rumors, well, let's take care of that uniform."

And she took me to the tailor.

One week later I found myself in the courtyard of the school in my new outfit, awaiting the dress rehearsal. The girls, seeming taller because of the long *áo dài*, which were more form-fitting on their young figures than usual, moved awkwardly, self-consciously, as if they had been partially stripped bare. The boys appeared almost virile in their pants, which were cut in a European style. We observed each other timidly. For the first time, we separated ourselves spontaneously into two groups, the girls on one side, the boys on the other, instead of mixing as we had done up until then, without affectation.

And the arrival of those responsible for the group, dressed in the same uniform, only increased our self-consciousness. We looked at them, dumbfounded.

Usually, the teachers kept the same distance from their students as a father from his children. That was evident from their strict way of dressing and in their manner of expressing themselves, full of gravity; in short, with a certain dignity. Those approaching us now didn't show any of these characteristics. Seeing him again, I found the music teacher very handsome. He looked like the actor Robert Taylor, whose photograph, displayed in the only movie house in the city, I never tired of admiring: the same scarf was tied under the collar of this shirt, and he wore the same expression of an upholder of the law, without fear and without reproach. The only thing he lacked to make the resemblance perfect was the wide-brimmed hat.

My attraction for this man, which I believed had been reduced to ashes, came back to life. As if he had guessed my thoughts, he directed an ironic smile my way. I reddened to the roots of my hair. Mortified, I wanted to chase him out of my thoughts; but I was already helpless before his power.

I slept poorly that night. The oppressive heat added to the heady fragrance of the jasmine coming through the open window, weighing me down with languor. My skin was moist, and the image of the teacher haunted me. I thought again of the afternoon session, when he had been standing a few steps away from me. It seemed to me that I wanted nothing more than the happiness of standing close to him. I had no hope that he would pay attention to me, even less that he would love me. I was perfectly conscious of the grave complications that an amorous relationship between a teacher and his student would surely unleash. No, I simply wished to live in his atmosphere, like an object, like that violin that he held absentmindedly in his hand and which moaned under the pressure of his fingers.

For the first time, I felt the desire to remain in Nha Trang forever. I mentally calculated the time that still separated me from the end of my secondary studies, marvelous years during which no one could prevent me from seeing him, since he would be my teacher.

My mother was surprised to find me "unusually silent." She plunged her acute gaze into my own but discovered only limpid waters there. I didn't yet have anything to hide, other than my reveries.

Finally, the moment came when we had to perform on stage. We were advised to use light makeup for the occasion. It was a preposterous idea. In our circles, no one ever put on makeup, except for actresses and whores, of course.

At first my mother was offended. But upon reflection, she thought that "polite society" would see me on this occasion and that it was necessary to look my best. There was already whispering that many mothers, attracted by the concentration of such a large number of girls of marriageable age, would come to choose a daughter-in-law to their liking.

As we had neither makeup nor powder, my mother had to use whatever means she could find. To begin with, you had to accentuate the contrast between the white and the black of the eye. With half a lemon in her hand, she resolutely pulled my eyelids wide open and squeezed. I had the painful sensation of a bolt of lightning, followed by a feeling of tearing. But the pain passed quickly, making way for a great feeling of well-being. It was as if I had opened my eyes upon a cleansed world. Then she put a little Vaseline under my eyelid so that it would give a shiny, moist aspect to my expression. To finish up, she crushed a splinter of coal, gathering the fine dust on a toothpick that had been moistened beforehand, and passed it between my closed eyelids. The velvety, wide look that the mirror reflected back at me was no longer my own. Cinderella had become a princess.

A sole flaw in this face: my coloring was too pale. A little color on my cheeks would make my beauty more reassuring. But where to find the makeup?

She searched in drawers and in trunks, hoping that something would make do. In the end, we saw her waving, with a triumphal air, the red paper that incense sticks are ordinarily wrapped in. It was a cheap and porous kind of paper that we drenched quickly in water. She rubbed my cheeks and lips with it. The effect was extraordinary; I looked like the color photographs of those striking beauties who decorate calendars. Faced with such an outcome, my mother no longer regretted the expense she had had to consent to for making my uniform. I had become so precious in her eyes that she refused to let me walk to the theater. I protested. Already uncomfortable with my sudden transformation, I was not anxious to make myself noticed perched on a rickshaw. Her enthusiasm humiliated me, for it seemed to turn me into a piece of merchandise for sale.

The whole way to the theater I had to undergo her interminable bits of advice about the conduct that a girl looking for a good match should observe, a speech I knew by heart for having heard it a thousand times. I let her talk while my mind was elsewhere. I arrived with a sullen look, angry toward the entire world.

The wings were a hive of activity. I noted in passing that the other girls were as dressed up as I was, their mothers no doubt following the same line of reasoning as mine. The excitement was at its height. One was looking for a ribbon for her hair, another couldn't find her score, a third was crying in desperation over her stained *áo dài*.

From the back of the room, the teacher was giving his instructions to the musicians. I had yet to look at him. I fiercely resisted doing so, as much from pride as from the fear of an overly strong emotional reaction. It seemed to me that in seeing him, I was going to get sick, as when I was small and my mother had dragged me, exhausted, to the waiting room of the hospital.

The wait was interminable. Finally, we walked toward the stage, stiffer than mummies. Behind the lowered curtain, my throat was little more than a parched desert. I contemplated the crimson velvet, wishing ardently that it would stay in that immobile position until the end of time. But the curtain went up.

The theater was full. I immediately saw my mother, then her husband. She had, thus, persuaded him to come. She had doubtless convinced him that the people he was going to meet could be useful to his business.

Standing in three rows, we squinted, grimacing, blinded by the brightness of the spotlights, shriveled up like mice caught in a trap. In front of us, backlit, was the dark silhouette of the teacher, baton pointed, ready for the attack. We waited for the first measure in a state close to hypnosis, so great was our anguish of missing it. So, when the teacher ended up giving the downbeat, the vocal trickle that we produced sounded ridiculously weak to us. I dreaded the moment of my solo more than anything, for the presence of my stepfather in the theater emptied out all my courage. When my turn came, I sang like a drowned person, like someone out of my depth. My ears buzzing, I wasn't aware of the orchestra or of the audience.

I was upset with myself when I reached the wings. I didn't like what I'd done. I thought with sadness that this was the last time we would sing together, that from today on there would be no more rehearsals, no more chorus.

My parents were waiting in the lobby in silence. In a gruff voice, my father said, "Let's go home!"

We walked in silence in the deserted, poorly lit streets. Eventually we were walking one behind the other, which reminded me of our exoduses of the past, but then we were unified by a collective fear, by the dangers there were to confront. Today, in these reassuring streets—the curfew would only take effect at midnight—we were strangers to each other. I would have paid dearly to know what my parents thought of the show and especially of my performance. They didn't say anything to me about it.

I was tired of the hostility that my mother's husband showed me, even more tired of the tense atmosphere he continually forced us to live in. Was my mother really putting up with it?

I watched her walking in front of me, slender and light. From the back, you could still take her for a young girl. Her husband, lean and skinny, always severe, could have passed for her own father. They were, however, only eight years apart in age. My mother had conceived me late, at the age of twenty-three. I was fifteen. She was thus no longer in the flower of her youth. However, despite a tormented life, she had kept an air of innocence. She resembled those women who preserve something virginal up until the threshold of old age, in the way that nuns do. I watched them move forward, one behind the other, sad and silent shadows. "I will not be like my mother," I thought, forcefully. "I will not live with a man I don't love."

We arrived home without exchanging a word. I spread out a mat on the daybed, under the window where I usually slept. Nearby, my stepfather was busy lighting the oil lamp, the prelude to his supper alone. He had maintained the Chinese custom of a supper composed of a single dish, delicate and nutritious: stuffed pigeon or turtle, cooked for a long time in a double boiler. He would taste it without sharing. In order to avoid our envious looks, aimed dart-like at his bowl, he would eat very late, when the children were asleep. From time to time, my mother would keep him company. They would talk for a long time about money while he ate, and she watched him eat. That's the way it was.

12

The Music Teacher

Now that rehearsals were over, I had nothing left to do.

Late one afternoon, when I was on the front steps plagued with boredom, the teacher came by on his bicycle. When he reached me, he rang his bell and offered me a radiant smile. Surprise and emotion made me speechless. He stopped. Afraid that people might gossip at seeing us together, alone, in front of my house, I ran to let my mother know in order to put an end to this ambiguous situation.

She was surprised to find him there but didn't let it show. But she became suspicious when she learned that he had come for no important reason. However, she put up a good front, inviting him to have "just a cup of tea." That was a polite phrase meant to dismiss him. But he accepted the offer with a spontaneity that was shocking for an Asian. I only appreciated him more for it; I couldn't stand the social restraint and hypocrisy practiced around me. My mother, though, with smiles and convoluted phrases, sought to make him understand that she did not wish him to accost me like that in the middle of the street. She insisted on the word "teacher," thanked him unsubtly for his visit "that we did not deserve in any way," and said that she was happy to see him behaving like "an affectionate father."

I was in agony. But the teacher didn't appear at all affected by her duplicity. He seemed quite at ease, saying that I was a gifted pupil.

"You must encourage her to pursue her studies, Madame," he added with authority.

They continued their conversation, all the while drinking little sips of tea. It was as if I didn't exist anymore. They chatted like old acquaintances, he a little condescending, she as if at confession. The more time went by, the more she let herself open up. She admitted to him that I didn't have a father, to which he answered, not without irony, that he had noticed it. That she would reveal my illegitimacy so bluntly hurt me. Why would she disclose my shame to the first man who came along? Naturally, I had forgotten that I wore my *métissage* on my face and that my "hidden shame," as I liked to think of it, was obvious to everyone.

I suddenly hated the teacher and his ability to gain my mother's confidence. From then on, I would send him packing to the camp of hypocritical and calculating adults. "He is too old," I repeated to myself, making use of my age, fifteen at the time, the only advantage I had over this man.

When he took his leave, my mother was effusive in her thanks, and I wondered what for. He stole a glance at me, as if we were complicit in something. I averted my eyes. He turned on his heel. We watched him. I noted with bitter joy that from the back he was completely uninteresting to me.

As he crossed the threshold, the teacher let out a resounding "Ah!" implying that he had just remembered something important. He retraced his steps and mentioned to my mother that there was a singing competition organized by the town, a competition he advised her to sign me up for. Without thinking, still under his spell, she promised to do it at the first opportunity. That meant that I could go out once again, taking advantage of long days of freedom. Later I understood the meaning of his falling all over himself to be charming; it was destined to obtain my liberation. Immediately, I again found that he had every skill and charm.

For a long time I stared at the empty doorframe, the imprint of his outline still lingering on my retina. When that image faded, I suddenly became aware of his disappearance as well as of my loneliness.

From that day onward, he took over all my thoughts. I didn't leave the front steps anymore in the insane hope of seeing his cream-colored bicycle. I would conjure it up with affection, like some dear girlfriend. Seeing him became an insistent need. I would jump at the metallic sound produced by each bike passing in the street. I had never experienced anything as intense. I didn't know that I could miss another human being to that extent. My nights were interrupted by awakening suddenly with a start. With my eyes open in the shadows, I would endure, powerless, the internal bite that wouldn't let go. It seemed to me that crying would have soothed me. But in spite of my efforts, the tears wouldn't come, and that, too, was a new experience for me. It wasn't the kind of suffering that wounds you like the tip of a knife and makes the tears flow; it was a fire that was consuming me.

I had only one hunger, one thirst, one desire, and that was him. I would call out to him with all my might, without trying anything to gain satisfaction. I was sick with a passive love, and I would be content with fading away.

My mother was monitoring my languor with a wary eye. She thought quite naturally of a passing fancy, was trying to figure out who the guilty party was but couldn't.

The hypothesis of a sweetheart having been set aside for lack of proof, she took me to the doctor, who diagnosed me as anemic, a likely malady in an undernourished country—almost everyone was anemic. He gave us a prescription written in a tight script. My mother ran to get it filled immediately by the nearest pharmacist. That very evening, she forced me to drink the bitter potion, a useless torment.

For me, time spun out its thread of gloomy days and sleepless nights. I was the prey of a sustained illness. The front steps tugged at me, irresistibly. I would go sit there at all hours, on the lookout for his silhouette, the memory of which, at once exact and burning, I retained.

When she noticed that the medicine did not dispel my melancholy, my mother decided that I was not sick but possessed by one of those unfortunate, wandering souls that inhabited the invisible world around us. She swapped the doctor for the pagoda.

With her arms loaded with flowers, sticks of incense, and amulets, she led me to the Buddhist temple at nightfall. It was from twilight on, that hour between the realm of the living and that of the dead, that you might hope to communicate with the supernatural world.

The Buddhist monk that she paid had as his mission to drive out from my soul the other soul that had me in its clutches. He recited long phrases in a monotonous voice. Sitting behind him, I saw only the dark mass of his robe and the bluish shadow of his shaved skull. The heavy perfume of the incense and the monotonous recitation of the prayers cast me into a kind of torpor. I knew which soul had taken hold of my own, but I didn't want in any way to be set free from it.

Soon, I was better, not because of the prayers or the offerings; rather, it was the hope of seeing the teacher again, for my mother, faithful to her promise, had just signed me up for the singing competition.

A little while later, I received news about the teacher from a friend from chorus. Of Cambodian origin, Mai was extremely kind and liked by everyone. He was an orphan and had been taken in by the teacher, who treated him like a younger brother.

My mother liked Mai right away. She found him amiable and had him stay for dinner. It was a charming meal during which our guest proved himself to be the life of the party. He had seen all the Laurel and Hardy films and recounted them to us in an irresistible way.

We discovered his quick-wittedness and especially his sense of humor, and we took him into our hearts. He brought to our family a relaxed masculine presence that it lacked. Mai never stopped praising his "adoptive brother," as he called him. He reported to us in detail the various expressions of his kind heart. I was grateful to him for it, for I needed to know that the man was without reproach in order to admire him. He brought me the air that the Other had breathed. I imagined that Mai's hearing still held the echo of my teacher's voice, that his sense of smell preserved the memory of his scent. Later on, when we knew each other better, I thought I might be able to confide my secret to him.

I accompanied him out to the street. We walked next to each other, without awkwardness, peacefully happy as a brother and sister might be. When we left each other, he slipped a note into my hand and ran away with a "See you tomorrow." I was dumbfounded. I was convinced that it was a declaration of love. A sudden anger rose up inside me against the one who had so quickly turned upside down an unadulterated affection. I could never see him again and would lose at the same time the only link to the Other. And he dared say "See you tomorrow" to me.

I was going to throw the note away when, changing my mind, I opened it. Two movie tickets fell from the folded paper. The message began with "Devoted little sister." It couldn't be Mai. We were practically the same age; he wouldn't ever adopt this tone of someone older with me.

Trembling, I looked at the bottom of the page where the signature was: "Older brother Duc." It was the teacher. He hadn't forgotten me. I leaned against the wall to give me time to calm my wildly beating heart. Then slowly, very slowly, I deciphered the message. It was an invitation to a film showing. He explained how to go about it in a fine, regular script, without erasures. The stratagem was simple: Mai would take responsibility for the invitation, would accompany me to the cinema, and would slip away at the beginning of the movie. In the dark, Duc would take his place.

I had ardently desired that he love me; then, I had abandoned this hope, considering my wish as pure folly. Now that I had my dream in my hands, now that I could either inscribe this story into reality or prevent its beginning, I felt completely helpless. I thought of all the girls he had made dates with. Was it at the same place? My mind passed in review all the ones that my friends Dô and Ghi had mentioned.

I didn't like the idea of being on the same list. My mother liked to repeat that it was "better to be the only love of a beggar than to be the hundredth concubine of a prince." Her words had never seemed so right. I tore up the tickets, scattering the pieces lying in my hand by blowing on them. I rejoined my family, proud of myself.

Two hours hadn't gone by when I regretted my deed. What evil spirit had pushed me to refuse a proposal that I had wished for so much? I didn't know how to make amends for my stupidity. One moment I was tempted to steal some money from my mother, but she always knew exactly how much she had and where she put it away. Steal from my stepfather? Impossible! I would rather die than give him reasons to despise me more. Mai remained my last resort. I would tell him everything, and he would lend me the amount necessary to buy two new tickets.

He arrived at about ten o'clock. Until noon, he was busy with my mother as if he had wanted to avoid me. When we were finally alone, instead of confiding in him, I remained silent. It was he who first asked me if I had read the note he had given to me. And then, forgetting my good resolutions, I attacked:

"With the other girls, was it also you who arranged the dates?"

He stared at me for a long time without answering.

I was extremely upset. I cried silently. I added in spite of myself, "Does it always happen the same way? In the same place?"

Mai sighed, then said, "Do you want me to tell you about the Charlie Chaplin film I saw recently?"

"No!" I yelled.

But Mai told me about the film anyway. At the end, we were both laughing. When the dishes were done, he asked me, "What should I tell him?"

"I don't know!"

Indeed, I didn't know any more. I wanted to and didn't want to. The existence of the other girls poisoned my feelings. I hated him with all my might. I spent the beginning of the afternoon wavering between yes and no. In the end, I went with Mai to the cinema. My mother let us go without worries as if we were both her children.

Mai left me at the door with a smile. "I'll see you tomorrow, won't I?"

Suddenly I found myself alone in the half-light of the lobby. It was still too hot, and the movie house was empty. There was still time to go. I left.

He was there, searching the darkening entrance with his eyes. We looked at each other. What his eyes said was tender and serious. My aggression melted instantly. I thought that I liked his eyes. He smiled at me.

I don't know how long we stayed like that, without words or gestures. Finally, he went toward the entrance. I cried out, alarmed, "I don't have the tickets anymore!"

My happiness collapsed in ruins: he was going to leave, and I was going to lose him forever! Indeed, he did go away, but it was to buy two more.

"Come!"

That informal command[1] was the first word of our intimacy. I listened to him as if it were music, I etched it into my memory, I repeated

---

1. Here the music teacher uses the familiar form with the narrator for the first time; in the original text, the "tu" form is used, or "Viens!"

it tirelessly until it created a murmuring noise in my whole being. We were alone in the balcony. I wasn't paying much attention to the film, but for ten years I kept the program that the usher gave me in the month of August 1950.

Properly huddled deep in the crimson seat, I made an effort to prevent my arm from brushing against that of my companion on the same armrest. In the half-darkness, I saw the outline of his head, held upright, as if he were solely absorbed by what was happening on the screen. I tried to get interested in the film: a tall, redheaded woman was going back and forth in a flower garden; an old man, looking very sad, was playing chords on a piano while contemplating her through the open window.

He was very near me and at the same time inaccessible. His bare arm next to mine tempted me painfully. Did he know it? He turned toward me. His tilted head brushed against mine. My heart overflowed. I closed my eyes. I felt very weak. "I am going to faint," I thought to myself. An eternity went by.

"Aren't you feeling well, little sister?" he murmured in my ear.

I smiled weakly. He took my hand, a wet, trembling bird, in his. I kept my eyes shut, incapable of making the slightest sound. The violence of love was hurting me.

"Don't be afraid; I won't hurt you."

His warm breath was burning my cheek. I snuggled up in the hollow of his shoulder, my mouth dry.

"I'm not afraid," I managed to articulate.

I had just been born. I opened my eyes to see his, immense, blurred. I cried for no reason like a glass running over. He took my face in his two hands and, leaning in the way people drink from a spring, lightly licked my tears.

A universe of tenderness opened up wide within me. My soul was a passionate bird, babbling its first song. Still, I remained frozen and passive. I knew neither the words nor gestures of love. Everything was surprising and enchanting to me. None of the books I had read—even clandestinely—had told of the wild trembling of your whole body when a fervent mouth moves across your face. I didn't know anything about the language of the senses.

Up until then, my body was an object that I had to keep in a state of cleanliness, nothing more. I had never contemplated myself in the nude. I had never seen anyone get undressed in front of me, save my sisters when they were very young. From the age of six on, girls and boys would hide to remove their clothes.

Thus, I was content to eagerly receive his kisses, like the parched earth soaking up a salutary rain. When he pulled away, it was as if he had been wrenched from me. Distraught, I looked at the screen without understanding. He got up.

"I am leaving before the end of the film. That way, no one will see you with me."

What a surprise. How cool he seemed! So, the whole time I was giving myself up to his embraces, without any notion of time and space, he had kept in mind the length of the film, getting up exactly a few moments before the end. Undoubtedly, we had not been through the same thing. Noticing this discrepancy gave me the feeling of being abandoned.

Alone, I lingered in the lighted theater, my mind confused, watching the scarce audience members leave from the balcony. I went out last, still on fire from the memory of his caresses. I didn't dare return home immediately. It seemed to me that my skin was still marked with his scent; my mother would have no trouble guessing my transgression. I wandered the streets, giving my heart the time to return to its natural rhythm, surprised to notice that nothing had changed. No one turned around as I passed; I was just an ordinary passerby. That a man had held me in his arms wasn't visible on my face! I was disappointed that such a violent feeling didn't have more luster.

My mother didn't ask questions. In spite of that, I found the family atmosphere irritating. I thought constantly of his hands holding my face, of his tongue licking my cheek, and of the taste of dark tobacco from his mouth.

A languid weakness made me want to go to bed and cry. I missed him desperately. Beside myself, I wandered in the house, my mind vacant. I would get up only to sit down again. I would go into the kitchen and there, with my arms hanging, not knowing what I had come to look for any more, I would retrace my steps.

"What's the matter? Why are you so restless?" asked my mother, aggravated by my behavior.

"I'm too hot. I don't feel well!"

"You must have gotten sunstroke coming out of the cinema. Take an aspirin tablet and lie down."

That was all that I hoped for: lying down to dream about Him. Reliving over and over the marvelous moments that I had spent in his arms. "... Little sister ..." His words like a ribbon of honey. His hand, hot. His mouth, so sweet. Suddenly, I got very hot. "I really do have a fever," I thought. Then I had the brutal revelation of having lived with a complete lack of love.

Mai arrived early, at about seven o'clock, when I was sweeping the house as I did each morning, just after jumping out of bed. My mother was preparing her husband's morning coffee in the kitchen. We were alone. He slipped a letter into my pocket. My heart was beating as if to burst. I became conscious of the dangerous path that was opening up before me. I thought of my stepfather's fury, of my mother's sorrow, and of the scandal that would stain the honor of my family. And if I backed off? There was still time. Only Mai knew about my lapse; all I needed to do was have him promise to keep it secret. I would not read this letter; I would give it back to its author. That wise decision lightened my feeling of guilt. It didn't last long. Soon the idea of renouncing a scarcely glimpsed happiness tormented me. From hour to hour I changed my mind. I would caress the letter deep in my pocket, resisting the desire to learn what it contained. And if I opened it, just out of curiosity? I could always give it back to Mai later. I closed myself up in the toilet, feverishly unsealing the envelope. "My beloved little sister ..." I closed my eyes. Now nothing could prevent me from running to him.

He proposed a second meeting to me, in one of our school's classrooms deserted during this vacation period. But how to justify a new absence? Mai couldn't serve as my cover anymore; another outing with him would have appeared improper in the eyes of my mother. If I only had a visit to make, to a sick girlfriend, for example, who needed my care during the whole afternoon. Unfortunately, all my girlfriends were in excellent health. The more the day wore on, the less success I had in finding a solution. I got to the point where I wanted my mother to guess my thoughts and detain me by force.

When the moment came, I was extremely agitated, incapable of inventing a plausible lie and equally incapable of resisting the urgent need that pushed me toward him. I had only one obsession in my mind, that of feeling his lips on my skin again. I was thirsty, so thirsty for love. Out of ideas, I took advantage of an inattentive moment on the part of my mother and went out without the slightest excuse. I left as if leaving for good, indifferent to the consequences of my act.

I ran toward the school, my face burning and my heart trembling. The entry gate was half open. I stopped, paralyzed by a great feeling of fear, the fear of getting mixed up in this affair, the fear of not knowing what I would have to do when I was facing him. I had no experience, and I wondered how a woman behaved when she was alone in front of a man.

I crossed the courtyard without running into anyone. With my nerves tense, I cautiously turned the door handle. The teacher, wearing white, cotton clothes, was sitting on a bench. I found myself in his arms without really knowing how. My fear evaporated instantly.

An extraordinary feeling of well-being ran through my body. Being there, against him, seemed like the most natural thing in the world to me. One might have said that I was born for that moment. I confessed to not knowing that love could be so marvelous. He burst out laughing. I did the same.

He spoke to me of his life, about an elder sister whom he loved fondly and who lived in Hue, the capital of Annam, where he himself had been born. His stories enchanted me; they gave me the feeling of possessing him even more.

He pecked at my mouth and my eyes in a greedy way. I fervently breathed in the smell of his chest, moaning softly, weighed down by a feeling so strong that it became painful. Suddenly, someone knocked repeatedly on the windowpane. We shuddered. On the other side, little kids, dressed in tatters, sitting on top of each other to get a better view, made obscene gestures aimed at us. Duc closed the curtain while I fled, sick with shame.

I ran ahead, distraught. Without realizing it, I had taken the road to the beach. I threw myself down on the sand, crushed. I cried for a long time. Little by little, fatigue took over my sorrow, and I fell asleep.

I must not have dozed off for too long. Still dazed, I looked at the ocean, my head empty. I thought I should go home. What kind of story could I put together to justify my absence? I believed I was lost.

I headed for Ghi's welcoming house. She was surprised to see me with my eyes red and my eyelids swollen.

"Did something serious happen to you?"

Before answering, I dragged her out to the garden, telling her the whole adventure without stopping.

When I had finished, Ghi declared, "First of all, you will tell your mother that you were with me. If she wants to verify it, I'll ask my father to cover for you. We won't mention Professor Duc's name. Furthermore, I will try to find out if those kids talked about you. In all likelihood, they wouldn't recognize you on the street."

"I'll never forget what you are doing for me."

I left, relieved. My mother took me at my word. She scolded me for form's sake. I was remorseful for deceiving her so easily. I watched out for rumors, but finally, no one knew about my clandestine rendezvous. If those children had talked, it was around people who didn't know me.

With that danger out of the way, I dreamed again of the teacher, avoiding, however, recalling the painful scene that had demeaned us. Now that my mind was calm, I wanted to know how he had taken my flight. Was he angry about it? I had no way of communicating with him: I didn't dare send a letter to his home. There was nothing left except to place all my hope in Mai, our messenger.

The latter finally gave me a long letter in which Duc regretted his carelessness. He swore to me that his feelings were pure and that our love was as beautiful and as sad as the one that joins the clouds and autumn.

From then on, we saw each other every day. We got into the habit of meeting at a place called The Rock Mounds. Immense boulders offered secret, cool caves where we liked to shield our meetings. One of them harbored at its center a vast, flat rock, smooth and perfectly round. One day, he undressed me, then posed me nude on that altar, an immodest flower offered to his gaze. Bothered, I let him do as he pleased, the muted sound of the waves in my ears and the dampness of the sea spray on my skin.

His fingers slowly traced arabesques on my body, lightly touching my breast and my thigh. I was learning about pleasure. I opened my eyes, rolled upwards upon my lover, and we embraced each other.

"I am dying of love for you," I breathed.

He pulled away, panting.

"Stop; you will take me too far."

I didn't understand. I believed he was angry.

"What did I do?"

He shook his head without answering, then suddenly held me very tightly. So, I hadn't offended him? I was reassured.

It happened that before we separated, Duc left a purple bite mark below my breast. He joked, laughing, "What will you say to your mother when she asks you how you got that black and blue mark?"

I laughed, too, with the feeling of having violated something forbidden. But we both knew that it was nothing but a pretense. I was at an age when you don't show yourself nude in front of your mother, let alone in front of a husband who would only take his wife with all the lights out. No matter! I left him, delighted with my unseemly secret.

I returned home toward evening, my hair messed up, my eyes shining, and an insolent look of happiness on my face. I was evolving as if in a dream, absentminded and airborne, indifferent to the world. My mother waited for an explanation that didn't come. I didn't have one and didn't want to look for one. She observed my haughty and inspired airs in silence, impressed by my sudden change. Her mother's heart had guessed the danger, for she avoided scolding me. On the contrary, she was very gentle.

Now she would propose short, private walks to me, initiating a kind of relationship she had never had with her daughters. We would talk about unimportant things while we walked, like two good friends. I could certainly feel her impatience to get my little secrets out of me, if not an outright confession. But I knew that she couldn't understand me, much less tolerate such a scandalous love. I concealed my secret, my mind made up to act as though innocent.

My mother spoke of life in general in an indirect way, of the dangers that lie in wait for a naive, young girl. She gave me advice on the way to choose my girlfriends and recommended that I respect my teachers.

"A respect that you should temper with a certain caution, for, unfortunately, a teacher is also a man," she concluded.

Her words awakened her suspicion, and when she asked for news about the teacher, I answered her that I had none. She looked me up and down, sadness veiling her gaze. I understood that she knew. I felt a pang of anguish, but I said nothing.

We returned home late that evening. In front of the house she gave me a final recommendation: "Be careful not to get pregnant; your life would be ruined forever."

And with that she put an end to our walks. The echo of her words, as terrible as a curse, haunted my sleep. Of course, I was firmly determined as much as my mother not "to get myself pregnant." But in what way? She would have done better to assert herself more explicitly instead of leaving me with that vague anxiety. I didn't know whom to ask for advice; the girlfriends my age were as ignorant as I. As for the teacher, broaching such a question with him seemed impossible to me. Taking an interest in sexual things...what degradation! I loved my teacher with an ideal, romantic love. I had given myself to him without reservation, confiding my virginity to his care, intimately persuaded that he would never take advantage of my lack of restraint. Hadn't he, up to now, shown proof of his respect?

However, my mother had succeeded in infecting me with the poison of fear. I was going to my rendezvous with him less blithely, and I was no longer entirely enjoying the sweet moments we were spending together. When he would lay me down on the smooth, cool rock, my body would tense up. Through my half-closed eyelashes I would spy on the movements of his caresses, ready to run away at the first sign of danger.

The beginning of the following school year did not hinder my love—far from it. I had the supreme happiness of seeing him every day, for he was at the same time our literature, mathematics, and music teacher. In front of the others we acted with indifference. I avoided encountering his gaze, and he didn't show me any special attention. This secrecy, which was not without its piquancy, stimulated my pleasure. I savored our secret and was condescending toward my schoolmates bent over their notebooks. I had pity for their passionless hearts, for their dull lives.

I had managed to get a seat at the end of a row, near the center aisle where the professor would come and go during class. Sometimes he would stand close by, just behind me. I could actually feel the heat emanating from his body. A slight movement would have been enough for my head to touch his chest. The proximity of his presence as well as the forbidden nature of the situation literally set me on fire. As if he had guessed my intense excitement, he would move away and soon I would hear his voice at the other end of the classroom. We would stare at each other, separated by the entire length of the room. My desire must have appeared blatant, for his gaze, once shattered, would turn away.

But this comedy of impassivity would get on my nerves. I could no longer stand my role as a student like the others. I could no longer stand his act as the honorable teacher. I had had enough of the hypocrisy that forced me to consider with coldness the man whose intoxicating odor and warm breath I had known. I wanted to rush into his arms and shout our love in front of everyone. I begrudged his fake indifference. I wanted to compromise him. I would look at him intensely, willing to provoke a scandal. But he continued his class with an even voice, without a look in my direction. A stranger. I cried from heartache. He didn't love me, not as much as I loved him, not to the point of taking risks.

But my anger would be short lived, for he always knew how to re-conquer me with just the right gesture to surprise me, like leaving a piece of candy furtively on my open notebook. I would feel a wondrous joy at this boldness. Thus unfolded my days in class: streaked with suffering, insane joy, pouting, and reconciliation. A turbulent, underground life ignored by my classmates.

Professor Duc was loved by all. Competent, modern, and engaging, he would speak to each boy and girl—especially to each girl—in a personal way, in a trusting tone, giving the unsettling feeling that you had been taken into his confidence. The girls would drink him in with their eyes; the boys would copy his bearing, his smile. As for me, I found him handsome like a movie actor. He was our hero, and we adored his teaching, particularly his music class.

When he would carefully take the violin out of its case, grasping the bow, a quasi-religious expectation would come over the class. Before beginning, he would dedicate a smile to us, wedge the instrument under his chin with his eyes closed, making affectionate adjustments.

Outside, the sun poured down a blinding, motionless light. The music would pierce the silence with its long, plaintive sound. His gaze would slide over me, return, linger. My heart would melt; I would think he was playing for me alone, and the music reached me like a gift.

During this period, I completely neglected my studies, getting done only what was absolutely necessary in order to spare giving the one who loved me the unpleasant task of awarding me a bad grade. The school had become nothing but a pretext that allowed me to see more often the teacher whom my girlfriends called "Master Four,"[2] since we had acquired the basic rudiments of the English language and because he was the fourth child in his family.

In this way we could make the most of each other until six in the evening, the moment when the doors were closed. I would go home to leave my school bag there, then slip out right away to throw myself into his arms. My mother was eaten up with worry, discreetly watching out for my period, scrutinizing my face as if she could read the name of the guilty party on it. But, indifferent, I didn't even notice her torment.

Little by little, our frequent meetings made me more familiar with Duc. He intimidated me less. Our relationship progressively shed the self-consciousness it had had at the very beginning. I let myself be undressed without being too embarrassed. He would contemplate me for a long time, short of breath. A vein on his temple would swell up, pulsing like a beating heart. He would make me afraid like that. I would turn my head away with a kind of disgust for the stranger I had just seen. I would then return home, less happy than the other times.

Despite myself I thought again about my mother's predictions of my ruined life. The letters he would slip under the covers of my notebooks became more urgent. They would speak of my "languid body overcome with sleep," of "tortured desires, difficult to express." This new tone, laden with innuendo, heightened my worry although I had no idea what he might be feeling, except that it must have been something reprehensible.

As for me, I was satisfied with our kisses and our caresses. They fulfilled me. I wanted nothing more. Was it so important to rob me of my virginity? That subterranean flower, that buried treasure that my

2. In English in the original.

mother kept harping about, I didn't know how it could be stolen from me. I didn't know how a man's body was made. I had never seen my lover with his clothes off. During our meetings, it was he who would undress me. That seemed natural to me and suited me in a certain way. For my great fear was that he might resemble my stepfather whose genital organs, once glimpsed under a pair of shorts that were too short, had disgusted me.

I liked his cheek next to mine, the happiness experienced in his presence, and the unjustified feeling that it would always endure. I had settled into a kind of eternity. For the moment, my greatest suffering was our being separated on Sundays and holidays when the absence of school would keep us from each other. On those days I would suddenly lose him, without any possibility of seeing him, even from afar. He would quite simply disappear, die, leaving me in mourning until the following Monday. Gloomy days during which I would drag around my languor, beside myself.

My mother would observe my absent air, sighing, her look full of reproach. She had decided to remain serene, but deep down, her suspicions only grew. She was waiting for proof. An imprudent moment, a false step, and that would be it for my love.

However, these dangers barely crossed my mind. I scarcely paid attention to the world that was around me. I wanted to see him at all hours of the day. I was becoming insatiable. We even agreed once to meet in the evening, on the beach, among the families who had come to take in the coolness. It was very foolish, but we were counting on the shadows of the poorly lit shore.

I had planned on my mother's not being vigilant. When I proposed a short walk to my sisters in an innocuous tone, she immediately imposed the maid on us as our chaperone. I should have been on my guard, but this tighter supervision was no cause for alarm; I don't know why. Unconscious, I was going to my ruin.

The maid led us to the busiest spot, the only one lit by streetlamps. In a straight line, toward the water, I could make out the dark outline of the teacher. He was waiting for me. What pretext could I come up with in order to join him? My sisters were playing with other children, but our maid was never further than a step away from me. Each minute that went by was a minute that was lost to me. Nothing seemed more absurd than sitting there while the man I loved was so close. And if he left, tired of waiting? That possibility was intolerable to me. Without thinking, I took off in the direction of the ocean, hoping that the darkness would hide me from the view of the chaperone. I could make out two open arms and threw myself into them.

"Miss . . ."

The maid was standing behind us. I freed myself from the teacher's embrace, ashamed.

"It's time to go home," she said in a harsh voice.

We looked at each other; there was contempt in her eyes. I thought of my mother's anger. Was she going to beat and run me out of the house? I wasn't afraid of the blows, which would be the lightest punishment I could think of. But where would I go if my mother didn't want me anymore? I wanted to fall on my knees and beg the maid to keep silent. But her coldness intimidated me. I said nothing.

Once back, I went to bed immediately; I wanted to avoid my mother, have a night of respite, and only confront the storm the next day.

But the day went by without the dreaded scene taking place. The maid had kept silent. I tried several times to catch her eye in order to read some sort of complicity in her gaze. In vain. She seemed to have no secret to share with me. She considered me with indifference. As for me, I had known her for too short a time to dare ask her any questions.

She had come to beg for work at our house two months before. Originally from one of the provinces around Saigon, she had arrived here with a three-year-old girl, very thin and covered with scabies; her immense black eyes were the exact replica of hers. The man had abandoned her. Now she had to work in order to raise her daughter properly. Didn't we want to employ her?

My mother examined first the child, then the mother, and remained silent. This woman's story was banal. It wasn't the first time that a woman seduced and abandoned had come to ask for work with her child on her back. They were dirty and neglected for the most part, their hearts overflowing with bitterness. They considered their kids as burdens they wanted to get rid of as quickly as possible. This one didn't resemble any of the others; she showed an uncommon passion for her daughter. She seemed happy with her lot, cursing neither destiny nor the man who had dishonored her. In that way, she seemed a little simpleminded to us. We didn't know if her optimism came from her virtue or from a congenital stupor. My mother was leaning toward the second answer as she observed her with a slightly ironic smile.

Without letting herself be intimidated, the woman continued enumerating her skills. Her naïveté was touching; in the end, my mother didn't have the heart to refuse. Maybe she had pity as well for a woman whose situation reminded her of her own. She hired her even though we didn't need domestic help; I was old enough to take responsibility for the household tasks. Without taking into account that in the future we would have to feed two more mouths . . .

Already my mother seemed to regret her all-too-hasty decision. As if she had guessed my mother's hesitations, the woman declared that she would give up her wages. She asked only to be fed and housed. The matter was settled. From then on, we were all satisfied with her service, including my stepfather, who found that she "was a hard worker."

I had little contact with her. Completely absorbed in my feelings, I had no attention to pay to others. Now that her silence had spared me a scene, I would have liked to be able to thank her. I would have liked to know the reasons why she had covered for me. But she hardly seemed anxious to talk to me. She conspicuously avoided me, thereby showing me that she disapproved of my behavior.

Despite this premonition, I behaved with total recklessness, now leaving for my rendezvous openly, insensitive to the grimaces of disapproval that the mothers of virtuous daughters directed my way from their doors. I was far away from them; I lived in a universe where I was free and loved. What did I have in common with that right-thinking and resigned herd whose lives were withering between the narrow barriers of social hypocrisy?

Of course, I knew that this whole affair would lead me in the near term toward some catastrophe. But the word *catastrophe* itself took on an exciting connotation in my mind. I envisioned it with a curiosity tinted with hope, as if it were going to sweep away everything and change the landscape of my life. As for the social consequences, I already knew them: no man would ever want to marry me. In truth, I did not consider it a privilege to serve a shrewish mother-in-law, to have a swarm of children, and to finish your life in resignation. I was living my adventure, caring little for what I was going to lose, but determined, above all, to seize the happiness that was given to me.

I continued to meet the teacher secretly. We would change locations almost every day. But our liaison was becoming the subject of comment from the whole school, whispering that would stop suddenly when I passed by, leaving a heavy silence in my wake. This society had strict ideas about morality, particularly in a sphere as serious as that of the education of girls. To whom would we confide our virgins if the teachers themselves proved to be delinquent?

We knew this and yet we continued. We were perfectly familiar with the area around Nha Trang. We had tried all the straw huts whose greedy owners would rent us a bed where we could embrace each other without being surprised. Despite appearances, our frolicking remained chaste. I was thirsty for tenderness above all, and his caresses never went beyond the limits marked out by my fears. Except one time, when his hand slipped between my thighs. I sat up in a movement of fierce defense.

"Don't be afraid," he whispered. "You will not lose your virginity with me."

I thought that no one would come to my aid if he wanted to take advantage of me. I imagined myself dead, lying in a pool of blood that continued to flow from my deflowered sex organs. Hadn't people murmured to me many times that losing your virginity was like a wound that bled?

"I want to go home," I implored.

Duc went out to look for his bicycle while I, sitting on the filthy bed, clearly saw the ugliness of the surroundings. From outside his cheerful voice called me: "Come, I'll take you to a plantation where you can pick all the fruit that you want."

I adored fruit. Often, I would munch green mangoes until I got sick from them. I joined him. He avoided touching me. I got onto the baggage carrier, restraining myself this time from wrapping my arms around his waist.

The plantation was a delight. Dense like a forest, it sheltered mango trees, guava trees, and starfruit trees, all laden with ripe fruit. I ran toward the trees with cries of joy, climbing high up in a mango tree before he even had the chance to dissuade me from doing so. I shook the long stems of golden mangoes in front of the flabbergasted eyes of the teacher standing at the foot of the tree.

"Come down! You're going to fall and break your neck."

I made fun of his concern and continued my climb. I was no longer a grown-up girl of fifteen; I had rediscovered the time when I was a little girl, when each tree presented a temptation I couldn't resist. Once again, I saw my mother's fright, her anger, and the blows I would get when I came down. Today, I was free to climb as high as I wanted. I shrieked with satisfaction, so much so that my sweetheart, bothered, asked me to be a little more restrained.

"You can easily see that you're not entirely Vietnamese," he declared as I munched a guava.

Even though the tone was kind, that remark hurt me.

"Why do you love me then?" I said, aggressively.

He was surprised and didn't answer right away.

"Because I like you," he murmured after a moment.

"But if I'm not Vietnamese, how could you like me?"

He looked at me without understanding, then burst out laughing.

"But I like you precisely because you aren't entirely Vietnamese. You see, you are Vietnamese without being Vietnamese; that's what's attractive about you. When I look at you, you are at once familiar and strange. And I like that. You should be happy rather than sad about that. Don't be silly."

And he held me close to him.

When I got home, toward evening, the deserted house was plunged in darkness. The maid cried silently, sitting on the floor. I immediately thought that some tragedy had befallen my family.

"Where is my mother?" I cried out.

The sound of my voice filled the silence.

"Answer me. What happened?"

I shook the maid violently.

"You can be proud of yourself," she sniffed. "The world is now upside down and it's your fault."

"It's my fault?"

"Your father discovered all the letters hidden under the cover of your notebook. He knocked over the inkwell on it and wanted to change the paper. When he took out the old one, all your letters fell out on the floor. There were a lot of them. They took a long time to read them; then, they went out. I think they went to see the principal of the secondary school. Your sisters are at the neighbor's house."

So, it had happened. The moment that was so dreaded, that I hadn't stopped waiting for down deep inside me. I knew that it would be impossible to hide my misdeed in a society where each life had to be an open book exposed to everyone's sight. However, I had not foreseen that my parents would discover my transgression through something as intimate as my love letters. At the thought of my stepfather bent over my mail, the heat of my shame set me on fire.

I tried to remember the tone, the words they contained. To think that they had read all that. My mother was my mother; she could peer into the bottom of my heart. But him, a man who didn't love me, so strict and so severe that it would be hard to attach the slightest feeling to him. Imagining his looking at my secret life sullied it definitively. I begrudged myself for not having burned the letters, which were at the principal's office right now. Was he, too, in the process of reading them? Might as well expose me naked throughout the city.

A sound of footsteps interrupted the course of my reflections.

"Is that whore back?" said the voice of my stepfather.

From the kitchen, the maid murmured a scarcely audible "Yes."

In the main room my mother moaned loudly, not knowing what evil she had committed in "letting a viper grow in her body like that." I had "splattered her with mud." "How could she show herself to the world from now on?" A daughter without honor, with no heart, who hadn't had pity for her own mother! I had torn her heart asunder.

My mother's moaning hurt me. I hadn't intended to make her suffer. I had only her; she was the only person who had shown me some affection. I loved her.

My stepfather was taking his revenge. "Didn't I tell you, mother of Dzung? She is deceitful and vicious. But you didn't want to believe me; you always tried to protect her. You are too weak with her. You have to be pitiless and control her with an iron fist."

They burst into the kitchen where I was standing, my stepfather in the lead, followed by my mother. He was foaming with rage, brandishing a whip that struck me immediately across the back. I swallowed my cries. My mother encouraged him, punctuating the blows with insults whose filthy character astounded me and wounded me more surely than the bloody stripes on my skin.

I was drunk with pain when my parents left the premises. Without witnesses, I let myself break down in tears, miserable in a way I hadn't been in a long time.

Daylight awakened me. I had fallen asleep on the floor, my body aching, exhausted by my tears. I stayed there, waiting for someone to decide my fate. I felt no pang of revolt against the treatment they had afflicted upon me. Hadn't I always known that my liaison would be discovered one day?

My back was in terrible pain. I inspected my wounds: my stepfather hadn't held back. The maid, who had come to prepare the master's morning coffee, did not speak to me. Neither my mother nor my sisters worried about what state I was in. They had thus refused to pity me at all.

At mealtime, the maid came back and lit the stove. She looked through me as if I were a ghost. I hadn't eaten since the evening before. I avoided looking at the steaming plates whose smells reached me despite myself. I didn't quite understand my mother's cruelty. After all, no one had deflowered me; I was intact, so why would she treat me as if I were a ruined girl?

With mealtime past, hunger had me in its grip. I hadn't left the area of hard-packed ground where I had lain down the previous evening, as if an invisible wall had forbidden me to cross its boundary.

A little while later my mother came to announce in an icy voice that "that unworthy teacher would be forced out of teaching. As for you, disgraced daughter, we will find a punishment equal to your transgression."

We were alone, and she was yelling as if she wanted to be heard by the whole world. I was lying at her feet.

"I only have you, my mother. If you abandon me, what will become of me?"

She looked me up and down.

"You should have thought of that sooner."

And she went away. I was shattered by the punishment inflicted upon the teacher. I hadn't yet thought of him. For me, he was part of the adult world, and nothing serious could happen to him. That he might be subjected to such a severe sentence troubled me.

During this time, my mother was proclaiming loudly that I was an "innocent lamb" (and not a horny slut, as she had vulgarly described me), diverted from the right track by a man with no morals who had taken advantage of his position as teacher to exploit my inexperience. As a consequence, she was going to file a complaint against him for corruption of a minor. The school principal, very worried by the scandal that tainted his establishment, recommended an amiable settlement to my mother. He was in favor of initiating the teacher's transfer, but quietly, without it having the appearance of a sanction.

The middle-class women of the city, while pretending to understand my mother's indignation, were exchanging knowing smiles. They didn't believe in my innocence. They would point out, not insignificantly, that that man had never lacked respect for their daughters; and that was because they were virtuous. My mother would have been better off saying nothing. Besides, what about her? Where did she come from?

All families talked about was the "secondary school affair." My classmates, their brains overheated by all that was being made up around them, would suddenly remember that they had seen me make "shameful advances" toward the teacher. Each one would then go on to make up more stories, encouraged by an indulgent audience.

My mother was not at all unaware of this malicious gossip. But she felt strong because of having the letters written in the hand of the "guilty party" and whose contents left no doubt about his immorality.

The principal, who had read them, had understood well the explosive character of such documents. That's why he suggested to the right-thinking women that their commentaries be more lenient with respect to me and that they behave more amicably toward my mother in order not to push her to commit an "irreparable" act. As for the teacher's wife, he advised her to overcome her aversion and offer my mother her apologies.

Since the evening of the drama, I had lived in confinement in the kitchen, eating the leftovers that were seemingly forgotten and sleep-

ing on a mat that the maid had left nearby as if by mistake. I didn't
know anything about the malicious rumors that were circulating about
me, nor of my mother's threatening steps with the school authorities.
Even though I hadn't been given the order, I never crossed the threshold of the kitchen, furtively escaping only to relieve myself in the la-
trines located at the far end of the garden. No member of my family
had ventured into my dungeon, and the maid, who came there of necessity, would move as silently as a shadow. They acted as if I didn't exist
anymore. I endured the first two days courageously, considering that
that was the price I had to pay to atone for my mistake. But the third
day seemed interminable to me. However much I cried myself to sleep
from exhaustion, the time wore on. I suffered especially from not having anyone to talk to.

I was aware that the ordeal was much harsher for Duc than for me.
He had to justify himself to the principal, to his wife, and to my parents. And above all he had to suffer the humiliation of seeing his love
letters handed around. The thought of this made me suffer more than
anything. I would have loved to be able to stand up for myself, to tell
him that I was not blameless in the display of our intimacy. But I was a
prisoner at my house, and the whole city had its eyes fixed on us; our
affair was definitely over with.

I was at that point in my thoughts when my mother called me.
The teacher's wife, having swallowed all her pride and shame, had come
to make amends. I was disappointed that her husband hadn't fulfilled
this obligation which, after all, concerned him first and foremost.

I went to join the two women. What preoccupied me was knowing
what they were going to do with me. I hadn't returned to the school in
almost a week. One might have expected that I would never return
there ever again. Now my stepfather could make me into his domestic
servant, and my mother would have no more valid arguments to oppose
him, assuming that she might still want to defend me.

"Sit down, my daughter," my mother ordered in a voice that was
intentionally sweet.

I guessed that this feigned affection was intended for the visitor in
order to show clearly that she considered her daughter to be a victim.

"How are you?" added the visitor.

I stammered an inaudible "I'm fine, thank you." She seemed to have aged, her mouth drooping in spite of her attempt to smile. I didn't want to be impolite and smiled at her in turn.

My mother triumphed. She was merciless. In the tone of a judge, she explained to the unfortunate woman all the harm that her husband had done to me.

"Of course, it's out of the question that the little one return to school. I fear it will be necessary for us to keep her at home."

A long silence followed this reproach. Finally, the professor's wife suggested in a hesitant voice, "I believe that the best thing would be to send the young lady away from Nha Trang . . . [A silence.] I know a religious establishment in Saigon . . . very suitable . . . with a good reputation . . . They give classes up to ninth grade . . . and the cost for room and board is reasonable."

"You are kind to take an interest in her future," whispered my mother. "You are lucky, my daughter; thank the lady."

The teacher's wife had taken the situation back in hand. Not only had she succeeded in getting me away from her husband, she had also put my mother in the position of owing her something. She seemed less downcast.

The two women separated, the game a draw. Neither one had lost face in this delicate duel. Honor was safe since my mother would tell others that the teacher's wife had come humbly to ask for forgiveness for her husband. As for the latter, in the future she could explain to the curious that the affection that Duc had shown me was nothing more than the interest that every teacher has for a gifted student. This was a "misunderstanding that a sincere conversation with the girl's mother" had completely cleared up.

For more plausibility, the two women went frequently to each other's homes, displaying a clear understanding. This back and forth lasted about two weeks, the time it took to calm down the malicious gossips. After that, it stopped for good.

On the occasion of this truce, I was allowed to take my place back in the family circle. But my prestige as eldest sister had diminished considerably. My sisters addressed me with no respect whatsoever, and it was not unusual that my parents, conspicuously ignoring me, would consult my younger sisters over my head.

It was all the same to me. What worried me was the question of my possible studies in Saigon. My mother hadn't talked about it yet with her husband. We now knew that the room and board were as much as four hundred piasters a month. She didn't have it. Getting such a sum would require skill and a sound strategy. Should she fail, nothing would be left for me but a humble existence while my classmates would continue their advancement.

I was ready to do everything to avoid this possibility. Not displeasing my stepfather was the first thing to do. I took pains to show him all the signs of sincere regret and painful remorse. At meals, I was content with just rice, not touching any of the meat or fish, thus punishing myself in front of him.

For her part, my mother sought to convince him of the advantages that he would have by financing my studies up to ninth grade. After that, they would force me to become a midwife.

"Obviously, all that costs a lot, but it's an investment whose benefits would be considerable. Her diploma would allow us to open a private maternity clinic . . ."

My stepfather remained silent. Without doubt he found that she was defending her daughter too vehemently.

"This will be a sure thing, for these days all women give birth in clinics," she added.

A renewed silence.

"All the more so since she seems to regret her past behavior; she will be more docile in the future. What do you say, father of Dzung?"

He didn't answer right away. But in the days that followed, we saw him come back loaded with documents that he studied with the greatest attention.

From then on, I had the right to go out once a week, accompanied by our faithful servant. As we passed, children and even adults would run to their doorsteps, devoured with curiosity. The girls shot me sly looks, then burst out laughing behind their handkerchiefs.

Our maid, doubtless uncomfortable to find herself in my company, took care to walk far behind me, meaning by that that she, too, condemned me. I was anxious for this agony to be over.

One day, we arrived at an intersection. A gang of kids, lying in wait behind a tree, jumped out, yelling at the top of their lungs. "Hey! The husband thief! Hey! The teacher's whore!"

I was ashamed, I was afraid, and I fled as fast as my legs would carry me. I ran, pursued by the hoots. Finally, I collapsed at the foot of a tree. I was very hot and especially very thirsty. The maid whispered in my ear, "Calm down. I'm here."

She wiped my forehead with her scarf, cradling me very softly as if putting a little child to sleep.

She helped me get up when I was able to catch my breath. We returned home without alluding to what had happened.

In the city people didn't tire of speaking ill of me. I became a kind of curiosity: *métisse*, immoral, crazy—those were the adjectives they attributed to me. I would listen with surprise to my story, a story that I didn't recognize.

So much ill will made me suffer, but I consoled myself with the thought that this affair would at least permit me to leave the city. Two more months and I would be far away.

❧ 13 ❧

At the Boarding School

My overstuffed trunk was closed and locked. I had never had so many clothes in my life. We usually had three changes that we washed frequently because of the dust and sweat caused by the climate. These outfits were an incredible expense for us, but since the French school required them, we had to rise to the occasion.

My mother accompanied me to Saigon, leaving my sisters, the youngest of whom was only three years old, in the care of the maid. On the platform, they clung to my mother, sobbing. The goodbyes were a trial; as the eldest, I felt ashamed, depriving them like that.

From the train station, we went directly to the private school. The nuns, all dressed in black with white cornets, welcomed us. Aside from the mother superior, who was French, the others came from South Viet Nam, their origins given away by their dark complexions and the roundness of their faces. They moved in rapid, small steps, making the wings of the cornets tremble like large white birds ready to take flight. I hadn't seen nuns since the orphanage. These ones seemed pleasant to me. For the most part from the working class, they had temperaments inclined to laughter and jokes, retained from an education that had not been very strict. Gathered around the mother superior, who was a good head taller, they made up an innocent picture of well-behaved children and would break out in fresh laughter at the slightest thing that was amusing.

My mother poured out a long litany of thank yous and said that she wished to see me treated with the greatest severity. She expressed herself in a pompous Vietnamese that was translated for the mother superior. When the mother superior had understood, she assured me, carefully articulating each word, that everything would turn out well if I was well-behaved and obedient.

Two nuns grabbed hold of my trunk, and another took me out of the office. I didn't have the time to bid farewell to my mother.

I was settled into a dormitory where I counted twenty beds. The furniture was basic, and they put my things in a communal armoire where each one had her shelf. A small nightstand made for the only private domain of the pupils. In any case, I had nothing of a personal nature.

Taking into account the modest cost of the boarding school, the clientele was composed of children who came from the middle class, small business owners or employees. The girls were kind and guileless. I found myself more relaxed and happier there than with my own family.

I liked being a boarder. It was extraordinary living exclusively with people who were the same age as me, with the same problems, the same dreams. For the first time, I could learn without having to hide, without being continually bothered by the dishes to do or by a sister who demanded to be taken care of. Studying was no longer a shameful act but a quality that merited rewards.

My French professor, Madame Moreau, was one of the rare lay teachers at the school. She was a tall, red-headed woman with flaming hair cut very short and whose unbelievably white skin was covered with freckles. Always dressed in a safari jacket and white skirt, she looked like those naval officers I had seen in American movies. And her husky voice further reinforced the illusion. We admired her masculine air, her reassurance. Watching her was such a fascinating spectacle that we would sometimes forget to listen to her. She would then get angry and point an accusing finger at random:

"Repeat what I just said."

The designated pupil would stammer miserably. I was the only one to find favor in her eyes for, despite my distraction, my memory would automatically record her words. I would repeat what she said.

"Good," she would say.

And the class would continue.

When she found out that I was destined for the profession of midwife, she said, "You disappoint me, my girl. You lack ambition. You have the capacity to continue up to a bachelor's degree and you're talking to me about studying to be a midwife. Wouldn't you like to be a teacher, for example?"

I timidly admitted that I would like to be a doctor or an engineer.

"No, no. You're not good enough at mathematics for that. Continue with literature."

Besides the possibility of becoming a teacher—a profession that was not "virile" enough for my taste—I didn't see how you could use literary knowledge in your working life. However, from her advice I retained the idea of pursuing my studies beyond the *baccalauréat*, a high school diploma. I knew perfectly well that my family would never want to support me for such a long time. But at fifteen, I had no sense of my limits; I would not be a midwife, even if it meant disappointing my parents. I imagined in advance my stepfather's triumphal air, telling his wife stiffly, "She is congenitally ungrateful; I've always told you that."

And he would be right. It would cross my mind that a twist of fate always led me to disappoint my mother. Still, I loved her tenderly and I only wanted to bring her satisfaction.

Everything that suited my temperament ran counter to her dreams. I suffered from the pain that I was going to cause her without being capable of renouncing my ambitions. I began working fervently.

I was very moved to see the Nha Trang train station again during summer vacation. My absence had lasted eight months. My mother and my two sisters were standing on the platform. Seeing them, I suddenly took full measure of how much I had missed them.

"You've grown a lot." I addressed my sisters in order to say something.

"And you, you have put on weight," declared my mother, satisfied. "That's good. Now you are really a pretty girl."

She accompanied the compliment with a sigh. From experience, she knew that beauty was not a synonym for happiness—far from it.

At home, the best place at the table was reserved for me and I was offered the best delicacies. All of them wanted to know what I had done during the long months of our separation. I painted the boarding school in attractive colors: my classmates loved me and my teachers appreciated me. I lied in saying that the food was decent.

My mother listened, happy. Her kindness having won my trust, I confessed my ambition to her, supported by most of the teachers but beyond what she had hoped for me. I expected her resistance, but to my surprise, she approved.

"I chose the simplest solution for you. But if you want to have a higher position, why not?" And she added, dreamily, "There is always a moment when the rich husband remembers that his wife is poor; that's when her beauty has faded. So, your profession will be useful to you."

For a long time, we discussed the ways to provide for my continued studies.

"The most difficult thing is to get to the *baccalauréat*; after that, I could work while being enrolled in college."

The university was at that time only a prestigious name, something like a dream that I would conjure up without daring to believe it too much. I was finishing up sixth grade[1]; six years separated me from college-level studies. The university was only an abstract goal. But my mother embraced it with a kind of enthusiasm that amused me and surprised me all at once. She regretted that because of a false step, she had had to make do with a mediocre life, sacrificing her more ambitious dreams.

"I was a very romantic girl. Who knows what I would have become had I not gotten pregnant with you."

"It's my existence that got in the way of your plans."

"It was destiny," she sighed.

I risked asking a question about the one who had spoiled her life, but she answered evasively that "he was a man of no importance."

The two months that followed were the best moments. I had rediscovered my mother's complicity again, and public rumor had forgotten its grievances toward me.

The teacher, incorrigible, had embarked on other adventures. Dô, Ghi, and I talked about it.

"The chosen one . . ." Dô began.

"Or the victim," Ghi corrected.

"In any case, now it's a rather ugly girl who had lost all hope of being wooed until the day when Master Four noticed her."

---

1. See Chapter 10, Note 1, p. 126.

We had found our secret code again to refer to the teacher.

"There were no more pretty girls on the shelf," said Ghi ironically. "The terrified parents took them out of the secondary school to put them in schools for girls."

I listened to this news without emotion. My memory retained the image of a man who had nothing in common with the one my girl-friends were talking about.

But if my heart remained serene, my pride was hurt, so much so that when I fortuitously had occasion to cross paths with him in the street, I intentionally burst out in laughter meant to be scathing. He didn't hear me. My laugh had wounded only me.

During our separation, Ghi had become engaged to the son of a friend of her father's. He was coming straight from the zone occupied by the Viet Cong. He was twenty years old, while we were only fifteen. Taking advantage of that age difference, he would give us advice in a dictatorial tone, harshly criticizing the petit bourgeois education we had received. He found us childish and irresponsible.

"You only know how to dream! Dreams are the opium that makes you stupid. Learn to see reality!"

He wanted to change his fiancée from head to toe. He wanted her to be athletic, to get interested in politics . . . For this reason, she was the only girl in our group who swam and played tennis. She had learned to ride a bicycle as well, greatly scandalizing the upstanding people who would look at that girl straddling the seat, flabbergasted. I admired her audacity. The only thing that bothered me was seeing her half-naked in a swimsuit. We didn't swim, and I didn't know the pleasure of the water, the assault of the waves. However, I was convinced that Ghi was right, that you couldn't disrupt the unchanging lives we led without occasionally adopting excessive behavior.

Thanks to the "fiancé," we sometimes managed to forget the difference between the sexes and to chat without too much restraint. We would talk about our favorite poets, but the boys preferred to broach the question of communism in Tonkin.

"My family came back to the South, because we thought that communism was not a valid solution for the whole country," declared the fiancé. "It's a system that's applicable in the North, not here."

"But that's treason! You well know that here you serve Bao Dai, who is only a puppet manipulated skillfully by the French," intervened Son, a rebel.

That I knew; it had been repeated often enough to me in my family. But I would have been incapable of saying it as clearly, and especially with Son's authority.

"I know," replied the fiancé testily; he didn't like to be contradicted. "One day we will run Bao Dai out."

"But why would communism suit the North and not the South?" Dô asked timidly.

That was true, but why? No one among us knew why. Dô was doubtless thinking of her father who was still fighting in Tonkin.

The fiancé looked around at all of us, shaking his head pensively. Evidently, he took pity on our ignorance. He gave himself some time to think, as if searching for the simplest way to explain a rather complex subject.

"Because, you see, Tonkin is an arid land where work in the fields requires collective organization precisely on account of the necessity for irrigation. In Cochinchina, the soil is fertile and each person cultivates his field as he wants to. Private property is thus the best solution."

An enlightening display. Ghi was drinking in the words of her sweetheart. As for us, we were speechless. Son tried to save face.

"I don't know if you're right. In any case, we will take care of that question later, between us men. For the time being, the urgent thing is to get rid of the French protectorate, which is nothing but disguised colonization."

A general outcry of approval accompanied his words.

A boy took me aside. "I think, for example, that you are wrong to study French instead of imbuing yourself with our language and our culture. You don't believe that it's serving colonialism?"

I reddened. I sought to defend myself, saying that it was not my fault and that I hadn't chosen to study French.

Protests arose from all quarters.

"It's up to us to forge our destiny," affirmed another boy.

I noticed that from the beginning, the girls contented themselves with listening or, at best, asking questions. Not one had come to my aid. I kept quiet for lack of arguments. But I didn't believe at all in that assertion. Neither my mother's experience nor my own had convinced me that a woman could shape her destiny. I thought, on the contrary, that a woman was the plaything of so many events over which she had no control that it was impossible for her not to put up with it.

But I didn't know how to state an opinion that my friends would have inevitably found traditionalist. So, I kept it for myself, leaving the others with the illusion that they had persuaded me.

Very often we discussed politics—or rather the boys discussed politics. We girls listened quietly, trying to assimilate some basic ideas.

In fact, apart from the fiancé, who had lived in the Viet Cong zone, the others held forth in a purely abstract way. Often, I was not in agreement with the unreserved enthusiasm they showed for Hanoi's Communism. I had seen the Viet Minh up close in the past, not counting several members of my family who had been eliminated during the great purges. Even though my theoretical ignorance was great, my feelings, nourished by the atrocious stories of survivors of the regime in the North, were tinged with horror. I wanted to communicate my experience to those who had none, but I didn't manage to organize my ideas in a satisfying way.

Despite what appeared to be a camaraderie without ulterior motives, the boys secretly hoped to dazzle the female audience with their knowledge, while the latter was devoted to charming them discreetly.

In this game where I had some chance of being considered a pretty girl, it was up to me to prove that I wasn't stupid. That's why I preferred silence to an inopportune contribution.

Some of the boys wooed me without seeming to, encouraged in their enterprise by Ghi, who was longing to find me a boyfriend, a "cavalier," in order to make our lives more similar. But I kept a polite distance on this subject. I still had a sensitive wound from my last adventure.

My mother considered my evenings out with a disapproving eye. But she knew that I would have to return soon to the boarding school and was reluctant to reprimand me. In addition, the thought that we were in a group calmed her worries.

The summer was going by pleasantly when I was stricken by a slight fever that returned every afternoon and left me languid from fatigue until the following day. In the evening I would become sweaty, on fire.

This situation lasted several weeks, during which I lost my appetite completely and a spectacular amount of weight.

The doctor we consulted diagnosed pulmonary tuberculosis. The word shattered us. Tuberculosis was considered a fatal disease since people didn't have the means to pay for a long stay in a sanatorium. Misfortune had entered our home. The most difficult thing was to preserve an apparent gaiety in order not to alert our friends and acquaintances. We knew that the fear of being contaminated would have terrorized people. I was isolated from the rest of the family: I had *my* bowl, *my* glass, and *my* chopsticks that my mother washed separately. She boiled the clothes I had worn. I had the feeling of being excluded from the society of the living.

Even so, I didn't have the appearance of being gravely ill, save a dry cough from time to time. We decided that I would return to the boarding school; we would hide my illness. It would be enough that I take care of myself, seeing to it that I fed myself decently—I wondered how: the food at the boarding school was so bad—sleeping enough and resting each time I needed to.

And so I returned to Saigon.

I loved the beginning of the school year because of the reunions with old friends whose absence had begun to weigh on me. The first day of class was always merry, all bathed in a warm friendship as if past quarrels had never happened. I met up again with the same friends and the same teachers, with the exception of Madame Moreau, who had followed her officer husband to Africa, to Abidjan, I believe. Her replacement, a young Indian woman from Pondicherry,[2] dressed in a tiny jacket that stopped just below her breasts, leaving her whole abdomen bare, scarcely veiled by a green silk sari. We avoided looking lower than her face, uncomfortable with this nakedness. But she moved so naturally and gracefully that we ended up forgetting this unseemly detail.

With great difficulty, I obtained permission to go lie down twice a day, once after breakfast and again after dinner. The rule was very strict on this subject, the nuns' main worry being to prevent the pupils

---

2. Pondicherry was also a French colonial settlement in India.

from meeting up in the dormitory privately in order to shield them from the temptations of guilty amorous adventures. But even so, some couples formed, and some girls were in love with each other. We were between fourteen and sixteen years old, and with our budding sensuality and no object for the impulses of our hearts, upon whom else were we to shower our overflowing emotions? The nuns themselves had their preferred ones for whom they declared a forbidden passion that did not rule out the sensual.

The one who preferred me, Sister Aimée—that was her name—became alarmed at my condition and forced me to go see a doctor despite my resistance. The X-ray revealed a "cavity" in my right lung. The doctor recommended three months of rest in the mountains; he was thinking of Da-Lat.[3] But apart from my parents knowing no one in that city, I didn't want to interrupt the school year, which had already begun.

Thanks to the protection of Sister Aimée, I wasn't sent home. I even got permission to attend two hours of class per day. For the rest, I could do what I wanted on the condition that I stay in bed to rest. For months on end Sister Aimée tenderly took care of me, combining the devotion of a mother with the zeal of a lover.

That year she was supposed to go home to her family for vacation. It was a favor that the rules granted to the nuns every ten years. She proposed that I come along with her. Together we wrote to my mother, explaining to her that such a stay could only be beneficial for my health. The poor woman, whom bonzes[4] (monks and nuns) had always intimidated, gave her consent in a letter full of gratitude.

Sister Aimée still had her mother, an aged woman whose face was furrowed with lines like the cracks in dry ground. Tiny because of her stooped back, which was folded almost in half, she still had a lot of vitality.

There was almost no one else in the house but this old woman. Sister Aimée and I found ourselves alone. I told her about my life, at least the episodes I judged suitable, not saying anything about my bas-

---

3. Da-Lat, a city in the Central Highlands, is famous in Viet Nam for its temperate climate.

4. Buddhist monks. Buddhist nuns would be implicitly included in this general term.

tard origins or my past loves. She confessed the difficulties of being a nun to me, the temptations and the pitfalls to overcome. Her love for me gnawed at her, filling her with remorse. She had taken a vow to give it up.

"But not before helping you pursue your path in life."

She remembered a friend in class from before, married to a doctor, a pious woman who gave a considerable sum every year to charity.

"That money would allow you to continue until the *baccalauréat*."

My imagination took flight; I would be placed in the best schools; I would succeed. the *bac*, the master's, maybe even the doctorate . . .

"Have you been baptized?"

I thought so, when I was in the orphanage, but I wasn't sure of it.

"Suppose that you are. Have you been confirmed?"

No, of that I was certain, for I didn't even know the name of the ceremony. She explained to me that it was a sacrament that required a godfather and a godmother, just like a baptism.

"We could confirm you; I would ask her to be your godmother. If she accepts, she will assume her responsibilities and help you continue your studies."

I told her that it was God who had inspired her, but she gave me a melancholic smile.

"God would have preferred that I have a purer heart."

She wrote immediately to her friend, Madame N.

My days passed in waiting according to an immutable and monotonous rite: the antibiotic Rimifon, a meal, rest, then more rest, a meal, Rimifon. I swallowed the food that was prepared for me out of duty, without appetite, and I didn't stop losing weight, to the distress of the women who were taking care of me. My condition didn't improve. I was afraid of dying, and I cried all the time.

At the end of the month, Sister Aimée went back to the convent. I went home to my family.

My mother broke down in sobs when she saw me get off the train.

"My poor daughter, you are nothing but skin and bones."

Then, breaking common practice, she hugged me close to her.

Indeed, my skeletal thinness was frightening to see. I had a grayish complexion and a dull look. I measured the extent of my decline by the fear that my sisters showed when they approached me.

That month of August was devoted to my condition as a sick person. My parents made the news known. From then on, friends and acquaintances came by at all hours. An unhealthy curiosity led distant friends to come see me close up.

Their assaults of friendship tortured me, and I could detect behind their smiles what their eyes were saying: that I was ugly and pitiful. There was also that way of standing very far from me, avoiding all direct contact. I formulated only one wish, that they leave me in peace.

On the contrary, my mother was visibly delighted at the number of visitors who came to bother me. As soon as it looked like a visit was shaping up, she prepared tea and put candied fruit on saucers. Those ladies would drink, munch, and encourage me for a few minutes, then would spend an hour or two speaking ill of me. One group wouldn't have had the time to leave when yet another would arrive. And then the ceremony would begin all over again. My mother kept a detailed list of all those who came by—it was always women; the men didn't bother—noting in a reproachful tone others' absence.

"Well, well, Madame Nu hasn't come by, and yet I sat up all night with her ill son!"

I testily answered her that I didn't want to see those gossiping women who were only there to chatter with her. She called me ungrateful, and we got angry with each other.

"Besides, I'm not dying. I'm going to the beach to swim."

My mother didn't have the time to stop me; I had reached the door with my swimsuit in my hand. I had bought it the previous summer when the style—copied from Esther Williams—had prompted some girls to take swimming lessons. At Ghi's insistence—she was already a good swimmer and wanted to have me experience the "incomparable pleasure of frolicking in the water"—I had picked out a one-piece suit whose cut, though classic, had a low neckline at the back. I had never worn it, unable to overcome my modesty and especially my fear of the water. I was well aware that this wasn't the best moment for me to put on a swimsuit. But I needed to do something that would compensate for the feeling of powerlessness that was crushing me.

There weren't many people on the beach, about ten including a few girls with plump thighs and broad shoulders, all beautiful and shapely. I sat down in an isolated spot, ill at ease. The girls were chatting and laughing; groups of boys passed by, then passed by again, making the most of the bare skin on display. Self-conscious, I kept my eyes riveted on the sand, whose reflection was blinding me. Three of them came toward me. I pretended to be absorbed in the arabesques that I was tracing mechanically with my finger.

When they reached me, one of them said loudly, "Ugh! What a bag of bones!"

All the heat in my body rushed toward my face. The muffled drum that was beating in my ears was my heart. I had trouble swallowing my saliva. The girls stopped talking and were looking at me. A heavy silence surrounded me as if the beach had emptied all of a sudden.

My pride required me to remain there a little while longer. I continued to draw figures in the sand that I didn't see. I begrudged myself for having brought on my own humiliation. Why hadn't I stayed at home? I was ugly, a cruel truth hurled at my face, stinging like a slap. I felt like I was a hundred years old when I finally got up.

I knew that the disease had changed me a lot, but I didn't know that I could inspire disgust. As a *métisse* of an unknown father, the only quality that people saw in me was what they called "my beauty." What was left once I'd lost it? More than ever I needed my education. I wanted to return to Saigon without delay. I told my mother, who didn't understand. Wanting to leave when she was taking better care of me than anyone was proof that I didn't love her. She cried, repeating tirelessly that she was the most unfortunate of mothers, and I the most ungrateful of daughters. Her pain tore me up, but I needed to be sustained by the affection and esteem of others, and that, neither my mother nor my family could provide. No doubt I should have told her about my misadventure, but modesty always prevented us from confiding in each other. Once more, misunderstanding and miscommunication separated us.

In the week that followed, our relationship was weighed down by unspoken hard feelings. The thought that what was essential for me should inevitably cause her grief made me feel guilty. The closer the moment of my departure got, the more I was relieved, whereas my mother expressed the greatest despondency. Her ostentatious sadness was unbearable to me. I tried to console her.

"Don't be sad; you know that they take good care of me there. Besides, I have to find a job, especially now that I'm frighteningly ugly."

But she continued to lament. "I could have abandoned you when you were little, and I didn't do it. Now that I need you, you only think of running away. I always knew that you were ungrateful!"

And then she cried. I was in despair.

"Alright, I'm ungrateful. It was in the cards, wasn't it? I can't do anything about it. Don't worry about me anymore. You have two other daughters; let them be your consolation. Without me, you will be happier. Your husband will have nothing to reproach you for, and he will even be kind to you, for I will no longer be here to remind him of your past."

That was the first time I had allowed myself such a blunt remark about my mother's past. I had had no intention of going so far. I would have wanted to tell her how much I loved her, not only because of what she had done for me but also because of the suffering she had endured. I regretted having hurt her. But it was too late; my mother slapped me twice. I really deserved it.

Such was my relationship with my mother. I loved her without ever knowing how to show her my affection. She reproached me for my harshness, and without doubt she was right. My feelings for her were complex; sometimes I was ready to do anything to make her happy; other times I had only one desire, to run away and erase the failure of her life from my memory.

The older I got, the less I could bear the heavy atmosphere of our family. I was tired of my stepfather's absolute authority. His presence transformed the house into a kind of austere temple in which all movement was prohibited. He didn't tolerate playing, laughing, or even conversations. He liked to see us separated from each other, bent over some useful occupation. Our joy burst out as soon as he turned his back; it was snuffed out upon his approach. I was impatient to see my classmates again and the books that opened up broader horizons for me. All things considered, the boarding school offered me more freedom. On the condition that you conformed to the rules, which weren't excessively strict, I could chat as long as I wanted or submerge myself for hours in reading, without feeling at fault.

In the boarding school, I was assigned the nicest bed in the dormitory, located under a window so that I could take advantage of a little fresh air when I rested.

I especially liked the morning, when I would get back to my bed at about ten o'clock, after recess. We were still far from the hectic noon activities with their noise of silverware striking the tables. In the silence, the slightest sound would have a distinctive quality to my ears, almost musical. In closing my eyes, I could distinguish the muffled hiss—like cloth being torn—of the bucket of water being poured on the flower beds under the kitchen window. Sometimes a shout would break the peaceful atmosphere; it was the mathematics teacher scream-ing, confronted by the unenlightened brain of some pupil.

I played at recognizing Sister Aimée's voice in the distance, a low, very resonant voice buried under thick parasitic layers of shouts and murmurs that sometimes managed to reach me. Finally, weary from my efforts, I would gradually slip off to sleep. The lunch bell would wake me up.

I dreaded afternoon naps, when it was horribly hot and not a breath of air alleviated the torpor of the dormitory. I would then curse the French bedding whose thick mattress increased my discomfort. I dreamed of a mat set right on the cool cement floor like at home, in-stead of a sheet that my sweating dampened in places and that made me constantly toss and turn.

Even so, I was working as much as the others, for despite my fail-ing health, I had been selected from among some of the pupils in eighth grade whom they wished to take the *brevet* examination.[5] For the insti-tution, it was a way of testing the level of their teaching.

Our responsibility was great. If we passed, other students could take it every year; if we failed, the experiment would end right there. I could have refused, but if I didn't take the test, I would have disap-pointed the teachers who were counting on me.

Still, I knew that in the event that I passed, I would have to leave the boarding school, whose teaching stopped at ninth grade. Where would I

5. The *brevet* is an end-of-term examination.

continue? It was useless to think about private establishments, whose fees were exorbitant. As for the public schools, there was the Marie Curie French *lycée* or Vietnamese secondary schools. Since I had stopped studying Vietnamese when I left Nha Trang, I didn't have any other choice but to pursue instruction in French. The French *lycée* was very difficult to get into, and I didn't know anyone likely to get me admitted there.

To my great surprise, I passed the *brevet* exam. My parents, whom I had not kept informed, learned the good news from the newspaper. They summoned me home. I mentioned some medical consultation in order to stay longer in Saigon, hoping for news from Madame N., who had promised to receive me.

The school was deserted now. As the only boarder, I ate my meals in the kitchen with the service staff. At night, I slept alone, surrounded by twenty empty beds. I was afraid of every unusual sound, of the shadows that the street lamps projected on the walls. Very often, I was unable to fall asleep.

I hardly saw Sister Aimée, who was living with her community in the central building forbidden to lay persons. Every now and then she would agree to see me. I would then meet her in the parlor like a relative who had come to visit. Our conversations would inevitably center on Madame N., who had given no sign of life.

Sister Aimée suggested to me that I familiarize myself with the tenth-grade curriculum to occupy my time, but, discouraged by the uncertainty of my situation, I didn't have the heart to study. I preferred to go back home.

What struck me first of all was my stepfather's change in attitude; there was a less rigid air about him and even a certain kindness. My success seemed to delight him, and I had the feeling that he finally accepted me. Perhaps he was content to have given me his name after all.

Later, when he broached the question of my studies to be a midwife, I didn't dare confess to him that I had no intention of committing myself to the path he had marked out for me. I tried to buy time with a silence that he could interpret as he wished. My mother supported me in this evasive action. The improvement of my condition filled her with so much joy that my studies became completely beside the point.

"Agree to what your father tells you. We will see what's advisable to do when the time comes."

I couldn't have asked for more; I needed peace after the long months of sustained effort in Saigon.

I renewed contact with my girlfriends in Nha Trang. Ghi had gotten married. She was fifteen. They lived with her parents while they continued school.

That left Dô, the least pretty of us all, the most level headed, the most intelligent. She hadn't gotten married, and she didn't have a fiancé. She was free like me. Together we went along the deserted shore, arm in arm, listening to the rumbling of the ocean, dreaming for hours on end, just like old times.

Impressed by my success with the *brevet*, Dô wanted to change schools.

"The secondary school here is not good enough, you know. My mother intends to send me to the Couvent des Oiseaux."

That was a school of great renown. People said that among its first boarders was the Empress, the wife of Bao Dai.

"You are lucky; me, I still don't know what's going to become of me."

My future was entirely in the hands of a charitable lady I hadn't seen yet.

"Don't worry. Everything's gone well up to now; why not again?"

Indeed, that was also the opinion of my family. My mother believed that a superior power was watching over me and that there would always be a solution to my problems.

Unfortunately, the invisible powers remained silent this time. Sister Aimée had not succeeded in contacting her friend, who was on a trip abroad, and the new school year was quickly approaching.

My mother was preaching resignation.

"Being a midwife is a good profession after all. Say yes and your father will pay for your schooling."

"That I cannot do. I hate childbirth," I cried out.

I remembered my mother's pregnancies, her paleness, her nausea that went on for months, her lack of appetite, her drawn face. She carried her stomach with fatigue, exhausting herself in making the child swelling up her abdomen grow.

That was when, in my position as eldest daughter, I had to take charge of all the work.

The approach of the delivery did not constitute a respite for her, quite the contrary. Anguish replaced the feelings of sickness: What if it's another girl?

I begged my mother, "Please, don't make me; I can't do it."

Tired of fighting, she agreed to give me a ticket for my trip and the amount of the first month's board. It was up to me to find money after that.

I arrived in Saigon ready for anything. I told my classmates about the financial impasse I was in, even if it meant losing face, such an important notion in the society in which we were living.

Soon Lan, who shared my table, proposed that I come live at her house. Her father had a clothes-dying shop, and there was plenty of work to do in the store. I could make myself useful on Wednesdays and Sundays in exchange for room and board. I accepted.

Lan's father lived with his two wives and a brood of six children, the majority of whom were very young. He was a man of about fifty, still very vigorous and always laughing. The first spouse, Lan's mother, appeared to be so old that she was frequently taken for the grandmother of her children. The second, and the favorite, naturally, was about twenty-two. She made me think of the sins of the flesh, no doubt because I always saw her stretched out, half-naked, nursing her last-born. That was her only concern. She would leave her bed only at mealtimes, displaying her naked breasts, which the husband ogled with possessive pleasure.

I shared the attic of the house with Lan. The bamboo ladder used to get up there was so shaky that it discouraged old and young, so that we enjoyed absolute peace. There wasn't any furniture at all. In a corner were hidden trunks full of magazines whose covers showed women in unbelievably languid poses.

In each other's presence, we pretended not to notice these provocative photographs, but I took advantage of Lan's least absence to immerse myself in the contemplation of those bodies swooning from invisible caresses. I was persuaded that Lan, for her part, did the same thing, so much so that finally, by a tacit agreement, we would slip away in turn, leaving the way open for the other.

I spent many a torrid afternoon in the attic, giving myself over to reading about carnal pleasures whose essential meanings escaped me but which still made me burn with desire. At night my dreams were filled with hands reaching toward me without ever managing to touch me. I would wake up at the height of frustration. Nearby, Lan shifted as if she couldn't manage to find the right position to sleep in.

"Are you asleep?" I whispered.

"No, it's too hot,"

"I'm covered with sweat. Too bad; I'm taking off my blouse."

She didn't answer. I threw my blouse far away. A wet rivulet tickled me as it ran down my back. In the nocturnal silence, the muffled cries of the second spouse reached us, sounds at once plaintive and wild. We remained with our ears pricked up for quite some time after calm had returned to the house. In the morning, we didn't dare look each other in the face, as shameful as if we had committed a vile deed during the night.

Working in the store, wrapping the clothes that were already dyed took several hours a day, without counting the ironing, which was extremely fatiguing because of the heat. The irons, heated red-hot by the embers, weighed heavily in our hands. We sweated profusely, our hair stuck to our foreheads, our soaked short-sleeved blouses plastered to our bodies. Lan worked as hard as I did, so much so that at no time did I feel like an employee. We ironed side by side, without a word, careful not to burn the clients' clothes. All the while I worked, I thought that I was lucky. If Lan's parents were satisfied with me, I could continue my studies without having recourse to Madame N.'s help.

But Sister Aimée did not consider the situation in that way.

❦ 14 ❦

Madame N.

By dint of persistence, Sister Aimée ended up getting in touch with Madame N., who agreed to meet with us.

There was nothing left for me to do but prove to this person that I deserved her help. Even though Sister Aimée constituted my trump card, I knew that her decision would depend on the warmth I could or could not inspire. I was in more anguish than at the time of the *brevet* exam. Together we reviewed the coming meeting, from the first greetings right up to the goodbyes.

"Don't be too timid or too daring," my protector advised me. "Seize the occasion to show your skills, but be careful! Do it with modesty."

We finally went to Madame N.'s, both of us very tense. We didn't breathe a word until the moment when a big, green-painted doorway appeared before our eyes.

"It's here," said Sister Aimée, after having verified the address written on the piece of paper she held in her hand.

A flowering garden formed a kind of bower for the house nestled in the background. Often, I would pass in front of similar houses thinking once and for all that this privileged universe was not within my reach. So now, here I was crossing the threshold of one of them.

Inside, everything was unimaginably luxurious. There were Chinese vases and lacquer; each object seemed to have its place for eternity in an immutable world. I was impatient to finally meet Madame N., hoping to discover in her the secret that had earned her such a fortune. I imagined my mother in a similar setting, waited on by servants.

Lost in my thoughts, I hadn't noticed the entrance of the mistress of the house, a bad beginning. Sister Aimée called me back to reality with a discreet nudge.

Madame assuredly deserved her destiny. She resembled the reclining ivory statuette that decorated the teak pedestal table. Her protruding black eyes, shaped like almonds, were expressionless, like two pools of still water. She made you think less of a real person than of a work of art.

The two friends greeted each other ceremoniously. I waited, standing slightly apart. Not once had Madame N. looked at me; she seemed to signify by this attitude that in no way did I enter into her decision. Whether she granted or refused her assistance was a personal affair between God and herself. If need be, the friendship she felt for Sister Aimée could weigh in her decision but in no case would my merits.

A servant entered, setting a large silver tray on the table. Madame N. distractedly handed me a cup of tea, which I declined; I preferred to stay in my proper place.

Embarrassed by my refusal, Sister Aimée chose to believe that it was a gaffe: "Forgive her. She's very shy."

I heard the clinking of spoons on saucers, the purring of the air conditioning. My silence had put off the two women, but a demon pushed me to continue. Again, I declined the cookies that were held out to me. I was aware of being unpleasant.

Irritated, Sister Aimée automatically stuffed a cookie into my hand. I felt a profound desire to go, leaving them there. The cookie was reduced to crumbs in my tight fist. I scattered the contents on the expensive carpet, a secretly vengeful gesture that did me good.

In the street, Sister Aimée couldn't stop praising the piety of her childhood friend.

"She's an excellent woman. She will help you," concluded Sister Aimée.

I would have wanted this "excellent woman" to have more consideration for me; I would have wished that her good deeds be done in a less inattentive manner. Unfortunately, I was only the path that would allow her to get into heaven. I owed her nothing, since nothing had been intended for me personally.

᙭

With confirmation in mind, I was sent to catechism three times a week. Once would have sufficed, but it was deemed that my whole religious education was to be redone and that it was necessary to take double helpings.

In the adjoining chapel, in front of an altar of blinding gold, I was initiated into the mysteries of the Holy Trinity in the company of little girls preparing for their first communion.

"Remember, my children, that the Son of God died on the cross to save your souls," the parish priest said solemnly.

He then told us about the suffering of Christ, the flagellation and the crucifixion, completely incomprehensible forms of torture for me. Why was so much pain necessary? I spontaneously communicated my reflections to the priest, whose eyes widened with horror.

"My child, the mystery of Redemption is fundamental. If you don't understand that, you will understand nothing about Christianity. Besides," he continued in a categorical tone, "it's a sin of pride to want to understand; you have to believe!"

"Yes, my father," I answered humbly.

I asked for nothing better than to believe. I was tired of being constantly out of place in the world in which I lived. I needed to feel at peace with something; why not faith?

Subsequently, I became the model pupil in catechism class. If it happened again that I had doubts, I shook my head hard as if shaking off raindrops after riding out a storm.

Finally, the long-awaited day came, a holiday when the future candidates for confirmation were pampered and enjoyed all kinds of favors.

The families were there early to share the children's joy. The women were wearing elegant *áo dài* of silk or crêpe de Chine. The men moved about in European shantung suits in white or a pale yellow known by the term "chicken fat." Many of the families knew each other. They exchanged greetings and joked, and the ladies laughed discreetly behind their fans. The gentlemen openly burst out laughing.

The parlor was full. The nuns, bustling about, passed from one group to another, arranging the pleats of a dress here, a lock of hair there. I stayed in my corner; no one was around me and that was for the better. I didn't really want to make myself noticed. For several hours, I had waited for Madame N., my future godmother, without excessive emotions. Even so, I considered the fact she was so late as going too far. I imagined her being annoyed at having to go out of her way for me, a chore among others imposed upon her by her acts of kindness. How much charitable work had she undertaken in order to buy her way into paradise? A strange religion. "And how do the poor get to heaven?" I said to myself. But I quickly dismissed that wicked idea.

The more time passed, the more my presence among those girls, several years younger than I, became incongruous. My being alone was especially puzzling. Others watched me: why was I alone? Who were my parents? I lowered my head, irritated, cursing my godmother

I thought of the discomfort that had always been my lot. Outside of the years spent in the orphanage, where my origins and my place had been clearly defined, I would often find myself in situations where I had to pass for what I was not: "So, your father is Vietnamese?" people would ask me, sometimes spitefully. "No, he's Chinese," I would answer coldly.

Behind that banal question, I easily saw that it was my mother who was being judged. I considered that I was saving her honor in avowing that my father was Chinese. Not that marriages between Chinese and Vietnamese were more encouraged; at least they weren't stained by the relationship between colonizer and colonized, between master and slave. With a Chinese man who was her equal, my mother would recover her dignity.

A peal of the carillon's bells interrupted the animated conversations in the parlor. It was time to go into the church. My godmother was still keeping us waiting. Sister Aimée didn't stop going back and forth from the door to the parlor. Finally, the candidates for confirmation were asked to line up. What was I to do?

"Get in the back row," suggested Sister Aimée. "You will be able to slip out without being noticed in case Madame N. doesn't come."

Indeed, her presence was indispensable: no godmother, no confirmation. We were very disappointed. Sister Aimée was not far from taking her friend's lateness as a personal affront.

The church was filled with an elegant audience and loaded with flowers, perfumed with incense, all of its chandeliers lit. The priest, in his chasuble embroidered with gold and precious stones, drew majestic movements in the air.

At the triumphal sound of the harmonium, the choir intoned,

> The Lord is my shepherd
> I shall not want
> He leadeth me . . . [1]

A sweet and consoling religion. There were no shepherds in my country; here, the keepers of the water buffalo were kids for the most part. But I, too, aspired to have a shepherd to lead me and provide for my needs.

In catechism, I had been taught that God knew each one of His creatures and that He could call each one by its name. And so I, too, was known by God, who was familiar with all the details of my life. My *métissage*—it was He who had wished it for reasons that I was incapable of understanding.

I loved to believe in this version, which absolved my mother completely. She was no longer guilty since such were the ways of Providence. I reproached myself for having resisted a religion that seemed particularly suited to my personal situation.

Already the first row was advancing toward the holy altar. Two more rows and it would be my turn. Should I wait longer or leave discreetly?

I looked for Sister Aimée, seeking her advice, but she, too, had disappeared. I left my place and cautiously advanced toward the door. An imperious voice stopped me:

"What are you doing, you poor wretch? Return to your place."

Sister Aimée stared daggers at me. "Madame N. is here," she hissed between her teeth.

"Finally!" I thought. My tense nerves relaxed and a sudden wave of nausea took hold of me like a black veil; I collapsed on the tile floor.

When I regained consciousness, I had a damp towel on my forehead. Behind me someone was saying, "The service is long, and she is fasting; it's normal."

I advanced, staggering toward the altar, guided by Madame N.

---

1. "Tu es mon Berger, ô Seigneur, Rien ne peut me manquer où tu me conduis" in the original.

The priest placed salt on my tongue and poured oil on my forehead. To the questions he asked, and which seemed shrouded in fog to me, my godmother answered "yes" for me. I especially wanted to lie down, but we remained standing because of the sermon.

To finish up, he gave me his benediction, telling me to go in peace. My godmother accompanied me back to my place.

I looked at Madame N., her porcelain face leaning toward the altar, illuminated by an ardent faith. Was she going to turn her head toward me amicably now that I had become her goddaughter? No. Undoubtedly, I did not interest her.

Even though I could not hope for her affection, my self-esteem had a difficult time accepting such total indifference. Was I that insignificant, or was she particularly lacking in sensitivity?

It was a subtle bit of trickery on my part, for I didn't need anyone to tell me that I was completely at fault. Excellent women—the various "grandmothers" of my childhood, my mother herself—had tried to become attached to me without managing to. Why would a stranger like Madame N. have succeeded in doing so? My flaws . . . I knew them by heart by dint of hearing them enumerated by my entourage: ungrateful, egotistical, violent. Sometimes storms of hate against the whole world exploded inside me. I would then be tossed by heavy waves of murderous violence that took a long time to quell.

Madame N. had done the right thing to lose interest in me. The opposite would have only caused heartbreak for her. And as for me, why wish to get involved when I was sure to disappoint her in the end?

At the close of the mass, those taking communion and those who were confirmed joyously escaped from the church. Cheerful laughter burst out here and there. It was hot. The gentlemen had wet circles under their arms. On the emotional faces of the ladies, sweat traced thin rivulets.

To my left Madame N. was chatting with Sister Aimée in a low voice. She was without doubt the most beautiful woman of all those assembled. Her beauty showed not a hint of makeup. I slowly advanced toward her.

On my approach, Sister Aimée turned around and addressed me with a smile of encouragement. Madame N. cast an expressionless look at me, her eyes like pools of still water. I blushed.

"How do you feel, Thérèse?" inquired Sister Aimée.

Since my confirmation I had been bestowed with a new first name. Hearing it used to address me left me speechless. So Thérèse was me. I would have to get used to it from now on. I answered in a weak voice, "I'm doing well now, thank you, my sister." Then, gathering my will with both hands, I addressed my godmother: "I am grateful to you for having accepted to be my godmother."

A banal formula. I was not pleased with myself.

"You will make me happy if you prove to be a fervent soldier of Christ," she said.

And she held out a box of chocolates to me. Without doubt it was a nice present. I knew that chocolate was expensive and the box she had offered me was enormous. I took it awkwardly with both hands, like a servant holds a tray, conscious of being perfectly ridiculous.

At my age, shifting from one foot to the other, weighed down with a box of chocolates! I suddenly hated Madame N. Why hadn't she offered me something more appropriate for a girl—a book, handkerchiefs, or a piece of jewelry, for example?

"Well, Thérèse, thank your godmother," Sister Aimée suggested.

That was too much; I was not Thérèse, and I didn't want a godmother anymore. In a sudden move of defiance, I placed the box at the feet of Madame N. and ran into the empty classroom, where I cried for a long time.

I did not see Madame N. again and did not hear from her, even though she provided for my expensive education for several years. From the first meeting, I knew that I occupied no space at all in her mind, and even less in her life. What difference did it make? She had helped me be what I am and I still have thoughts of gratitude for her.

I would go to mass every day and I took communion regularly. Sister Aimée, charmed by my piety, made regular reports about my spiritual metamorphosis to her friend, insisting on the necessity "not to leave fallow such a fertile field." She spoke of my soul as well as my mind. "Through myself as intermediary, Providence has sent you this child; I dare to believe that you will not turn away from her," she wrote.

Madame N. did not turn away from me. What's more, she dazzled her friend with a spectacular act of generosity: she decided to send me to the Couvent des Oiseaux, the place where her own daughter was a boarder.

I immediately wrote a thank-you letter. I was at the peak of excitement: what was happening to me was wonderful. I already saw myself with a *baccalauréat*, a master's, and a doctorate *ès lettres*. I would be known and admired; I would be someone to be reckoned with. No one would dare mention my *métissage* anymore.

And if I failed? Succeeding was becoming a necessity and especially a duty toward Madame N. I raided the school's library, weighing down my nightstand with volumes on mathematics and on the methodology of essay writing, as if this rampart of knowledge would protect me from failure.

I oscillated between fire and ice, between happiness and despondency. I ate poorly and slept little. Summer vacation came. I was not sorry to change ambiances; the emotions I had felt since becoming certain that I would continue at the Couvent des Oiseaux had exhausted me. I longed for nothing but rest within the family circle. I returned home.

My prestige increased from one year to the next; it was apparent in my being welcomed more and more warmly by my parents. During the long months that separated us, they had had the time to build a legend around me. My success on my exams—I didn't inform them but they ended up learning about it from the newspapers—created a radiant aura around me as a chosen one. And now the incredible news that a stranger was going to pay for my studies at a renowned school! In the minds of my mother and my sisters, my life was a tale in which they could embellish the events according to their fantasy. My uncompromising stepfather ended up feeling a certain esteem for me. I couldn't resist the temptation of proving them right. If luck had smiled on me, didn't I deserve it? I was thus worth something.

That morning, when the train entered the station at Tuy Hoa, coughing up its shower of incandescent sparks, the sun was already high in the sky. I was the only passenger to set foot on the arrival platform. As always, the heat bothered me. I was repeating to myself that I would indeed never get used to the climate of my country.

The platform was deserted, and the suitcase was getting heavier and heavier for my arms. No one had promised to meet me, and yet, I was disappointed. I went toward the exit, crossing the cluster of concrete and corrugated metal huts.

To my amazement, my entire family was waiting for me in front of the entrance. I was overjoyed. In my mind, I flew into the arms of my mother even though in reality I only offered her a smile.

"Your sisters are happy that you have finally come home. They missed you," said my mother.

That was the custom: we never expressed our feelings directly. But I knew that my mother was speaking for herself. A flow of cool water inundated my heart.

"Let's go home!" said my stepfather, going toward the shiny automobile whose door he opened.

The car was a red Fiat, the color of Tết, the new year of the lunar calendar. It was really quite garish. I was surprised that someone as austere as my stepfather would have chosen such a conspicuous color. He had to have earned a lot of money and doubtless really wanted to show it.

The six of us piled in, the little ones sitting on the knees of the older ones. We were proud even so. My stepfather drove at an exaggeratedly slow speed, as much from lack of experience as from his wanting to give others the time to admire his new acquisition. People came out of their houses to watch us pass by. Some greeted my parents with a slight bow of the head.

Soon we were in front of the house, a house I had not yet seen. They had had it built during my absence, a two-story house overlooking the main street. On the second floor, a curved balcony attempted to confer an opulent air upon the building. As for the ground floor, it was in what we called "American style," quite in vogue during those years. It was extravagantly colorful, resembling a child's toy: a pale pink façade with pistachio-green shutters and a sky-blue railing. In Saigon, I had had the chance to see houses in this style, considered the very symbol of modernity.

Unique in its category, ours aroused all sorts of feelings. Some had a quiet laugh, finding it dreadfully parvenu; others conversely were open-mouthed with admiration. But everyone recognized that it had cost a lot of money. That was the only thing that mattered to my step-father. He had renewed his tobacco business with the French, and this house was meant to prove that he was solvent. It had an exclusively promotional function.

It was all the more true that the inside had nothing in common with what was on display outside. The walls were bare, and the rooms nearly empty, save the few unpretentious pieces of furniture that my parents had had for a long time: a large platform daybed that served as a bed at night and a place to sit during the day once we had put a mat with flower motifs on its smooth surface; a table; and a few chairs. No armoire or chest of drawers. We put away our clothes in woven bamboo trunks. Taking into account the urge to move that seized my stepfather periodically, we could leave more easily in this way. We continued to sleep on cots; in a word, we lived in almost the same way as before.

In terms of food, this "almost" translated first of all into the fare at our table as is inevitably the case in poor countries where being rich meant more food. Our meals consisted of five dishes instead of the usual two. Enough of salted and dried fish. Now we had two kinds of meat and fresh fish. In addition, a variety of vegetables instead of the inevitable water spinach. My mother bought the highest quality rice, over two hundred pounds at a time, and my stepfather permitted him-self the luxury of paying a small fortune for *saucisson* and Camembert imported from France. Our table bore witness to our opulence.

That was the first step. The second consisted of forging a new so-cial image. My stepfather hired a chauffeur part time who would come to drive us to mass on Sundays. As the car was too tight for all the members of the family, the chauffeur had to make two trips. A first, very early, when the church was almost empty, for my parents and my youngest sister who was still a small child. And a second at eleven o'clock—rush hour, so to speak—to leave off the girls, that is, my three other sisters and me. We would go there as if to a performance, with the goal of seeing and especially of being seen.

A short while before, my parents had converted to Catholicism. I assume my mother did it because of a natural inclination toward spiri-tual things. Without doubt, she had also been seduced by the pomp of Catholic ceremonies. My stepfather had more material motivations. Catholicism was then the religion of President Ngo Dinh Diem, so his embrace of that religion meant that many doors would open for him, particularly to the administration which he often had to deal with in order to obtain a trading license or a permit for shipping merchandise. He had already renounced his Chinese citizenship and opted for Vietnamese citizenship. A certain number of his compatriots had done the same. Doing business was their strength and raison d'être. Many had lived in Viet Nam since childhood. By and large they had maintained no ties with their families living in China. Going back there was quite simply inconceivable: what would a businessman do in Communist China? Moreover, they had created a veritable Chinese city in the heart of Saigon, with its businesses, its gambling parlors, its whores, and its trafficking, as well as its laws, its codes, its traditions, and its secrets. A kind of capital within the capital where a stranger was welcome when it meant spending money, but where an invisible barrier prevented any further penetration.

When he wanted to see his family, my stepfather went alone most of the time. Sometimes, however, he allowed us to go along with him. The feeling that I still recall is that of a tight-knit community that was especially rich, even though that wealth remained discreet. My "uncles"—I called them that without knowing the precise relationship that bound them to my stepfather—were not spendthrifts and dressed modestly like any other small restaurant owner. But their safes were full. I remember the considerable sum they offered my parents to alleviate their expenses when they learned that I was going to study in France: a million piasters. At the time, the salary of a young teacher in a secondary school was about seven hundred piasters. I stammered my thank-yous when one of the "uncles" stopped me.

"It's not worth the trouble to thank us. Consider it as an investment we are making. Upon your return, when you are a scholar, it will be up to you to do us a favor. No one speaks French in the family; you will be useful to us."

Considering the import of these ties, my stepfather kept from revealing his conversion around where his relatives lived. He led, so to speak, a double spiritual life. In Tuy Hoa, a city where he was the only representative of his clan, he could practice his new faith without fear. What's more, it constituted his business card. But when it happened that he returned to Cho-Lon, he didn't hesitate to bow before the altar of the Spirit of Commerce or to light incense sticks to pay homage to Buddha.

That kind of hypocrisy revolted me. Lacking the power to tell him so, I attacked my mother. We had violent quarrels during which I accused her of superstition and obscurantism. She didn't understand. Of my reproaches, she remembered only the sadness of noting that I had lost all sense of filial piety. In her turn, she blamed the European education instilled in me at school. We were both bruised from these fights. My mother managed to reconcile her Catholic faith, her invocations to Buddha, and the cult of the ancestors with a disarming naturalness. In her mind, a human being was the prey of so much misfortune; it was better to reconcile several protectors instead of only one. Why renounce one for another? As for the cult of the ancestors, it was the foundation that no religion could ever replace; it was part of our country, of our soul, "like the river that runs toward the ocean without losing contact with its source," as she was fond of saying. My blessed mother. But for me, who were my ancestors?

Otherwise, we lived rather happily. The servants had received orders to brag about my merits each time they had the occasion to do so. They did it skillfully at the marketplace during the long customary process of bargaining. In a few weeks, the entire city was informed of the scholastic success I had achieved, of the liveliness of my intelligence, and especially of my stepfather's wealth, assumed to be quite considerable since he could afford to send me to the most renowned school in the country. Of course, my family had neglected to mention that an unknown woman had taken on the expense of it.

In the meantime, we attended to my outfits. The whole family was requisitioned to sew. Other than these preparations, we had an important problem to resolve: the purchase of a ticket for the airplane that would take me to Da-Lat, the city where the Couvent was located. The telegram that we had received indicated that a nun would come wait for me at the airport. Was it because of the inherent lack of security of trips by train? An attack by the Viet Minh on the way through the mountains was possible. For whatever reason, I was to arrive by plane.

My stepfather balked at the expense. However, we could not back out. Contrary to her habits, my mother refused to sell her jewelry to save the day. It was because she knew that this time her husband was caught in a trap. The whole city believed that he was sending a girl who was not his own to a celebrated school. Everywhere his generosity was praised. Was he going to contradict such a fine reputation? He gave in. I had not finished getting on his nerves.

❧ 15 ❧

The Couvent des Oiseaux

My trunk was ready. My mother had taken up her knitting needles again, abandoned since her youth in Hanoi, and tried to make me one last cardigan. From the time we had begun bathing in the humid heat of the South, she hadn't needed woolens anymore. With a nostalgic air, she contemplated the beautiful ivory needles lying in their case of old cloth smelling of mothballs. With a lost look, she recited from memory the elements of the moss stitch or the honeycomb stitch. The cardigan of angora wool that came to life in her hands was as light as a soap bubble and as soft as a bed of velvet.

I had been assured that it would be an indispensable piece of clothing, for Da-Lat was at a high altitude, and the temperature didn't exceed sixty degrees during the entire year. It was a city that was well-known to the French, who went there frequently on vacation. Its temperate climate and the carrots and potatoes that were grown there brought French people something akin to a whiff of France. The rich Vietnamese from Saigon came to take refuge when the scorching heat made life in the capital unbearable.

Although it was my first, the trip by plane left no imprint on my memory. I only remember it being very short. The moment I got off, a French nun, quite short with bushy eyebrows like those of an old mandarin, came toward me, welcomed me in a voice that was almost masculine, took my travel bag from me, and then gave me a peck on each cheek. I blushed. I wasn't used to such demonstrative receptions. Without delay, we climbed into a small van that Mother Marie-Claire drove herself.

The trip seemed very long to me. The rocky road made the vehicle jolt constantly. Inside we were shaken like dice in a cup. Everywhere my eyes saw only gray rocks and forests of pine trees thick with needles. The overly cool air made me shiver. I felt displaced, as if I had left Viet Nam for another country.

A bit anxious, I wondered if I was going to adapt to this environment, so different from what I had known up to then.

As if she had guessed what I was thinking, Mother Marie-Claire reassured me: "Don't worry. Everything will turn out well. It will be three o'clock when we arrive. The pupils will be in class, and you will see no one. I'll take you to your room where you can rest. You will meet your teachers and the pupils a little later on."

Learning of this rest time calmed my worries. I could thus get a feeling for the place and adjust my behavior.

The van climbed a hillside, then stopped in front of an ordinary-looking doorway. I was expecting something more impressive. Mother Marie-Claire rang the bell, and the door opened immediately. We took a wide staircase that led to the upper floors and walked along two long corridors before reaching a room.

"From sophomore year on, pupils have single rooms," she explained to me. "They are a little smaller but you will have much larger ones in junior and senior year."

As she was talking, she opened the door. The waxed parquet floor reflected the light like a mirror. Opposite me, a window overlooked the park. Mother Marie-Claire advised a "little nap," wished me a "good rest," and closed the door behind her.

I found myself alone. In my room. It was unbelievable; I was on another planet. Everything had changed in so little time: the climate, the landscape, the everyday setting. I approached the window. In front of me was a pine tree, very similar to the ones I had seen on postcards coming from France in the days before Christmas. Beyond, rows of pines with bare trunks stretched far away. Not a sign of anyone walking. Everything was silent. Suddenly, something struck a branch, then another, then stopped. It was a squirrel, the first I had ever seen, similar to a delicate flower blown by the wind from tree to tree. I remained filled with wonder at that dancing ball.

I jumped when someone knocked at the door. I didn't know whether to answer or not. What was the custom? Holding my breath, I stared, immobile, at the white door handle; it still hadn't moved. A long time went by. When I finally made up my mind to open the door, no one was there. But my trunk was. The people who had put it there had left for lack of a response. I dragged it inside, then nimbly closed the door. I felt better protected in this closed room.

I stretched out, but sleep didn't come. A thousand practical questions bombarded my mind, really silly questions: were you to shake the hands of the nuns or bow your head in the Vietnamese way?

The sound of shoes hitting the wood floor interrupted my thoughts. A cascade of laughter resounded in the hallway, then fell silent in front of my door. Ten hands knocked at the same time. This time I answered "yes." The door opened partway, revealing a row of smiling faces that welcomed me. My new classmates burst into the room, jostling each other and laughing. Some wore uniforms while others had kept the Vietnamese *áo dài*. Right away they asked me what city and which school I was from. I appreciated their speaking to me in our language, Vietnamese. Besides, it was quite natural, for there was no foreigner among us. It hadn't been like that before when the school had a majority of French girls.

Younger than I, they seemed more carefree, more cheerful, and more spontaneous. You could see that they hadn't suffered yet and that they weren't lacking anything essential, so that they could take life in a confident, optimistic way. I delighted in sharing the company of these happy girls.

Finally, they left me to get to their studies, promising to come get me at dinnertime. Right at six-thirty I put on my most beautiful *áo dài*, tied my long hair with a ribbon halfway down my back, and then waited. The same joyous flurry led me through endless hallways and hurtling down several flights of stairs. I followed them, preoccupied by the idea of not finding the way back to my room when evening came.

We arrived at the refectory. Just outside the room, groups of pupils chatted quietly in low voices. What a surprise not to see them in rows like everywhere else. I said as much to my classmates, who burst out in mocking laughter: I still took part in those outdated practices? One of them explained to me, "Here we don't line up, and there are no punishments. They think that sophomores should be able to behave reasonably."

"And no one has ever behaved in an unreasonable manner?"

"It can happen. In that case they point it out to her, and it's up to her to mend her ways."

"And who points it out to her?"

"Anyone. Me, someone else, or a nun."

At that moment, a nun entered the refectory. As if it were a signal, the pupils followed close on her heels. Each one sat where she wished. I sat down with my classmates at a table for six. This was a far cry from a cafeteria. There was an appetizer, a meat course, and rice in abundance. I was surprised to see the familiar rice in place of bread, and someone explained right away: "From the time that there were almost no French boarders anymore, our mothers consulted with us and in response to popular demand, they replaced the bread with rice."

"That's fantastic!" I exclaimed.

"And that's not all. Do you know that we are the only school where they try to use our Vietnamese given names with us? If you had been at a *lycée,* they would have automatically stuck you with a French name because it's easier for the teachers."

"Can you see yourself as Jeannette or Cécile?" said another, giggling.

From one moment to the next I realized how lucky I was to be at such an extraordinary school.

The meal took place in an ambiance of amiable civility, each one being extremely polite in passing on the food to her neighbor.

After dinner, we went to the room where evenings were spent, a room where some kept busy with games while others read, still with no supervision whatsoever. Not liking games, I used my fatigue from the trip as a pretext to retire to my room. I needed to be alone.

Stretched out on the bed, I savored the pleasure of having a room of my own, like a lair. I would have liked for my mother and sisters to see the calm and luxury that surrounded me. On the night table was a branch of mimosa that a friendly hand had put in a glass of water. I had never known anything like this before. In my mind, I reviewed the different boarding schools I had known: the orphanage, the years spent in Saigon. I thought I had overcome the harshest trials. I fell asleep, at peace.

The tinkling of a bell awakened me. In the hallway, the deep voice of a nun intoned the *Benedicamus domini,* to which sleepy voices answered

Deo gratias. Warmly tucked into my covers, I looked at the light that lit up the neighboring rooms, for the walls of each cubicle stopped about eighteen inches from the ceiling. All the faucets began to murmur at the same time. Everyone was cleaning up all around me. The noises of tooth brushing, of glasses clinking against washbasins, of gargling. I had been mistaken last evening; there was no lair here and my solitude was an illusion. I now had the feeling of being in a public square where my slightest movement could be heard. It seemed as though my neighbor on the left or on the right could suddenly say to me, "So, you didn't brush your teeth this morning!" "You are going to have to be careful!" I thought, all the while washing up with my invisible classmates.

There was just enough time to get dressed, and someone knocked at the door as if a hidden eye had been constantly spying on me since I woke up.

"Are you coming to have breakfast?" someone whispered.

I opened the door. All my new friends were there, freshly washed and dressed like me. So that was what collective stimulation was. You brushed your teeth as soon as you heard your neighbor brushing; then silence: that meant she was getting dressed and you could do the same; and so on and so forth . . . The morning ritual done, the pupils spontaneously went down to the refectory together. And so it went; no need for exhortations.

The ambiance in the refectory was as pleasant as the evening before. The café au lait left me indifferent; I would have preferred a good bowl of noodle soup. My friends chatted and seemed quite happy. But I had lost my state of grace. Certainly, I continued to think that I was benefiting from the best school, like a mouse falling into a jar of rice. But the feeling of having discovered a corner of paradise where everything was devoted only to the intellect had already begun to fade.

In French class I saw my dear friend Dô again. She was not a boarder, and thus, I hadn't seen her when I arrived. We directed a discreet smile of complicity at each other over the bowed heads. I was impatiently awaiting recess; I needed to hear her opinion of the teachers and the pupils. Did she feel the same malaise as I?

I joined her as soon as the class was over. We went toward the grounds. The pine needles crackled under our feet with a dry sound, and a strong odor of resin filled the air.

"How beautiful it is!" I cried out. "How different from what we knew in Nha Trang."

"It's true. But I prefer Nha Trang."

"Aren't you happy here?"

"I'm neither happy nor unhappy," she declared. "I'm here to learn. The nuns are nice, but I do not embrace their religion. As for the pupils, they have nothing in common with us. They know nothing about our history or our literature. They are incapable of citing the name of a single poet. It's a wonder that they know who Nguyen Du is."[1]

"That's indeed strange. Are you sure you aren't mistaken?"

"Certain. You will see for yourself."

"So, what do they know about, then?"

"Things you don't know," answered Dô, smiling. "For example, who are the 'in' singers in Paris, what is the color in style in France this fall . . . I'll bet you don't know anything about all that."

"You win! I can't even imagine what Paris is like. Do you believe there are houses along the sides of the streets like here?"

"I don't know. You see, I'm happy being a day pupil. That saves me from having to see people I don't have a lot to say to." And then she added after a moment of reflection, "Even their characters seem foreign to me. At fifteen they still clap their hands together, jump up and down, and laugh loudly like little girls."

"Don't they get reprimanded for that?"

Dô burst out laughing. "Not at all. On the contrary, they find them open and spontaneous." Then she said in a low voice, "You know, what we were taught as virtue takes on the appearance of vice here. If you 'count to ten before you say anything,' they think you're concealing something. And if you don't say the bad thing that you think of someone to avoid hurting her feelings, they say you're a hypocrite. They don't like me very much here in this place. That will probably be the case for you. Be very careful."

Her revelations left me dumbfounded. My mind grasped with fright the multiple difficulties I was going to have to overcome.

"You did well to warn me. Too bad that you're not a boarder; the two of us could fight with more courage. Why aren't you?"

---

1. See Chapter 10, Note 4, p. 128.

"The room and board are too expensive. So, tell me, is it your parents who are paying for this luxurious school?"

I remained silent. It bothered me to confess to Dô that I was benefiting from the good deeds of a Catholic lady who despised me enough to take care of me without wanting to get to know me. Finally, I confessed. "No, it's not my parents who are paying for it. My presence here is due to a fortunate twist of fate."

And I told her the whole story of my encounter with Madame N. Dô listened to me attentively.

"You are very lucky," she concluded. "Doubtless thanks to the good deeds you accomplished in a previous life."

Dô was a Buddhist and believed in metempsychosis. I hadn't shared her point of view since my confirmation. But I valued our friendship too much to initiate a discussion on that subject. All the more so because my new faith was still shaky, and I was certain that I would be at a loss for arguments in the face of the solid convictions of my friend, convictions whose validity I had shared not so long ago.

We experienced a peaceful happiness in each other's company that recalled what we had known before.

"Did you know that Madame N. has a daughter in ninth grade?"

"Yes," I answered. "Her name is Marie-Paule, I believe."

"So, she has a French given name? Yet her parents are both Vietnamese."

"She's a Christian; that's her baptismal name. You well know that there are no Vietnamese names on the calendar of saints!" I added in defense of Madame N. Regretting my vivacity, I continued, "I went to say hello yesterday, at mealtime. Isn't it my duty? But she treated me coldly. I don't believe that she wants to spend time with me."

Dô managed an enigmatic smile. "You still have a lot to learn. You went to say hello, because you are indebted to her mother. 'The one who drinks the water remembers . . . its source,' yes?"

"Yes, that's it precisely! 'That girl is of no interest to me; I am not trying to make friends with her.'"

"Well, you made a mistake. In my opinion, she found your attitude obsequious, and she looks down on you."

I opened my eyes wide. "But the world is upside down."

Suddenly, we were seized by the giggles. When we had regained our composure, Dô continued, seriously, "You see, expressing one's gratitude is a duty for us, while for them it's proof of servility."

Her words deprived me of all hope of being happy in this place. How I appreciated her presence; at least I could confide in someone. "You know," I told her, "I will work with all my heart to get good grades; as for the rest, I will remain as neutral as possible."

As we chatted, we went deeper into the park without realizing it. We had lost track of time. I suggested that we head back.

"Do you believe that we have missed the resumption of classes?" asked Dô.

"I don't know. Too bad we don't have a watch! Let's go back, even so."

We ran through the deserted walkways. Not one pupil was in sight. We were surely late, but how late? We remained outside the classroom without daring to enter. In a single movement heads turned in our direction. I was furious with myself: getting yourself noticed from the first day—how stupid!

"Come in!" said Mother Véronique in a voice devoid of anger.

We took our places again, murmuring banal excuses.

"So, what happened to you?" Mother Véronique inquired, almost affectionately.

I was still trying to find a pretext when Dô answered, "We forgot what time it was in the heat of discussion."

Her French still had a strong Vietnamese accent. She had looked directly into the eyes of Mother Véronique. I was really proud of her.

"You just meet and already you are having passionate discussions. The subject must be worthwhile. Could you let us know what it was?"

I observed my friend, worried. The pupils looked at Dô, then at Mother Véronique, in the way that you watch a ping pong game.

"We've known each other for a long time," she answered simply. "We were in primary school together."

"Very well," said Mother Véronique, smiling; then she turned to me. "I'm pleased that you have met up again with an old friend here. You will feel less out of place. Try not to forget what time it is next time." Then after a pause, she added, "I hope that this friendship won't prevent your making friends with your new classmates. We value a great deal a unified class, without cliques or preferences."

Mother Véronique took up the literature lesson once again, at the place where she had been interrupted. We were broaching symbolism. With the help of photographs, she tried to instill in us the notion of a symbol. One after another we contemplated the radiant image of a girl representing youth or a field of poppies whose goal it was to express summer.

I dreamed of the Chinese paintings whose landscapes, often misty and melancholic, are always completed by a short poem. Were they symbolic? I didn't dare ask the teacher that question. If Dô's revelations were correct, and I didn't doubt that they were, not one pupil here had ever admired a painting from the Song period. It was useless to bring up a problem no one was interested in.

Dô's presence brightened my stay. My only regret was that she was a day pupil, and I couldn't suppress a twinge of sorrow when I would see her leaving.

However, I did not feel unhappy. The cultural gap that Dô had highlighted was real but submerged. Superficially, life in the boarding school seemed harmonious and pleasant to me. In spite of everything, I had great admiration for its educational system, of a kind that was entirely new to me.

The school provided classes from sixth grade up to the philosophy courses taken in senior year. There were about three hundred of us pupils, divided into three autonomous groups, each one having its place to live and its own schedule. The youngest, in sixth to eighth grade, lived in small teams. The ones in ninth grade, who were about fourteen, that ungrateful age as one says, were organized in groups limited to six people called "families," each one obedient to a "mother of the family" chosen unanimously. As for the "philosophers," as they were called, they were judged well-behaved enough to live without a rigid structure, just like the future university students they would be tomorrow.

Such an organization gave us the feeling of being always responsible for our behavior and our actions. Each one thus behaved in the best way possible. As a consequence, our life together had a kind of lightness to it.

In this respect, the nuns provided plenty of examples. In my four years as a boarder, not once did I see a nun lose control of herself. That's why, when it would happen that one of us would let herself get angry, the sincerely stunned looks of the nuns mortified her more surely than a severe punishment.

Such was the ambiance at the Couvent des Oiseaux. We lived in the middle of nowhere, in a magnificent setting, far from the noise of the real world that died out at the foot of the grounds.

On the condition of agreeing to an "independent plan," a kind of moral contract that bound us to use our free time to study and not to gossip, we could work in our rooms, on the grounds, or anywhere, without anyone coming to supervise us. We only had to promise one thing: not to go beyond the enclosure around the grounds. But who would have dreamed of going out? The grounds were so vast that no one had the impression of being imprisoned.

I adapted easily to my new situation. I had excellent relationships with my classmates and never tired of listening to the wonders of Paris they extolled to me: Sacré Coeur, the Place des Ternes. Some had record players. We would listen to the latest hits imported from France: Mouloudji, Line Renaud, and old Duval. Together we would hum *Coeur pour coeur, dent pour dent* . . . or *Pourquoi viens-tu si tard?*

I discovered how important everything that came from France was for them. You would have said that France was where they had been born. They kept the slightest object as if it were a precious treasure. One, filled with emotion, showed me a dead leaf that her uncle had picked up in the Luxembourg Gardens the previous fall. I contemplated the brown patch lying between the pages of a book. Montmartre, the Luxembourg! Those places were no more real in my eyes than the towns of antiquity, dead cities whose essential attraction was to make you dream. I did not feel any desire to visit them someday.

To my great surprise my classmates seemed to maintain familiar, even intimate dealings with France, as if colonization hadn't existed.

Sometimes, animated by the desire to prove to them that I, too, could have something to teach them, I would recite contemporary poems in a fervent voice, ones by Vietnamese poets whom I admired. But they didn't understand a thing about them and made fun of my ridiculously serious airs. Hurt, I kept my knowledge to myself.

We continued to be friends to the extent that I shared their tastes, while mine were shoved definitively under the carpet. Dô witnessed my concessions with undisguised irony.

Since our having been late, we hadn't had the opportunity to be alone. In front of the others our conversations took on a banal turn. I suffered from this situation without finding a way to remedy it. Once again it was Dô who found a solution. One day, she led me toward the grounds at the first sound of the bell that announced recess.

"Come, I borrowed a watch; we won't be late this time."

I followed her, joyful. I felt a bit alone despite appearances. Admittedly, being less serious than Dô, I was delighted to laugh and listen to music with my new classmates, but my life experience, the education I had been given, and my sensitivity were poles apart from theirs. My liking for them was not feigned, but it was superficial.

The silence of the grounds enchanted me as always. The sun pleasantly warmed our untied hair.

"How good it feels to be here," I sighed.

Dô gave me a mocking smile. "This park is a screen of illusion that prevents you from seeing life. Do you know that we have defeated the French army at Dien Bien Phu? I do believe that this is the end of colonization."

"Victory!" I yelled without restraint, hurtling down the slope at full speed.

Dô followed my lead. We collapsed at the foot of a tree, breathless.

"How is it that no one has talked about it here?" I asked, catching my breath.

She did not answer. With our faces turned to the sun, we listened to a bird singing at the top of its lungs on a low branch, very near our heads.

"What's going to happen now?" I asked.

"There will be a meeting in Geneva to divide the country. The North, down to the seventeenth parallel, will be Communist under the presidency of Uncle Ho."[2]

"And the South? After all, that's what interests us the most, no?"

"The South will be under the leadership of Emperor Bao Dai. It seems that they are going to organize elections to allow the people to affirm their support for the Emperor."

"How have people reacted?"

---

2. The use of the word *uncle* here to refer to Ho Chi Minh is a sign of respect in Vietnamese.

"You can imagine how happy they are! Yesterday my uncle took us to a restaurant to celebrate the victory. There were other families there and everyone congratulated each other."

"You're lucky to be a day pupil. I would have liked to be with you last evening."

With her eyes gazing into the distance, Dô recalled the evening of celebration, smiling.

"Let's go. It's time," she said, shaking off the pine needles stuck to her sweater.

I got up with regret. We climbed back up side by side, keeping our secret despite the strong desire to announce the good news to the whole class.

The more I thought about it, the more I was worried for my parents. If only these upheavals didn't disturb the peacefulness of Tuy Hoa. My greatest fear was to be completely cut off from them. Dô harbored the same fears, for, like me, her family was far from her. She promised to find a map that would show us exactly where the seventeenth parallel was.

In class, Mother Véronique noticed my lack of attention.

"You are not with us today. Is something wrong?"

"Yes, I don't feel very well."

"You can go up to your room if you think it's necessary."

"No, thank you; it will be alright," I affirmed.

I tried to get interested in the class, but my mind returned continually to the seventeenth parallel. If Tuy Hoa ended up in the North, I would be separated from my family forever. It wasn't the financial insecurity that frightened me; my studies had been paid for by Madame N. up to the *baccalauréat*. I was thus sheltered and free of financial worries. No, it was above all the possibility of finding myself alone again in life. That I could not bear. I had had to put up with everything up to now; now it was up to me to set the limits of what was tolerable. I would do anything to get back to them.

My edginess and anxiety ultimately made me sick. Mother Véronique sent me to my room.

"Go rest. A nurse will come by to see you this afternoon."

I knew that the nurse's visit would incur some additional expenses for Madame N. That would be the last straw, if I were costing her more than her own daughter. Toward the end of the afternoon, the nurse took my temperature. My fever was real without being considerable.

"At 100.4, I'm afraid that you should stay in bed another twenty-four hours."

Another day of expense. "That excellent woman," in the words of Sister Aimée, could very well tire of me and withdraw her support. The fragile edifice of my future would then collapse all at once.

The nurse came back the next day. I went through a night's sleep filled with bad dreams. I was coughing a little. The fever persisted.

"A hundred," she declared. "How do you feel?"

"A little tired, but I don't hurt anywhere. Why this fever?"

"I will take you to a doctor who will clear all this up."

A doctor. Was I really sick again? I didn't feel up to beginning the cycle of medicines and rest periods again. I had thought that I was completely cured. I sobbed, emptying my anguish in a flood of tears.

When my classmates came to see me during recess, they found me very weak with reddened eyes. They stepped up their attentions, one awkwardly wiping my face, another bringing me a glass of water. I was angry to be looking like that. I thought of my mother, who would make fun of my "easy tears": "Go and urinate; you'll cry less!" The thought of these words made me smile despite myself.

"I prefer to see you smile," said one of them. "It's not so bad then!"

And they withdrew, reassured. Dô managed to leave last. Before crossing the threshold, she slipped a piece of paper into my hand. That familiar gesture took me back to the time when, locked up because of my affair with the teacher, I had had no contact with the outside world except for the notes that Dô and Ghi slipped me. Four years had gone by since then, four years that seemed to have happened in another life, so much had my ideas and my being changed.

With the message held tightly in the hollow of my hand, I put off the moment when I would have to see what it said. I knew that Dô had drawn the line marking the seventeenth parallel. Soon I would know what was waiting for me. I listened as the sound of footsteps going downstairs faded. The piece of paper was getting wet in my moist hand. Was Tuy Hoa in the North or the South? The answer that I didn't dare unfold was there. It was enough for me not to open my hand, not to read the note, to prolong this moment for as long as I liked before the catastrophe. For knowledge was a poisoned fruit. Hadn't Adam and Eve paid the price? My apple lay in the hollow of my hand in the form of a tiny ball of paper.

I opened my hand and let the paper roll onto the sheet. I carefully unfolded the wrinkled missive, taking the time to smooth it with my fingertips. Dô had summarily scrawled a map where the north of the country was colored in red and the south in yellow. The dark line of the seventeenth parallel placed Tuy Hoa on the side of the South. I was saved. I contemplated the map, incredulous. Once again, luck had smiled on me, and like each time, I was deeply astonished. Why me? I was no more deserving than any of the hundreds of little *métisse* girls who had shared my misfortune in the orphanage.

At the bottom of the note, Dô had added maliciously, "I hope that this good piece of news will make your fever go down." She was mistaken. My fever continued. The nurse came in, a tray in her hand.

"Here is your lunch; I'll come back at about three o'clock to take you to the doctor. Be ready."

Worried about what this supplementary care would cost Madame N., I wanted to ask for more information. But a direct question about money would have seemed in the worst taste. I would have to get around to it, and quickly, for she was already preparing to leave.

"I'm being waited on like a princess," I remarked blandly. "I suppose that my parents will get an additional bill this month."

"Oh yes! And if this keeps up, they might well be paying double by the end of the trimester."

I was embarrassed. Double. How was Madame N. going to react? After all, I was only a stranger for whom she felt nothing. I looked at the food without any appetite. My mother would often repeat, "Eating well is the secret of good health." I carried a piece of meat to my mouth; it was tasteless. I tried to chew it conscientiously, but the more I chewed, the more the meat increased in size. I threw the chewed-up mass on the plate and fell asleep, exhausted.

"Let's go, let's go, wake up," the nurse said, shaking me. "We are going to be late." Then, pointing at the untouched tray, "And you didn't eat anything. So, how do you expect to get well?"

I got dressed in haste and followed her to the van that took us to the city.

I hadn't seen Da-Lat since the day of my arrival nearly two months earlier. I was happy to see the houses, the streets, and the shops again, and especially to see once more the comings and goings of the colorfully dressed crowd of Vietnamese people. Going from the Couvent to the city was like changing countries. Two months spent in that protected place, in a kind of cultural vagueness where we were studying the language of Racine but communicated among ourselves in Vietnamese, had made me forget these familiar images.

The van let us off in front of the doctor's office. In the waiting room, an elegantly dressed man and woman leafed through magazines. A vase of artificial flowers was sitting on a large bronze drum. From the first glance, you could see that the doctor's fees were not within the means of just anybody. "Still more expenses," I thought with an unpleasant twinge. We sat down on a Chinese banquette, awaiting our turn. Through the window a patch of blue sky was visible.

Suddenly, the doctor opened the door and, with a wave of his hand, invited us to come in. The elegant lady lifted her eyes from her magazine and raised an eyebrow in surprise. He explained to her, smiling, "She's a young boarder who must not return too late to her convent. Besides, it won't be long."

The door closed again behind us. The man pointed out a dark room to me.

"Take off your clothes."

I was embarrassed. Take my clothes off, just like that, in front of a man? And what did I have to take off? The nurse could have told me, but she was in the other room. I awkwardly removed my *áo dài*. I was ashamed to exhibit my thinness, my bony shoulders, and my flat chest. I wasn't a little girl anymore; I was nineteen years old, and the man was still young. I dreaded his opinion.

Without a doubt, he had guessed why I was hesitating, for he yelled, as if I were far away, "Stand against the metal plate, naked from the waist up. I'm going to take an X-ray of your lungs."

I did what he said. The cold touch of the metal on my breasts sent a long shiver throughout my entire body. A bluish light lit the room.

"Take a breath and hold it."

That half-light and that masculine voice, almost sweet, were disturbing.

"Hmmm. Some spots remain."

I scarcely heard his remark. With my eyes closed, I was thinking with emotion about my teacher's caresses not long ago. I hadn't thought of him since our separation. Suddenly, I missed him achingly. It seemed to me that if the doctor had tried to touch me, he would have encountered my consenting flesh.

"Cough."

I was speechless with disappointment.

"Cough!" he repeated.

I coughed.

"OK. Get dressed then join me in my office."

Was that it? I could have wept with frustration.

In the office, the nurse wrote down the doctor's orders. He noticed my unhappy look.

"Don't be so worried. Overall, it's good. The large cavities are gone. In two months, you'll be cured."

I smiled weakly.

The return trip was rather sad. Neither the nurse nor I wanted to engage in conversation.

I started the inevitable Rimifon treatment again, the rest periods of lying down with an extra meal at four o'clock in the afternoon. I avoided thinking about the expense of this regimen, about Madame N.'s reaction.

During the school year I lived in isolation because of my illness, attending two hours of classes per week and, as a result, having only infrequent contact with my classmates. My mood turned morose; I didn't care about my studies. I spent hours doing nothing, without even opening a book, my eyes staring into space and my mind a blank. Or I would wander in the pathways of the grounds, alone, when the others were leading studious lives in classrooms. I thought constantly about my teacher and was suffering after the fact, four years later, from the break-up that had separated me from him. I regretted having done nothing to explain to him the situation of powerlessness I was in, nothing to reassure him of my attachment to him. For he had remained alive deep inside me. I would think about our happy moments with infinite regret as time passed, and would thus become more conscious of the affective void I found myself in. I knew that he had scarcely shed a tear at losing me; other pupils had taken my place in succession. But it was my fault: I had accepted our separation too easily. Consequently, why wouldn't he have wooed others?

An insane idea crossed my mind: what if I wrote to him? Dô would get his address for me. I would tell him that I needed him. No, that was crazy. Too much time had passed, we didn't live in the same city, and hundreds of miles separated us. He had surely forgotten me.

A discreet gesture, just an allusion, was needed, nothing more. What if I sent the program from the movie theater back to him, a souvenir of our first date? The title of the film was *I Have Always Loved You*. He would understand my appeal. The only thing was that I wasn't at all sure that he remembered the film, let alone the title. How many girls had gone with him to the theater since then? The best thing was to forget, but I couldn't. I was suffering more keenly than the day when the event had happened. I had lived four years without pain, without regret, and now that previous break-up was becoming intolerable. I didn't understand. Was it because I was sick and lonely? Or was I, by nature, the kind whose suffering, sown like a seed, would only begin to grow a long time afterwards? Whatever the answer, regret, like a refrain you hum automatically, occupied me day and night.

Nevertheless, the state of my health, apart from my frame of mind, improved. True to her promise, Madame N. took responsibility for all the expenses. I learned about it from Mother Andrée, our head nurse. I sent a letter to my godmother praising her generosity. She didn't answer. I swore to myself never to bother her again. Dô was right: we were from different worlds.

Summer took me home having put on weight and almost as white as a European for having been sheltered from the sun. My family found me more attractive.

My stepfather's business was prospering. We now had a permanent chauffeur and two servants. I spent a leisurely summer, dividing my time between reading novels and chatting with my family. I became fascinated with Dostoyevsky. Reading *The Idiot* disturbed me. I was surprised that an author so foreign to me, so distant in time and space, would have found words whose aptness and acuteness touched my heart with such force. My own profound discontentment found a fraternal echo there. I was not alone but in the company of beings whom suffering elevated above the ordinary. I considered my family, whom I found very down to earth, with nothing but condescension. I was irritated with my mother's overly materialistic preoccupations, and I could no longer bear hearing my stepfather talk constantly about money and profits. I thought of myself as the noble lotus blossom, forced to soak my roots in sludge. I felt nostalgic for Da-Lat's Couvent des Oiseaux. Up there, everything was beautiful.

By comparison I found Tuy Hoa's climate too hot, our house ugly, and the life we led stripped of elegance. The shrill voices of the maids hurt my eardrums. As for the chauffeur, he was downright vulgar. I made it my duty to bring my family a little of the beauty and refinement that I had recently learned about.

To this end I went to pick wildflowers early in the morning, doubly protected from the sun with a scarf under a straw hat, avoiding any suntan that would have made me look too working-class. I would return with my arms full of branches intended to decorate the house as I had seen done at my aristocratic boarding school. But as we didn't have a vase, I gave up on the flowers.

After that, I wanted my own room like at the Couvent des Oiseaux, a strictly private place that I could decorate as I liked and that would be my peaceful haven. My family was stunned. A private room? What for? Of course, my parents had a bedroom at their disposal, but that was easily explained: they slept together. As for me ... well, my request seemed like a caprice. Even so, my mother tried to please me. After all, she only enjoyed my presence for two months a year.

For want of anything better, she allocated to me the unused passage that connected the kitchen to the main building. Three mats hung up at right angles closed up the space like a box. Such was my bedroom. It reminded me of the time of our exodus when, with no roof over our heads, we had had to suspend mats vertically to shelter ourselves. My cheap-looking tent didn't resemble in any way the bedroom I had imagined.

My mother tried to console me: "I know how you feel. Now that you are back from the Couvent, you want to live like the French. Be patient. If your father's business continues to prosper, we will build a larger house where you will have your own room. As for me, I'll live as I always have."

Her words slid right off me without leaving a trace. I was weighed down with rancor, and I thought she was a peasant, a bumpkin, a *nhàquê*, and that she would stay that way forever.

To dissipate my bad mood, she spoiled me in a thousand ways. I was ashamed of myself. How could I disown my family? I didn't really feel comfortable at the boarding school either. I didn't understand anything anymore, but that's the way it was: when I was in Da-Lat, it was my family and my lifestyle that counted for me, and as soon as I found myself among them again, this life seemed devoid of interest to me. I only had one desire and that was to return to the Couvent.

The same nun met me at the airport. I couldn't repress a smile hearing her welcome me in the exact same way as the year before, word for word. I looked at the already-familiar landscape of pine trees and rocks with the feeling of having returned home. What a difference from my family, about whom I could never tell ahead of time if their welcome would be relaxed or tense! On the contrary, I relaxed in the company of that nun, at once affectionate and indifferent. No more excessive feelings, no more revolt. I was as vacant as a mirror in which nothing is reflected. And that void put me at rest.

The nun drove attentively, her eyes riveted on the twisting road. I said nothing. Silence seemed natural to both of us. For once I was in the presence of an adult, without asking myself what decorum might require me to say. I was part of another system of values, and to my surprise I liked that. There was something simple, something refreshing about it. Dô would have surely found my character easily influenced. But why did you always have to be on your guard, hindered by rules and duties? I was no longer entirely in agreement with my friend.

From the moment of my arrival, a gaggle of pupils rushed to meet me. With one week to go before school started, the class was almost all there, leading me to believe that my classmates were bored at home as much as I was. I felt great pleasure in seeing them again. At that moment I forgot our differences, retaining only the warm élan that drew us toward each other. It had been a long time since I had felt so happy or so in tune with a group. Their energy contagious, I became as much of a kid as they. Yelling, we ran after each other through the paths of the grounds, disheveled, with our cheeks made pink by the chill, and when we caught each other, we hit each other like boys fighting. I didn't dare imagine what my mother would have thought if she had seen me like that, with the result that I considered with some embarrassment the twigs stuck to my *áo dài* when peace and quiet returned. The others were laughing with delight, but I was already far away from them.

During that idle week, I became friends with An. She was two years younger than I. Her parents, originally from Tonkin, had settled in Saigon well before the division of the country, doubtless because they had anticipated the French defeat.

That year I dreamed of creating a high-level private school whose teachers would be recruited from among the best students at the Couvent. Contrary to the schools we knew, the tuition would be low in order to provide access to children from poor families. An listened to me without comment, nodding with approval at each one of my assertions, interrupting me only to point out a few tactical problems.

"Where will you get the money to finance all that?"

Her question caught me off guard; I hadn't thought about it.

"I don't really know. Maybe you have some rich friends who would like to invest in the enterprise?"

An laughed at my naïveté.

"How do you get someone to invest in a business that wouldn't be profitable? Your idea is great, but you will have to find the funding."

"In any case, we have the time to think about it," I said evasively. "Exactly five years: two to finish our secondary studies and three to get a bachelor's."

This plan, as well as preparing for the *baccalauréat* exams, occupied all my time.

Since the beginning of school, we had swapped our cramped cubicles for larger rooms. In addition to our beds, we each had a beautiful chest of drawers and, most importantly, a real desk. The rules were more flexible for juniors. Once classes were finished, we could go up to our rooms as if going home after school if we wanted, without needing permission. We were treated like adults, and we took this distinction very seriously. Even the most unruly had renounced their former games. From then on, our leisure time was devoted to useful reading: *Emile*, Voltaire's short stories, or even *Rameau's Nephew*. I would have preferred reading *The Nun*, but Mother X opened her eyes wide in horror: What? Didn't I know that it was a work put on the Index by the Church? I would do better not to touch it if I didn't want to lose my soul. So, I didn't touch it.

On the other hand, she recommended Lagarde et Michard, and I made it my bedtime reading. I learned the names of the authors whose names I had never heard before. I strove to retain everything—the birth and death dates, the titles of works. I studied in an abstract way, almost automatically, like a pill you swallow because your health demands it. On the one hand, I found neither the climate nor the landscapes of my own life in the books I had to study; on the other hand, there were simple words like "hollyhock" and "wild rose" that triggered no image in my mind. Involuntarily, I caused great mirth one day by taking the Reine-Claude[3] for a queen of France. I think the most difficult thing was that we were supposed to learn this literature not as a foreign literature but as if it were one in our native language. We felt obligated to make others believe that we were familiar with things that in reality we had just discovered.

I shut myself up in my room like a nun at prayer, going out only at mealtimes. I felt exhausted. To this excess of work was added the anguish of possible failure. I studied until late at night, and once asleep, nightmares aroused me from sleep.

To the great surprise of my teachers, I failed. For me this was a catastrophe. I remained prostrate for several days. My classmates, who didn't know about the delicate financial situation I found myself in, condemned my despondency, which they found excessive.

Mother X, our principal teacher, summoned me to her office and, without giving me the time to take a seat, scolded me: "How long do you intend to wallow in your defeat?"

I looked at the floor.

"Get ahold of yourself! It's not worthy of a Christian to give up hope at the first ordeal."

---

3. A kind of plum.

A dike broke, and I burst into tears. She let me cry.

"This is the end of my studies," I tried to explain between two hiccups. "Madame N. will never accept my repeating the year."

"Who's said anything about repeating the year? Isn't there a second round of exams? It will be enough that you review during vacation. What do you say about that?"

"Of course," I murmured, without believing it.

"Here is what we propose: We have first- and second-year pupils who need tutoring. We will agree to keep you for the summer in exchange for three hours of lessons that you will give. There will be enough time left for you to prepare for the second round. I'll let you think about it. You will give me your answer tomorrow."

And she dismissed me.

The second round . . . how had I not thought of it? I went toward the grounds and walked a long time among the pines, filled with an immense sense of relief. I felt myself up to learning the entire curriculum by heart. In my impatient ardor, I besieged the school's library without delay, scouring the shelves and grabbing all the volumes related to the examinations. Some had been checked out by my classmates. So, I went to bother them as they toiled in the refuge of their rooms. I nearly tore the books from their hands with a lack of consideration that was unusual for me, arguing that the rule forbade checking out a book for more than a week. I did the same thing when it came to the answers to the homework, and the mathematics and physics booklets. The nuns supported me. They liked active and determined personalities. In any case, I wanted to conform to the image that was expected of me, without taking into account my gratitude toward Mother X who, with one word, had pulverized the obstacle that blocked my access to knowledge.

It was as if I had gone mad. I demanded a classroom for my exclusive use in order to review in peace and quiet, and I picked a fight with anyone who dared bother me. I made myself so odious that even An abandoned me during this period, unable to endure my frenzied egocentricity. I drew up an exact schedule of my two months of work for each day and each hour, determining the lessons to learn, the exercises to do, and the moments of relaxation necessary for good mental health. I deliberately inflicted three "essays" a week upon myself, each falling within a four-hour time frame, according to the rules. The question of their evaluation remained, something I couldn't take responsibility for after all. For that, I went to ask for Mother X's help, with my review schedule in hand, firmly determined to ask her for the most severe grade possible.

Mother X attentively examined my pieces of "graph" paper, marked out in squares on which the subjects whose grades counted most were underlined in red. She was the one who showed me the most understanding and friendship. People said that she had come late to religious life. After obtaining a bachelor's at the Sorbonne and wanting to give herself a year off, she undertook a trip to Asia, a continent for which she had felt a deep attraction for some time. She ended up first in Saigon where she stayed for a few months; then, her peregrinations took her to Da-Lat. There she discovered, with a feeling that was instantaneous and absolute, her love for both God and this country. Immediately, she came to the Couvent to offer her services and was sent to France, to the mother church, to fulfill her time as a novice. This was the first wrenching, the first test, the first renunciation of all earthly love, even if it was the wrenching from a country. Soon she was judged worthy of putting on the habit of the order and taking her final vows. She stayed in France, offering up all her desires to God, including her infatuation with Viet Nam. But soon her superiors sent her to Da-Lat. Her joy must have been immense, and without doubt it was that joy that continued to give her appearance an inner exultation.

The older pupils of whom I was a part preferred her to all the other nuns. Rather than going to confession, we preferred to reveal our secrets to her in the benevolent silence of her office. All the older ones asked her for appointments and sometimes quarreled with each other over the privilege of going first. As for me, I liked her because of the genuine interest she had in Viet Nam as well as for her efforts to learn our language and to pronounce our first names with the acceptable accent. I trusted her, and her opinion had great value in my eyes.

Worried, I observed the special attention to detail she used in studying the schedule I had submitted to her. She slowly put the pages down on the desk without looking at me.

"Very good," she said. "I'm delighted that you accept my offer. I am certain that you will pass the second round, because this," and she indicated the papers, "is the proof of your determination."

She paused. I waited. I had guessed, from the start, that she didn't entirely approve.

"But, for your own good, I am forced to disappoint you. We will only keep you here for a month. Our Mother Superior, as do I myself, thinks that you need rest above all. For that, it is preferable that you rejoin your family during the month of July. You will come back in August."

My disappointment was beyond words. The efforts that I had deployed during a whole week with the goal of establishing a faultless program, and the nervous tension that had accompanied them, flagged all at once. My spirits sank.

"Did you hear me?" She explained to me in a calm voice, the kind used to make a difficult lesson understood by a pupil who was not very bright, "I am familiar with your excessive character. I've put up with it until now; remember that. But you are wrong this time. Believe me, your failure is simply an accident. One month of review is sufficient. Take a restful vacation with your family. You will only study better the month after."

I got up, seized my papers, and went out. Inside me was a cold anger. I went toward the grounds, took a sturdy stick, and with intense, hateful blows laid waste to the ferns along the pathways, breaking all the branches of the pine tree within my reach. I collapsed at the foot of the tree, exhausted by that fit of violence.

I decided to leave the next day.

The train was approaching Tuy Hoa. I recognized the jagged coastline fringed with green water, moved at the sight of this rediscovered landscape. The wheezing locomotive crawled along endlessly, belching showers of sparks. Finally, two long whistle blasts similar to two moans: the train was entering the station. I imagined my mother stopping her work and lending an ear.

A red-tiled roof appeared; it was the Tuy Hoa railroad station, which had exchanged its old roof of rusted corrugated metal for these charming tiles.

The train came to a halt. It was near noon, and the streets were completely deserted. I contemplated this city that I had known long ago, devastated by a gigantic fire, then transformed into an expanse of sand with a few basic shacks. Today its villas and its streets lined with young trees were laid out before my eyes.

A cyclo driver stopped, very content to find a client. I told him the address, but the man interrupted me: "Monsieur, the Bastos cigarette salesman, I know him."

And he pedaled toward my parents' domicile.

I hadn't been back in a year and didn't know that my stepfather was known by the title of "Bastos cigarette salesman." In a city that had been entirely reconstructed, things had changed quickly. I wondered if my parents hadn't moved yet again.

To my relief, the house was the same, but its appearance had been modified. The store window displayed an enormous sign representing a blue pack of cigarettes with the word *Bastos* across the middle in gold letters. The first floor had been transformed into a store. The four walls were well-lined with shelves offering the complete range of cigarettes of the same name. Armchairs and ashtrays scattered on small tables gave it the appearance of a smoking room. At the far end reigned a solid wood counter behind which my mother was standing with some sewing in her hand. There were no customers; it was slack, afternoon naptime. I observed her for a few moments before paying for the ride . . . She was holding the piece of cloth far from her eyes in the way a painter judges the last brushstroke of a painting. "Her eyesight has weakened," I thought to myself. From where I was standing, I was able to notice the abundance of gray hair, now salt and pepper. Two years before, she had still been conscious of her appearance and had made me pull out her gray hairs with tweezers during the long, naptime hours. The idea that she could get old or die someday hadn't crossed my mind. The image of her decline, which I had just seen without her knowing, filled me with sadness. I generously paid the cyclo driver, who thanked me.

Our voices disturbed my mother; she raised her head, with her needle suspended in midair, astounded.

"Yes, it's your daughter who has returned," I cried out with joy.

She didn't move a muscle, but her eyes welled with tears.

"Here you are," she said simply; then, turning toward the interior of the house, she said, "Come, my daughters, your elder sister is here!"

Three dark-haired heads appeared. I hugged them close to me with a single thought in my head: I, too, had a family that loved me.

My mother celebrated my impromptu return. The dinner tray held my favorite dishes: shark's fin soup and sautéed water spinach dusted with garlic. My standing in the family circle had improved considerably in the last few years. Without showing me any sign of friendship, my stepfather didn't reject me altogether. That day the look he gave me lacked malevolence.

"Hello, Father."

"I was waiting for you," he answered, getting up. "I have some work for you, some important letters."

That innocuous sentence carried more importance in my eyes than some grand declaration. It showed that he accepted me enough to call on me, that he held me in enough esteem to draw me into his business. I realized that he was imperceptibly offering me the position of his only son who had disappointed him. I felt a sense of triumph: he had thus been forced to recognize my merits; his prejudices would reveal themselves as unfounded. "People of my race" were not all as "wretched" as he thought. The esteem that he showed me that day cleansed the humiliation from before when I was a child and he would focus his hate and scorn on my brow.

"I thank you for the confidence you have in me," I said.

He didn't answer, but his silence didn't affect me. A long period of hostility is not erased in an instant. I had simply escaped from his grip. I knew that he could never make me suffer again.

While I was eating, I looked at his emaciated face: his cheeks had become hollow, and he didn't have all his teeth anymore. He would have looked much older than my mother had he not kept his naturally very dark hair. I contemplated the face that had been terrifying to me long ago, without rancor but with indifference.

With a glance, he noted the abundance of the food that an ordinary meal would not have warranted, but he refrained from making any disagreeable comments. Doubtless he thought it necessary to show me some consideration if he wanted to get conscientious work from me. He was mistaken, because I would have worked hard anyway. I was not driven by vengeance but by pride in proving to him that I was worth more than his son—me, the bastard daughter of his wife.

The meal progressed, as usual, in total silence. My stepfather had always been a taciturn man. As for the children, we did not have the right to speak without being invited to do so. That was the way things were, and it didn't bother anybody. From time to time, I directed a smile of complicity toward my mother. She seemed happy with the consideration my stepfather was showing me. An era of family peace was opening up to us.

"Did you get your *bac?*" my stepfather asked.

His question took everyone by surprise. Since my return I had forgotten my failure and the worries of the second round. My mother, completely wrapped up in the joy of seeing me again, hadn't thought about it either. Besides, the ambition she had nurtured for me had stopped definitively with the *brevet*. Whether I obtained the *baccalauréat* or not was of no concern to her. It would have been a luxury and nothing more. She continued to regret that I hadn't become a midwife.

As for my stepfather, he had gone in the opposite direction. For a long time he had obstinately opposed my education, on the one hand because I was a girl and on the other because he intended to reserve that privilege for his own son. But destiny had decided otherwise. The *brevet* that I had gotten a year ahead of time had first put him in a bad mood, all the more so because his son had been trying to get it for two years. In the end, he had given up pinning his hopes on a boy who showed neither gifts nor inclination for his studies. And so he turned to me. After all, the name he had given me was officially displayed on the diploma I had brought back home. Legally, I was his daughter; it was enough that he give this status some reality.

The question he had just asked was proof of his interest. But it put me ill at ease, for the more he paid attention to me, the more I feared disappointing him.

"I kind of failed it," I admitted. "But I'm going to take the second round, and I'm sure to succeed then."

I immediately regretted my foolish affirmation.

"I permit you to work in my office on the second floor if that can help you prepare for your examinations with more peace of mind."

We looked at him open-mouthed. I couldn't believe it. I knew for certain then that he had shifted his hopes to me. I was proud of that but also afraid. His indifference had left me free up to now. I studied the things that interested me, and I could drop them if I wanted as well. What would happen if he intended to manage my future? As a child, I had hated him. Today my fear and my hate had dissipated. He had become an old man for whom I felt nothing anymore. I wanted to be of service to him on the condition that I not belong to him. My greatest wish was that he make my mother's life more comfortable and more pleasant. As for me, I had finished with him.

I tried to make my answer as gentle as possible: "You are good to me, but the nuns advised me to return to Da-Lat in order to prepare for the second round. I am only home for a few weeks."

"You've scarcely arrived and you're already talking about leaving," my mother said reproachfully.

My stepfather acted as if he hadn't heard me. We continued to eat in silence. I was relieved to have dared express myself in front of him; I was free once again. But my mother's sadness spoiled my joy. The fortune teller of long ago had been right: I was just ungrateful. I was sorry about it; nevertheless, I could not act otherwise. Each day my path took me further, and I didn't know where I would end up. However, I held the firm conviction that one day we would be separated from each other. It would have been better had she taken more of an interest in my sisters, in my sister Dzung, for example. She had just turned fourteen. Her face was fine-featured, of a kind of beauty unnoticed at first but that becomes enchanting to the eye the more you look at it. She was intelligent, but her intelligence had been neglected, for, like me, sometimes she was sent to school and sometimes she was kept at home if domestic chores needed to be done. I promised myself to bring her to the Couvent as soon as I had the means to allow me to pay for her room, board, and schooling.

My refusal had broken the charm. My stepfather had put on his mask of bored severity again, while my mother displayed an air of mourning as if she had already lost me. I was tempted to stay just to please them. After all, who cared about my *bac*? I had sufficient knowledge to serve as my stepfather's secretary. My mother would then have me nearby. On the other hand, I would become the guilty witness of her wasted life. I would constantly repeat to myself that her condition would have been better if I had never existed. As a consequence, I could do nothing less than repair the damage by marrying the man she would choose for me. And that would have been my happiness, a happiness that would have destroyed me.

The weeks that followed were painful. Every day I devoted myself to writing my stepfather's business letters. His pleasant mood bothered me more than unconcealed anger. When, my tasks finished, I rejoined my mother, her reproaches prevented our mutual understanding. The family atmosphere was becoming suffocating.

I welcomed the end of the month like a liberation. My mother helped with the preparations for my departure in silence, a silence that was conspicuously disapproving. Even so, she offered me a ring "that I could sell if need be."

"Don't wear it, for your father might see it. Put it away in a safe place."

The mention of the little secrets she had to lower herself to in order to offer me this gift revolted me.

"I don't need it. Keep it for my sisters."

"But what if something happens to you?"

I smiled. It had been two years since she had had to worry about my living expenses. She was counting on Madame N.'s providential aid. I didn't hold that against her. Otherwise, I had nothing to complain about: the money that was coming in from the classes I gave met my expenses fully. Two or three times a year I could even spoil my mother and my sisters with a few gifts. The pleasure I derived from that was priceless.

"Don't worry about me, Mama. I have everything I need. Soon, when I have my *bac* degrees, I will be able to earn some money and send you some each month. Then, you, too, will have your financial independence; you will no longer be entirely dependent on your husband."

She was touched to see that I still thought about her. Confidence was re-established between us. I told her about my plan to open a high-level school in Saigon.

"Listen, Mama. I want to succeed on my own. Marriage doesn't interest me, and a family doesn't either. Look at yours; do you believe that it's a good example?"

"I do my best, you know," my mother said, defending herself.

"I'm not reproaching you for anything. If you knew how much I understand you . . . But, understand me, would you? Help me follow this path. Don't be sad when I go."

She smiled.

"I will come live with you, your sisters will study in your school, and as for me, I could take care of the cooking, the housework . . ."

She seemed younger, and I found her beautiful. My sisters, who had been following our conversation, broke in: "When are we going to live with you?"

I calmed their impatience.

"In just four years. I have to get my *bac* first, then my bachelor's."

I talked to them about my partners: An would go to law school, for she would take responsibility for managing the school, and Dô would study mathematics. I was lacking many other teachers, but I knew that it would be easy for me to find some when I, myself, was in college. The more I thought about my project, the more it took shape. My mother wanted to invite Dô and An for the next vacation "to get to know them." She helped me close my suitcase, now almost happy to see me leave. She held out the ring again to me.

"This is a contribution to your project."

I accepted it this time. My sisters decided to keep a piggybank whose contents would be allocated to the school. Even the maid begged me to take her with me "for the unpleasant work."

"I won't ask for a salary provided that my daughter can study with you and that she will have a better life than mine."

No member of my family accompanied me to the airport, and it was better that way.

My room had remained as I had left it. I had to tell the school's authorities that I was there, and I went to see them. The halls were empty, and silence reigned, like an abandoned house. The smell of floor wax hung in the air. I climbed the deserted staircase and reached the foyer: no one. I knocked at the door of the nun who was the bursar; no answer. I went out on the front steps.

Without the presence of the pupils, the grounds had a melancholic air. I sat down on a bench. The air was pleasantly bracing. The monastic life of this place resembled an oasis of peacefulness. The nuns who lived there seemed happier than many lay people I knew. They were always cheerful and busy.

Suddenly there were steps on the gravel, jokes, laughter: the nuns were coming out from vespers. They hadn't seen me. Away from our presence they had dropped their customary reserve. It was vacation for them, too. I listened to their chatter, surprised to see that the subjects of their conversations were like those of schoolgirls.

Later on, I entered the office of the Mother Superior.

"Welcome. You are the first but your classmates will arrive from Saigon in an hour. Did you have a good vacation?"

"It was excellent, but I'm happy to be back."

It was true. Nevertheless, the Mother Superior shot me an incredulous smile as if I had just said something flattering. I knew she didn't like flattery.

My relations with her were often unsettled by misunderstandings. I rarely said what I should have. Either I talked too much or I didn't talk enough. She didn't trust me. She seemed to suspect me of concealing who knows what. Not having the same code, we had great difficulty communicating with each other. It took me a very long time to understand that. At the time, this lack of trust hurt even more because I admired her without reservation. I envied my classmates who knew exactly how to behave in each situation.

I made reference to this awkwardness with Dô, who commented, "The cause of their failure to understand comes from the fact that you are Vietnamese and they are French. Why must you always try to be liked?"

Because I needed it, quite obviously. But it was a weakness that I didn't dare admit to.

"I don't try to be liked. I just find the way they judge me unfair."

Dô laughed.

"They are as they are and we are as we are. We are here to learn, nothing more."

More than ever I wanted to work relentlessly, get my diplomas, and leave as quickly as possible.

I still retain the feeling of being fed up with the month-long review. I was working from morning till night, allowing myself only a short walk after dinner. I was dead tired; my head was burning, and my memory in turmoil, with a knot of anguish deep inside fed day after day by my dread of failure. Only my evening walk would bring me some relief. I would walk aimlessly, my mind a blank, sensitive only to the sound of the crickets, to the sound of the wings of a night bird frightened by my approach.

I passed with honors. My classmates who also succeeded in passing screamed with satisfaction. But I felt only a great weariness. Mother X was surprised by my silence.

"Aren't you happy with your success?"

"Of course I am," I answered. "I'm just tired."

"You'll feel better starting tomorrow," she added, patting me on the cheek.

Her gesture felt overly intimate. I was like a lost dog tamed by the slightest caress.

Without delay I sent a telegram to Madame N. I felt better. I had gotten over the first obstacle. Later, when the certificate attesting to my success was given to me, I examined that ordinary piece of paper, astonished. I had imagined something more spectacular.

The nuns gave the award-winning graduates a dinner in celebration. The teachers took part, something rare that we awaited with curiosity, for they seemed so abstract to us that we could scarcely imagine that they could eat and drink. We were congratulated, one by one, individually. My tenacity was praised, giving the impression that my merit was even greater because I was the poorest. This public revelation distressed me. I was suddenly irritated by these girls for whom the *bac* did not represent the same stakes as it did for me. Failure would have wounded their pride; it would have changed my life drastically.

A little while afterwards the Mother Superior summoned me again. I prepared myself for the worst. She took an envelope out of the drawer.

"We received a letter from your godmother," she said in a neutral voice. "It concerns your studies at our school."

So, it had finally happened; I was being dismissed. I was seized by a fit of nausea and collapsed. I was carried to the infirmary. Behind me a voice said, "It's all an act." I hated them all. I was happy to be alone again in my bed.

With the rustling of a rosary, the Mother Superior appeared after a moment.

"How do you feel?"

"Better, thank you."

My voice was firm; I had nothing left to lose.

"I assume you don't want to keep me here anymore," I said. "I will leave when you want."

She looked at me, stunned.

"We haven't yet made a decision about you. Your godmother tells us that she finds herself forced to withdraw her support for you, considering the financial difficulties she currently finds herself in."

I had nothing to say. When all was said and done, it was less offensive for me to leave under these conditions than to be dismissed for unsatisfactory behavior.

"What will you do if we let you go?"

"I don't know. Anyway, I will carry on. I will look for a day job and study in the evening."

It was not a decision that I had thought about in advance, but it was obvious at that instant as the only solution. The difficulty resided in the fact that I had to go to Saigon even if I knew no one likely to put me up. My stepfather's family was indeed in Cho-Lon, but I wasn't certain they would want to accommodate me.

"What are you thinking about?" the Mother Superior questioned.

I answered without thinking: "About the difficulties awaiting me."

"We can offer you a solution," she proposed. "We need a sixth-grade teacher. You could easily accomplish this task during the day and work for yourself in the evening. We will see to it that you can attend the philosophy classes and perhaps those in the major subjects, too. Your salary will be useful in paying for your room, board and schooling. What do you have to say about it?"

"It's a miracle," I cried.

She ignored my enthusiasm.

"Think about it. It's a great responsibility."

I had already thought about it. I would live off my work, I would owe nothing to anyone, I would be free.

From that moment on, my days were completely devoted to the classes I gave and to those I received. In the evening in my room, I worked till late without any nun coming to ask me to put out the light. I had acquired adult status. I saw less of my schoolmates, who from then on considered me with a combination of envy, because of my status, and contempt, because of my station.

But their opinion mattered little to me. What's more, I took their immaturity with condescension. I no longer had the time to worry about such trivial questions. It was my first salaried job, and I was anxious that the nuns be satisfied with it. I liked my pupils, who felt the same about me. The Mother Superior sometimes favored me with a smile, a sign that she did not regret having kept me.

That year I had given up the idea of going on vacation, taking advantage of the peace and quiet of the boarding school to review better. Christmas, then Easter went by. Then came the time for examinations. The teaching I had to do, added to my anguish, exhausted me to the point that, in the evening I fell asleep on my lessons instead of learning them. At the time, there was a supreme remedy: the amphetamine Maxiton. Because of my situation, I was the only person authorized to go to the city. I bought a great quantity of it and gave it to all those who needed it.

For an entire month I took Maxiton; thanks to it I triumphed over my sleepiness. I failed the first round, like the previous time.

When I returned home during summer vacation, no one asked me any questions. As for me, I deemed it unnecessary to reveal that Madame N. had stopped helping me, thinking that it was none of their business since they couldn't do anything about it anyway. I was independent. I no longer had to ask for permission about what I should do or about where I should go. On the other hand, my parents could refrain from any duty toward me except that of putting me up at home. I was free to do as I pleased, but on the condition that I not hurt the reputation of my family. As far as that was concerned, there was only one thing to do: behave like an impregnable fortress. No weakness of the flesh or the heart. The life of a girl was a narrow path that had to lead her from virginity to marriage. Always saying "no" at an age when the heart asks only to open up, when the mouth calls for kisses, requires a kind of heroism. I lived this refusal until I was in pain, drawing my strength from the determination to prove that, on this point, I was worth as much as a woman of pure Vietnamese blood.

Like the previous year, I passed the October round with honors. I had thus cleared the great obstacle represented by secondary studies. My teachers advised me to register for the foundation classes for first-year university students, because a bachelor's in arts and letters was what I was most capable of doing. But there was no college in Da-Lat, and I couldn't enroll in Saigon without some assurance of finding the means to support myself. I could always resort to the solution of taking correspondence courses, but that was only possible if the Couvent consented to keep me as a teacher. After all, the pupils were satisfied with my teaching, and the nuns had been able to see the seriousness of my work. I asked the Mother Superior about it, and she accepted.

Contrary to the preceding year when I had worked as a kind of au pair, I received my salary every month in due form. With my room and board taken care of, I still had a lot of money left over. Each month I sent some of it to my mother, and I used the rest to pay for school for my sister Dzung, whom I had brought to the Couvent.

I intended to pamper my little sister. In reality, I only made her unhappy. Up to then she had gone intermittently—like me—to a Vietnamese school and didn't know a word of French. The Couvent's atmosphere, which had intimidated me so much upon my arrival, disconcerted her. She went from the classroom to the refectory and from the refectory to the dormitory, not daring to say a word to anyone. She seemed not to understand anything about what was being taught to her. My pride wounded, I scolded her harshly every evening. Her face impenetrable, my sister would look at the floor without defending herself, with nary a complaint. Her passivity would infuriate me even more, and I would heap more violence on her, stopping only when tears ran down her cheeks. I reproached her for her obstinacy, for her lack of drive, for what little sociability she had. I loved her with a kind of tyrannical affection, which only aggravated her feelings of helplessness and unhappiness. She endured this situation for the entire school year without ever rebelling. She didn't direct any reproach toward me, but then she didn't say anything else to me either. I still harbor remorse for not having loved her enough.

The passion I had for my sister's education took a lot of my time. I was not preparing well for the first-year university certificate examinations. I was caught short when the time came for the examinations in Saigon. As the school year was almost over, I sent my sister back home to the family. I had one week before the day the written tests were scheduled. I closed my suitcases for the last time. Starting with next year, I would have to live in the capital if I wanted to continue at the college of arts and letters.

I bid the Mother Superior farewell.

"I hope you have been happy with us here."

I didn't answer. My eyes welled up. My interlocutor took my tears as an expression of sadness caused by this final departure.

"Don't be upset. You know well that you can come back to see us when you wish."

I didn't disabuse her of that notion.

"Thank you, my mother."

We parted upon that misunderstanding.

❧ 16 ❧

Saigon

I got my first-year university degree in Saigon. My former classmates, the ones who had taken a liking to me, invited me to their homes and introduced me to the female friends of their parents, especially to those who were looking for a tutor for their children. I got many offers for work that I accepted without hesitation. Soon, my schedule was so full that I had to turn some offers down. At a fee of a hundred piasters an hour, I was earning a good living. The only thing left for me to do was find a suitable place to live.

At that time, there was only one residence hall for female students. The director whom I had approached told me right away that there was no room available. I admitted to her that having no family in Saigon, I didn't know where to go. Faced with my lost look, she consented to let me stay during the vacation.

"When school starts again, we'll see if we can register you here. However, the fact that you are already here gives you a better chance."

I was so happy I wanted to throw my arms around her neck. Life was beautiful. It had rained outside, and the air was still cool from the dampness. I walked straight ahead aimlessly, laughing out loud. I had resolved the problem of work and housing in the space of a week, without difficulty.

Everything was going my way. In the street, a young man blocked my path. He was smiling timidly.

"Hello, Mademoiselle."

In other circumstances, I would have beat an angry retreat. But today my mood made me inclined to be cheerful. The young man was emboldened.

"Don't you remember me? We were sitting next to each other during the written part of the first-year exam. My congratulations on your success. I assume you're returning to Tuy Hoa for vacation?"

He was speaking very fast, like someone who was reciting a lesson he had learned at breakneck speed for fear of having a memory lapse.

"How do you know that I live in Tuy Hoa?"

He traced a complicated design with the toe of his shoe, then stared at me suddenly.

"I know a lot about you."

I pretended not to hear him.

"You are very beautiful," he added.

I blushed.

"I'm in a hurry. Goodbye," I said coldly.

And I left him there.

Toward dusk when I arrived at the residence hall with my suitcase, the young man was waiting for me in front of the gate. Noticing my irritation, he hastened to explain.

"Don't assume that I'm trying to bother you. But you are alone and people are often mean. If you need anything, call on me. Here is my address."

He held out an envelope that I put in my pocket without reading the contents. Even so, I was intrigued to find him there just at the moment I arrived.

"Tell me, you wouldn't be a wizard, would you? How did you know I was going to arrive at this time?"

"Actually, I didn't know what time you would return, so I waited."

"And how long have you been waiting, if it's not indiscreet to ask?" I said ironically.

"Since you left me, early in the afternoon."

"The whole time? Good heavens, you're crazy!"

He smiled. "Maybe. But you know, I always have a book with me. I read and don't notice the time going by." He showed me the one he had in his hand, a paperback. "*Nausea* by Sartre. Have you read it?"

"Oh no!" I cried out disapprovingly. "At the Couvent we were strongly advised against it."

"So what did you read, then?"

"Other things," I replied, evasively.

"So, what else?"

He was starting to annoy me.

"Oh, I don't know . . . Claudel, Péguy, Gabriel Marcel . . ."

He smiled again.

"If you would allow it, we could exchange our readings."

He didn't lack nerve.

"You're jumping the gun. Who told you I wanted to see you again?"

"We are condemned to see each other, Mademoiselle. I'm registered for the diploma in French literature like you. My name is Ho. Don't say anything; I know yours."

I turned on my heel, furious. *Don't say anything; I know yours.* I didn't like how this boy had turned the situation to his advantage. I would have liked to be scathing instead of finding myself at a loss for words, like a silly goose. No proper Vietnamese man would have allowed himself to approach me in such a direct and crude manner. He would have tried to see a good deal of one of my girlfriends, who would have introduced him to me. He would have courted me discreetly, indirectly at first . . . To be frank, I would not have liked that hypocritical way of behaving any better. I didn't know what to think any more. This boy had ruined my beautiful day.

The director wanted to do the honors and show me around the residence hall. I followed her, still in the grip of my bad mood. We crossed a nondescript dining room and then a dreary hallway before ending up in the dormitory. I was shocked: twelve iron beds were facing each other, separated by metal armoires like you see in hospitals. After the luxury I'd known at the Couvent, the narrow, stained mattresses with their springs showing through made the room especially grim.

The director made a sweeping gesture.

"Here is your home. Settle in wherever you like since you are the first to arrive. I'll leave you now. Have a good stay. If you would like to have dinner here, you can buy meal tickets in my office."

I stood motionless in the middle of the room. From one of the windows I could make out the groves of trees in the garden. I eventually chose a bed under a window, unfolded the mattress, and put my suitcase on it. The armoire had been a khaki color, but was now chipped here and there. Rust had formed large patches on the surface. The unoiled doors made a squealing sound. But everything was clean. I stretched out on the mattress. On the ceiling, translucent geckos scurried. In spite of everything, I was content to have a roof over my head.

In the dining room, I was surprised to find about ten students. They were no doubt staying in the dormitories on the upper floors. Some knew each other, and were chatting among themselves; others were eating alone, like me. At a remote table, two young girls were caressing each other furtively. I averted my eyes.

"It's the couple from the third floor," murmured my neighbor. "They're pharmacy students. Obviously, they prefer to spend their vacation here, in bed, rather than going home."

She let out a little unpleasant laugh. I didn't answer.

Once dinner was over, I went out to sit in the garden. It was dark there. Up high a thin crescent moon appeared, cut out of the sky. A white *áo dài* moved toward me. It was my friend An.

"Are you dreaming?"

"I'm just getting some air. How did you get in?"

"Through the gate."

"No one asked you anything?"

"No."

"So, anyone can just walk right in here. What if it had been a boy?"

"Well, he would have come in just like me," answered An, laughing. She sat down.

"So, do you like your new room?"

"It's a sordid dormitory. You'd think it was a hospital ward."

I told her about my encounter with Ho. She already knew about it. He had talked to her to get my name and address.

"Why did you give them to him? How careless you are!"

My comment hurt my friend. "Put yourself in my place. He told me that the secretary's office at school needed your address, and he wanted to do you a favor."

"You must be joking. I went by this morning. They have my address."

Remembering the envelope that he had given me, I took it out of my pocket. We examined it in the light of the street lamp near the gate. His address was written there; it was in a part of Saigon we didn't know. Inside was a glossy piece of paper, like a business card. There was a drawing on it. A long line sketched in India ink marked the horizon.

Below was a wiggly line that could have been a snake, and way up on the card was a star. In careful handwriting Ho had put down these words: "You are the star, and me, this earthworm." The text was written in French. We both burst out laughing.

"He copied this drawing from *The Little Prince* by Saint-Exupéry," I said spitefully.

"Perhaps," said An, examining the card once again. "But he does have beautiful handwriting."

"Why do you believe he wrote it in French? He's a snob."

"To show you that you can be proud of him. It looks like he received highest honors from the jury on his exam."

"So what? What does that have to do with me?"

An smiled without answering. We spent the rest of the time comparing our respective schools. When she left me at ten o'clock, I went right to bed.

I awakened early the next day and got dressed with care: a tea rose *áo dài*, black satin trousers, and high heels. Here clothes made the man. I checked that my nails were clean. My mother used to say that it was enough to look at people's hands to know their social origins.

My first student lived in a residential neighborhood, far from the center of town. The taxi ride was expensive for me. I calculated that with that fare there wouldn't be much left of my pay. The lady of the house received me warmly, and the little girl, who had already been my pupil at the Couvent, threw her arms around my neck.

We settled ourselves in the living room. A tiger skin covered the black and white checkerboard tile floor. A pitcher of orangeade had been put on the table. But I was careful not to touch it, suspecting that was a way to judge my manners.

I briskly conducted my lesson for two hours. The little one did her best to keep up, a bit out of breath. But I cared little about it; I was eager to show off my talents to her mother.

When we were all done, the mother accompanied me to the door, delighted.

"I'm lucky to have you. My daughter hasn't had a good teacher in a long time. If you are interested, I could recommend you to my friends."

"Thank you," I said, without committing myself any further.

"Where do you live?"

"At the women's residence hall. Goodbye, Madame."

"The chauffeur will drive you back," she said, and without giving me time to refuse, she ordered, "Ba, drive Mademoiselle back to the women's residence hall!"

I sat in the back of the car. The chauffeur dropped me off without my even hearing the sound of his voice.

"Thank you," I said, slipping a few piasters into his hand.

Ho was waiting for me in front of the residence hall. His eyes followed the automobile, the shadow of a smile on his lips.

"You're keeping rich company," he remarked.

"I don't see a lot of them. I'm tutoring their daughter," I said, defensively.

I was annoyed with myself for being weak. After all, I wasn't accountable to him.

"Goodbye," I said, turning into the path.

He followed close behind me.

"Wait, wait . . . I came to give you some information that might interest you."

"That would surprise me!"

We had reached the garden where I had been sitting the night before. I didn't like the idea that people might see me with him. Gossip spread quickly when it was about a young girl's reputation. It would have been enough to be seen together a few times for me to be taken for his fiancée. I was quite irritated about it.

"Hurry up and tell me what you have to say. It's very hot out here."

Indeed, the noonday sun cast a blinding light, and the conical hat I was wearing wasn't enough to provide soothing shade.

Ho explained precipitously, "Alright then. For two years there's been a college of education to train secondary school teachers, something like the École Normale Supérieure in France. They have just created a department of French literature. Recruiting is done through a competitive exam that will take place in October. If you pass, you get a scholarship of 3500 piasters per month."

"Three thousand five hundred piasters per month?" I cried out. "That's a lot."

"I brought you the application papers," he added, pulling a folder out of his schoolbag. "Fill these out; I'll drop them off myself. It's a little late to sign up, but I'll manage."

So, I filled out the papers. Ho took care of the rest. And thus began my relationship with Ho. He loved me. I didn't love him, but I always needed his help.

We took the entrance exam, and both of us passed.

I stopped giving private lessons for lack of time. I wasn't sorry about it. All things considered, I preferred receiving my funds from the state, like a salary. I had never liked the furtive way those ladies stuffed what they owed me into my pocket, as if it were a tip.

Since the beginning of university classes, the dormitory had gradually filled up. Nevertheless, my presence there was not in question anymore; I was admitted definitively.

I went to the school of education every day, fearfully perched on the luggage rack of the moped that one of my bolder classmates would drive. Our arrival in the courtyard caused a sensation, for we were the only women to get around on such a contraption.

Our teachers, Vietnamese people who had done their university studies in France, nostalgically evoked their garrets in the Latin Quarter. They recalled their courses at the Sorbonne and talked about the turbulent political discussions in the cafés. Our lives, by comparison, seemed quite dull to us. In fact, none of us cared much about politics. Hadn't colonization ended with Dien Bien Phu? Wasn't the country independent? President Diem was thought of as an upright man. His willingness to appear in public wearing traditional clothes flattered our national feelings. As for Madame Nhu, the role she played in state affairs filled us with enthusiasm, for we interpreted it as a sign of the emancipation of women.[1]

---

1. Madame Nhu was President Diem's sister-in-law and an increasingly controversial figure on the political stage of South Viet Nam in the late 1950s and early 1960s. Known especially for her disparaging comments about the Buddhist monks who were self-immolating in Saigon intersections in the early 1960s in protest of the ongoing war, she was forced into exile after the assassination of her husband and brother-in-law in 1963. Additional references to President Diem are found in Chapters 1 and 14.

In the high schools and colleges, classes were conducted in the local language. Foreign language departments were gradually replacing French volunteer teachers with Vietnamese who had gotten their diplomas at the Sorbonne or at the university in Montpellier. There were other signs, too, that Viet Nam had been given back to the Vietnamese. A certificate in Vietnamese history was established, and students in French literature were allowed to opt for a certificate in Chinese.

What bothered us at that time was that the books we needed were scarce and extremely expensive. At school, the newly created French literature department didn't yet have a library. The few books we had were passed around until they were falling apart. As a consequence, we read little. In the context of this shortage, Ho was considered a generous prince. Housed and fed by a well-off mother, he could use his scholarship to purchase numerous books. Without question, he was the most cultured of the class. His papers—documented, thoughtful, and brilliant—provoked the admiration of the professors, who would read them aloud. I admired him despite myself. In any case, I benefited from his generosity. In time, I became familiar with Gide, Sartre, and Malraux. He introduced me to French poetry, to Baudelaire, Rimbaud, and Verlaine. He offered me fine editions of art books from Skira, and I learned to love the impressionists and the fauvists. I discovered Van Gogh, Gauguin, and Degas.

We never talked about our feelings. We would have seemed to be just friends if not for his presence everywhere I went. I would only retrieve my solitude in the dormitory of the residence hall. But even there I was not safe.

One morning at dawn my sleep was disturbed by a strange presence. I opened my eyes; through the mosquito net I saw Ho's face leaning over my bed. He gave me a dreadful fright. When I finally recovered, Ho had disappeared. Was that a dream or reality? I was certain of having seen him. I asked my neighbors, but they had not seen anything; they were sleeping. I was about to blame my imagination when I saw a book on the floor; it was his. So, he had come after all. What exactly did he want? I was suffocated by fear and anger.

During morning classes, he avoided my gaze. I stopped him at the front door.

"How did you dare come right into the dormitory? And with what bad intentions?" I cried out, on the verge of tears. "I warn you that I will complain to the dean and even to the chancellor if need be."

He went pale.

"Don't do that. I swear to you that my intentions were pure. I just needed to look at you, nothing more. Besides, you must have noticed that I did not touch you."

I didn't answer.

"Forgive me."

"Listen, you scared me. Don't ever do that again."

I looked at that seemingly submissive boy, wondering what I needed to do to protect myself from his urges.

"Please leave me alone. Look for another girl. I am not a 'star,' as you said. You're mistaken about me."

"No, let me love you. I won't scare you anymore."

He made a move to grab my hand.

"No," I cried out, running away.

From that day on, I was haunted by my fear of Ho. I didn't dare talk to anyone about it. Besides, they wouldn't believe me. The girls in our class, already irritated by his wooing of me, would have liked nothing better than to put all the responsibility on me. I avoided going around alone, and I refused to join the group of students at the end of classes when they would go have ice cream in the cafés on the Rue Catinat.[2]

I finally told the story to Bich, a schoolmate from the Couvent des Oiseaux. We didn't see much of each other at the time, but we had grown closer since running into each other at the college of literature. She knew Ho.

"Last year he was sighing after me," she declared, laughing.

"Really?"

"Yes. But it seems much more serious with you. He's bothering you more."

I hadn't asked for his attentions. In order to calm me down, she

---

2. The Rue Catinat was the most fashionable street in Saigon during the colonial period. Renamed Tu Do during the Viet Nam War, it is now known as Dong Khoi and is again the most upscale street in the city.

proposed that I come live at her parents' house. I put together a few things and followed Bich, without abandoning the residence hall, however.

Her house was large and comfortable. She introduced me to her two brothers: the older one was nineteen, the younger fifteen. She also had two younger sisters. As for her parents, they adopted me instantaneously.

Her mother, a short, thin woman, energetically ran the family business, which consisted of supplying food to the communities in the central highlands. Every week she would accompany the truck loaded with provisions over the mountain roads up to the city of Ban Me Thuot. Her father, a handsome, distinguished man, took care of the accounts, a less tiring job. He showed me an affection tinged with gallantry, as if to remind me that I was a pretty girl—I had just turned twenty-three—and he a man who was still young. I had difficulty considering him as my father, and when I happened to call him "Bác," a polite term meaning the brother of my father, we would smile with complicity, expressing our derision of that appellation.

His idleness made frequent private conversations possible during which we passionately exchanged our points of view on the meaning of life, happiness, virtue. We often ended up agreeing with each other. I admired his open mind, his nonconformist points of view. He gave the feeling of understanding me so well that one day I entrusted him with the story of Ho's bursting unbelievably into the dormitory of the residence hall. He listened to me attentively.

"That's a beautiful story," he said when I had finished.

I was greatly surprised.

"What? Don't you find that his behavior was unspeakable?"

"Yes," he admitted. "But understand me: if I were your father, I would give him a good thrashing to rid him of any desire to do it again. But if I were in love with you, I might have done the same thing."

"You? You would have done the same thing?"

His voice became fatherly. "Obviously, he acted badly. Excuse me if I offended you. We are your family here, aren't we? We're looking out for you."

Indeed, in his home I felt surrounded with more affection than in my own family.

It happened that Ho would follow me to the street where I lived, only to disappear about fifty yards from the house. I shared my fears with the father, who offered me his younger son Ma as a chaperone.

"He's young but strong. He will defend you," he said, laughing.

Ma was in tenth grade. Athletic and well-built, he was tall for fifteen. He took his role seriously. Every day he took me to school on his bicycle and came to pick me up when classes were over. Seated on the luggage rack, I held him tightly around the waist. No one could find fault, since our age difference ruled out any suspicion. I happily gave in to this physical contact whose fraternal character put my conscience at ease. I hadn't experienced such feelings since the break-up with my teacher from Nha Trang.

Like all girls from good families, I had practiced refusal in the name of virtue. We kept ourselves intact for marriage, whose social status swelled us with pride but whose carnal aspect frightened us. With a mysterious air, the oldest girls would say, "It really hurts." We were over twenty years old and still didn't know exactly how babies were born. Asking about it was like confessing to a hidden vice. We waited in anguish for the first girl to marry and reveal the mystery to us. We were in holy terror of sexuality. What we wished for was the physical tenderness that had been taken away from us too soon.

Parents did not lavish kisses and cuddling on their children once they were no longer young. Then began the arid phase when all touching was banned. Constrained by her rigidity, a girl practiced at never again letting herself go. At puberty, it became a constant struggle with herself, but we weren't alone in this struggle against evil. Morality, religion, and unwavering social surveillance supported us. Successes were praised, and failures severely reprimanded. The supreme reward was acquiring a reputation as a "difficult," "inaccessible" girl. These qualifiers, like so many jewels, enhanced our luster and increased our market value, so to speak.

I had a handicap in this competition: my *métissage*, the mark of immorality, an atavism I, too, believed in. Knowing that my past was not without reproach, I redoubled my efforts. I had not forgotten the scandal provoked by my guilty love for the music teacher. Even though no one knew about it in Saigon, I had harbored a secret shame that made me more distant than other girls. But I wasn't going to wait much longer to find out that playing hard to get was a very tough form of discipline. For a short time, I had been courted by an aviator who had finished school in France and who loved to paint. He was looking for a model, and we were introduced to each other. All the while he painted, he talked to me about Paris, about the banks of the Seine in the spring when the buds show off their green tenderness. That was a marvel I had difficulty imagining, not being familiar with the change of seasons. Sometimes we would go have dinner in one of the numerous fashionable restaurants on the banks of the Mekong. He would take me back, properly, to the residence hall before midnight. More rarely we would walk side-by-side, chatting. His company distracted me from my college classmates. I didn't love him, but he said he didn't give up hope of my changing my mind someday. Sometimes, we would joke about that matter. I loved the casual nature of our relationship, and I believed myself invulnerable until the day when he stood right behind my back to show me the moon in its first quarter. A magnet-like strength pulled me toward the man whose breath was burning the nape of my neck. My torso naturally encountered the chest of my companion, like a branch leaning toward the water. I became dizzy. With all my might, I managed to step to the side, pulling myself away from temptation. With my head thrown back in a position of someone admiring the sky, I took advantage of this subterfuge to regain control of myself. The man noticed nothing except my motionless back.

"What a beautiful night," he sighed.

"It's late; let's go back," I suggested.

We separated. My virtue was safe.

This painful frustration, this ongoing war against my oversensitivity, ceased from the day I was able to find platonic satisfaction and complete peace of mind in Ma's company. He was looked upon as my little brother, and the friendship that linked me with his sister along with the affection that her parents felt for me only reinforced that idea. In all innocence, Ma himself took pride in the chivalric role his father had assigned to him. For this reason, we became inseparable. I loved to put my cheek against the rough material of his shirt while his bicycle took us through the shaded streets of Saigon. By closing my eyes, I could go back in time, substituting for this back the teacher's against which I would press my cheek during our past escapades. Ma didn't know anything about my reveries. As for me, I was content to enjoy his presence without his knowing it.

The status quo lasted until the Mid-Autumn Festival, a festival for children. On that occasion, the streets were brimming with a noisy and laughing crowd. That year I went along with Bich's family, her parents, her brothers, her sisters, and me, a group of eight people. We held each other's hands, careful not to lose each other in the crush. But despite these efforts, the tide of humanity, in waves, separated us from each other. In the end, I had only Ma's hand in my own.

We walked through an ocean of lanterns held up high by hundreds of hands. Their flickering flames were so many fireflies in the darkness. The young children were on the shoulders of their fathers and proudly waved the fragile sticks holding the lanterns in the shapes of fish, stars, and familiar animals.

People trying to clear a path for themselves pushed us against each other. We let out cries mixed with laughter, drifting from side to side with the currents, our bodies squeezed against each other by the crowd. A gang of unruly children cut through the tightly packed pedestrians with their flimsy lanterns shaking so much that they risked going up in flames at any moment. Ma held me close to him, creating a rampart against the pushing passersby with his body. Our faces touched. We looked at each other, distraught. A violent feeling of the kind you encounter in a society full of frustration and taboos engulfed us. Nothing else existed except the attraction that drew us together. We kissed each other breathlessly. As for what happened next, I have retained only the memory of a magnificent celebration and a burning passion.

I returned home alone, affirming that I had lost sight of "my little brother," while he deliberately wandered the deserted streets to give more credibility to my lie. They believed us.

What we were feeling was not love but a constant and irrepressible desire to touch each other. Each day, as soon as classes ended I would fly home to where Ma was already waiting for me.

Like two young animals we gripped each other in a fury that was as much part of the game of love as it was a struggle. We constantly craved each other, so much so that living under the same roof became a real test. I could not be next to him without my hand lingering in a furtive caress despite myself. As for him, he was always in my way, "under foot," as his sister would tease him.

"Be careful not to fall in love with your big sister," she would joke without really believing it.

"Incest is an unforgiveable sin," the father added.

We got scared. In the days that followed, we stopped seeing each other, displaying a respectable indifference in front of the family. Worried, I tried to get into the good graces of the head of the family. I was seen often in his company, asking him questions about his youth, soliciting his advice. At the same time, we changed our routine, seeing each other around ten in the morning when family members had gone out. I skipped some classes, and Ma did the same. He followed me like my shadow. He sat next to me at the table, and at naptime, when I had dozed off on the platform daybed in the living room, he would spread out a mat and sleep at the foot of my bed.

It was in that position that Ho surprised us one afternoon, on the pretext that he had an important document to give me. I was still sleeping when he rang the doorbell. It was the father who opened the door for him. Ho took in the scene with a penetrating gaze. Instinctively, he had guessed the unseemly bond that connected me with the young man sleeping. His eyes lingered on Ma, then met my own; I detected a cruel glare. I became afraid of his hate in the same way that I had been afraid of his love.

I returned to the residence hall the next day in the hope of calming his jealousy. I explained to the astounded family that I needed to be alone to prepare better for the upcoming competitive examination. Indeed, I had to work relentlessly if I were going to get a job in the capital. Otherwise I would be assigned to a far-off province where my *métissage* would surely come up against the narrow-mindedness common in small towns. It was a high honor when the father, who never went out of his way, drove me back in his car. Ma proved that he could remain cool, consoling himself with the idea that he could always visit me at the residence hall after nightfall. Bich watched me leave with a distracted look, completely absorbed by her secret love for a pharmacy student. In the end, my departure satisfied Ho, who left me in peace.

I devoted the next month to two activities: my work and my nocturnal encounters with Ma. I didn't linger to chat with my classmates like before. But no one was offended, for everyone was committed to preparing for the competitive exam that would decide their future. Even Ho seemed to lose interest in me. In contrast, Ma was scandalized by my passion for work. He disapproved of my social climbing, a major flaw in a woman whose ambition should be limited to contracting a good marriage.

"I don't like the way you're behaving," he said, begrudgingly.

My efforts bore fruit: I came in third, with Ho at the top of the list, of course. In some ways, we were pioneers. We were part of the first class at the school of education, which was newly created by the Ministry of Education and was intended to train the teachers of independent Viet Nam. Our diplomas were given to us solemnly in the presence of the minister and the dean. They shook our hands. With the exception of my features, I didn't feel any different from the young men and young women standing next to me on the platform. I considered myself fully a child of Viet Nam, a citizen of Viet Nam. This was my country: it was my homeland, my soil. I wanted to live there until the end of my days. My diploma attested to my status as a state employee. It was a fact that couldn't be contested. I was conscious of turning the page on rejection and humiliation. A new life was waiting for me. I swore to myself to become a good teacher: I would train young people to be responsible and would inspire the girls with the desire to live autonomously. I was anxious to be deserving of the new dignity that had been vested in me. I was anxious to get my first job.

The interminable summer vacation discouraged me. What was I going to do during all that time? The best thing would be to return to my parents' home. I announced this news to Ma who, disappointed, reproached me for what little affection I showed him. I didn't take the trouble of justifying myself. Without doubt he was right. I had the ambition of increasing my worth through professional merit.

I left Ma on the station platform without remorse, saddened less by our separation than by his powerlessness to stop me. We left each other without promising to see each other again. He favored me with a forced smile. His dark hair, cut very short, made his face look extremely juvenile. He had the freshness and purity of a landscape after the rain.

Compared to other men who were rather slender, he had the appearance of a wrestler. I found him very handsome. Suddenly, I had the irresistible urge to touch him. Getting off the train at the risk of missing it, I drew him into the shadow of the train car. My wild mouth moved over his face.

"I love you," I breathed between two kisses.

He held me so tightly it hurt.

"Stay then!"

The two of us cast a single shadow, elongated clearly upon the platform by the lamplight. I freed myself; the situation was becoming dangerous. We risked being picked up by the police. Worried, I looked around. A child, a boy, stared at me insolently as if he knew I were at fault. His mother, whose attention he was trying to attract—without doubt to show her this scene—was busy checking the good condition of her bundle. I jumped on the train. When the woman raised her head in my direction, I was innocently in the window resting on my elbows. The child, who was still trying to tell his story, got a slap. At the same time, an employee in uniform gave the signal for departure. People cried out last bits of advice, exchanged last adieus. With his hands up to his mouth, Ma tried to yell over the general hubbub.

"I will write you."

The train started to move.

❧ 17 ❧

The Turning Point

Having decided to return home at the last minute, I hadn't let anyone know. Upon seeing me, my sisters stared wide-eyed, dumbfounded.

"Don't you recognize me?"

They immediately ran inside, crying out at the top of their lungs, "Elder sister is back!"

My mother ran to the door and froze at the sight of me, emotion brimming from her eyelids. My stepfather raised his head from the account ledger he was examining.

"You could have told us you were coming. I would have sent the chauffeur to the train station."

So we still had a chauffeur. That meant that his business was doing well.

"Forgive my absentmindedness."

The shadow of a smile lit up his austere features.

I rested from a year of effort while waiting for my first assignment. I secretly wished for a position in Saigon without really daring to believe I would get it. We all had our eye on the capital. Naturally, my mother advised me to request Tuy Hoa; that way I could live with her. I promised her I would, but did nothing about it. I had lived too long without a family to put myself under their supervision again.

Ho wrote to me regularly with news of our classmates who were staying in Saigon. Taking my interests to heart, he went regularly to the Ministry, watching out for the appointments, ready to do everything so that I wasn't sent off to languish in some province. I let him do it out of laziness, persuaded that he could defend my interests better than I.

Toward the middle of August, I received an imposing dossier regarding a scholarship in France. "An unheard-of stroke of luck," Ho wrote. The French government was offering some twenty scholarships to teachers whose specialty was teaching French language. After a long interruption, Franco–Vietnamese cultural relations were picking up again. Those in the know attributed these happy circumstances to Monsieur Meillon, at the time a professor at the School of Oriental Languages in Paris.

Without Ho, I wouldn't have known anything about this unusual opportunity: twenty scholarships for some two hundred candidates. I filled out the application and sent it in, registered, enrolled, applied almost mechanically, choosing Paris. I had so little hope of being selected that I didn't tell my parents about it. But my imagination danced in spite of myself. Bits and pieces gleaned here and there jostled in my mind: snow, impossible to imagine when you were familiar only with the scorching street sparkling with the dust suspended above it catching the light; the booksellers along the Seine; the Luxembourg Gardens; the autumn leaves . . . And what if I got that scholarship? What if I were to leave?

I didn't want to stay, and I was afraid to leave. I waited passively, without excessive emotion, reassured at the thought that once again fate would decide for me.

In the meantime, I was assigned to a secondary school in Saigon, a coed school located at the edge of the zoo. My wish was fulfilled. Ho sent me a congratulatory telegram, adding that the whole class was waiting for me in order to celebrate the event. I returned to take up my position. I had a lot to do before classes started again: courses to prepare and, above all, finding a place to live.

In the course of my many visits to rooms, I had the opportunity to become aware of the difficulties encountered by a girl alone. Quite often, landlords would raise the rent when they saw how inexperienced I was. Others, taking advantage of my credulity, proposed a moderate rent that they presented as a favor while patting my thigh with a falsely paternal air. I would free myself, frightened. I came back from these expeditions exhausted and discouraged. For several years I had had the illusion of having fought in order to survive. But the life I had led as a student had been protected. Now life outside the reassuring circle of my relationships seemed strewn with pitfalls.

I was close to giving up when I finally encountered a young couple. They seemed open, and I liked them right away. I learned very quickly that they had traveled a lot, something still quite rare. When I told them that I hoped to obtain a scholarship to study in Paris, our conversation took a friendly turn, as normally happens with people who have known each other for a long time.

"We've had many people come to see us," said the woman, "but I confess that we prefer you."

I smiled, flattered.

"That's why, if you want us to keep you at the top of the list, it's preferable that you give us a deposit."

"With pleasure."

They were so different from the hard-headed or lustful landlords I had seen, and their apartment was very pretty, furnished with taste.

"How much do you need?"

"Six hundred piasters will be enough."

The sum was large, the equivalent of a month of my future salary. Of course, I didn't have the first cent of it. But I didn't get discouraged.

"I'll bring it tomorrow," I affirmed.

I had thought of my stepfather's generous cousin, the one who lived in Cho-Lon. He was rich, and I hoped that he wouldn't refuse me the six hundred piasters. In any case, I would have the means to reimburse him as soon as I received my first paycheck.

My hopes were not disappointed. My "uncle" readily lent me the required sum, even being so kind as to offer me an excellent meal.

I took the money to the couple. It was the 25th of August, and they promised to give me the keys on the first of September. The wife offered me tea while the husband told me about their marvelous stay in France, in Marseille. When I left them, I was convinced that I had acquired some new friends.

The days following were devoted to buying books that were indispensable to my teaching as well as making the traditional courtesy visit to the principal of the school where I was going to work.

He was an affable man, simple in manner, contrary to the custom requiring that the head of an establishment display coldness and severity in order to put teachers in their place right away. Our conversation was rather amicable. The principal was full of advice, "as someone who was older," he clarified, as to the way to impose discipline on a class with a majority of boys "sometimes as old as you." Then, using a little French to test me, he asked about my literary tastes. To my credit I had the feeling of having cleared a hurdle.

I sent a telegram to my mother, telling her that I had found an apartment to my liking. I also wanted to take on the education of my sister Dzung, who needed to join me without delay if she really didn't want to miss the beginning of the school year. Three days later, I welcomed my sister at the Saigon train station.

On the first of September, I went to take possession of the apartment, as agreed. To my great surprise, the front door was closed. I knocked but got no response. The house seemed uninhabited. I waited, then knocked again. I was worried: had I make a mistake? I went to ask a neighbor for information.

"They have left for good. They took everything with them."

I was speechless. They had robbed me! I couldn't believe it. They had seemed so nice, and they were so cultivated. I couldn't understand how someone could be cultivated and dishonest at the same time. In my mind education, of necessity, was supposed to engender high moral actions. I was greatly disappointed. Where would I go now? I didn't have the courage to start all over.

I went back to the convent, sad and angry with myself. I told my sister Dzung about my misadventure, and she repacked her bag, ready to take the train back to Tuy Hoa. She, too, was accustomed from a tender age to reversals of fortune and sudden changes of residence. My classmates were sincerely sorry for me.

"What are you going to do now?"

"Go file a complaint," someone suggested.

I shook my head. I had been stupid, and that was too bad; that would serve as a lesson to me. My problem was to find a roof over my head quickly, but I didn't want to look anymore. The deception had taken everything out of me.

"This morning I saw a lady talking to Mother Laetitia. She was looking for a girl to tutor her children, three hours a day including room and board. I turned it down, because I have too much to do. But maybe you would be interested?"

I made a face. A room in someone's house wasn't exactly what I had in mind. I had just acquired my freedom, and I wanted a place of my own.

"Go and see anyway," my classmate insisted.

I went. The elegant woman who let me in was about thirty. Her husband was a "shareholder in Shell." So he was very rich.

She introduced me to her children, a boy and a girl, aged ten and eight respectively.

"Here are your pupils. You will take care of them from the end of school until dinnertime. My daughter has many gaps in her knowledge of mathematics, and my son is very lazy and must be closely supervised. I hope they won't make your life too difficult." She smiled. "Do you want to see your room?"

We crossed a garden with paths bordered by marigolds. All the way at the back was a small house that must have been used as a servant's room in the past, doubtless for the cook since the kitchen was close by. The room was large, lit by a wide window beyond which was the outline of the branch of a tamarind tree. A shower and washbasin were in a corner.

"You can enter and leave through the small door in the garden, just in back. That way you'll feel free to come and go as you please."

That last detail convinced me.

"Do you want to move in as soon as tomorrow? I'll let the cook know; he will serve your meals here, in your room."

I thought of my sister. How could I tell her that there were two of us? I put in timidly, "I will have my young sister with me. She's fourteen, and I intend to enroll her in the nearest secondary school. Of course, I will pay her board."

She stopped me with a wave of her hand.

"It's not at all important. I will feed your sister as well. The essential thing is that my children get along well with you and that they make progress."

"I intend to do my best."

I moved in the next day. We had only our two suitcases. We needed to buy a bed, a table and chairs. I dragged my sister on long expeditions to Saigon's central market, amused at acting like an adult. I finally had a place of my own. To inaugurate this new life, I bought myself my first alarm clock, an expensive Swiss one in a green leather case.

I enrolled my sister in the neighborhood school.

The first day of school was as big an occasion for her as for me. I was nervous. I had no experience with coed classes. I had only taught at the Couvent des Oiseaux, young, well-behaved girls whose psychology and reactions I was familiar with. How was I going to deal with boys in their senior year?

The principal accompanied me to the classroom and introduced me with high praise to the pupils. During his speech, I observed those tall adolescents, some of whom seemed quite old to me. I felt a kind of panic when the principal left the room. The pupils were still standing, awaiting my orders.

"Sit down."

My voice seemed hoarse to me. Putting on a severe mask, I said coldly, "Take out your notebooks. Here is the list of books you must buy for the year."

I naturally expressed myself in French like any self-respecting teacher. The perfection of my accent, a feature that earned me praise from the principal, seemed eminently comical to my pupils. They were used to instructors who still had their Vietnamese accent, and considered me with alarm, as if they had found themselves in the presence of a foreigner, in short, a real Frenchwoman.

"That seems to surprise you, but this is the way French is spoken," I added.

I then wrote Rimbaud's lines on the board:

> "I went off, my fists in my torn pockets
> Even my coat was becoming ideal . . ."[1]

And I required my pupils to read them correctly. None managed to, and so I took my revenge. I was still wondering how to best teach them when the shrill cries of monkeys suddenly broke the silence. I jumped, and laughter burst forth.

"The windows overlook the monkey cage at the zoo, Mademoiselle!"

Keeping a straight face with great difficulty, I wrote down the whole poem on the board.

---

1. "Ma bohème," Arthur Rimbaud.

"Copy this and practice reading it in an acceptable fashion for the next class. I will give grades."

The bell rang; the hour was over.

My sister came back delighted from her classes. She was happy with the school and with the freedom I gave her. She liked Saigon, the noise and the bustling life, so different from the provincial lethargy that she had known.

We had never felt so close to each other. I wanted to initiate a new relationship with her. Taking my example from Dô's family, whose practice of trust I had admired in the past, I declared to her, "I'm your elder sister, and I have authority over you, as you know. But you are grown up now. So, I would like to share everything with you. My salary is seven hundred piasters per month. I need to take out two hundred to reimburse our uncle in Cho-Lon. I will put the rest in this drawer. Take what you need; you don't have to ask me for permission. But keep in mind that that's all we have for the month."

My sister was left open-mouthed.

After a shower, I crossed the garden toward the main house where the children I was responsible for were waiting for me.

"So, what do you have to do for tomorrow? Show me your schedule."

The little girl obeyed immediately, but the boy looked at me without moving.

"What are you waiting for? Do like your sister."

He smiled. "I don't have anything to do for tomorrow."

"Even so, I'd like to see for myself. Show me your schedule."

"I don't have it here; it's in my bedroom."

"OK, then. Go get it."

"You go get it."

The test of wills was beginning. I looked at him for a long time in silence. He didn't lower his eyes. "The insolence of rich kids," I said to myself.

"Listen, I'm going to talk to you as a grown-up. I am your teacher, not your maid. I'm here so that you do well in class, the best, if possible. And if you want, with my help, you will beat them all. So, go get your schedule."

Then I busied myself with his sister. They went to the French school like most of the children from the cultivated middle class. The boy brought back his schedule, and I made him do a dictation. Without being outstanding, I acquitted myself reasonably of my task. A few weeks later, Ho burst into the living room where we were working. Absorbed in the explanation of the problems of distances and speeds achieved by a bicyclist who had the bad idea of pedaling faster on the trip out than on the way back, I hadn't heard him come in. My explanation was singularly lacking in clarity, and the little girl was listening to me with a confused look.

"To find the distance, you use the rule of three," said a voice behind me.

I raised my head. Ho favored me with a smile of triumph. What was he doing here? In a flash, I envisioned the anger of my employers. I looked at him in horror.

"Hello, uncle," the children cried out.

"So, yes, you're working at my cousin's."

He smiled again. I had recovered my courage.

"Well, good," I said, "for if you had come to provoke a scandal, I would never have forgiven you."

"Why do you distrust me? I love you."

I looked at the children, wondering if they had understood.

"Be quiet!" I hissed between my teeth. "Don't talk like that in front of them."

Ho changed his attitude.

"I came to announce a piece of good news to you. Your file was accepted and mine as well. Paris is ours! The first ones leave next week."

"Already?"

I hadn't had the time to think about that departure. Certainly, I wanted to leave, but later, in the indeterminate future, or maybe never. The idea of being able to leave Viet Nam was enough for me. It constituted my protection against a society that had silently rejected me from time immemorial. It was my armor, my way out. I was content with this dream of revenge. Reality caught me off guard.

"What do I have to do?" I asked.

"I believe that you must inform your principal no later than tomorrow. He needs to find someone to replace you quickly. As for me, it's already done."

"OK, I'll do it. All this is too fast," I added. "Deep down, I don't know if I really want to get this scholarship."

"Ah! If you stay, I will, too," declared Ho. "But that would be too bad. In any case, you have until the end of October to think about it."

I informed the principal.

"Your presence with us will have been like a shooting star," he commented.

As for my pupils, they didn't hide their disappointment. I told myself that, after all, we could have done some good work together.

"We have a month left. Let's make good use of it," I suggested.

Everyone approved. We agreed to devote all the classes to "conversation." Learning to speak French was what they wanted. A chorus of monkeys accompanied our words, but I didn't jump like the first time.

I still had to let my mother know, a difficult task. For a long time, she had nurtured the fear of losing me. With my departure, the last remnant of her past would fall away. She had lost her father and her mother. Her sister, the one from the same marriage as she, had left home at about twenty and had never come back. My mother had not returned to Tonkin, her birthplace, since 1947. I was the only witness to her past, even if a sad witness. I reminded her that she had been young, happy-go-lucky, and free. Her past freedom was also her mistake.

My mother replied to my letter by return mail. She announced her imminent arrival, for she was anxious to be near me during the days that were left before my departure, "without doubt the last we will spend together." I was irritated by her propensity to dramatize things. I had a scholarship for one year, renewable each year, with a limit of three years. My mother's alarm seemed exaggerated to me.

"Don't make my departure more difficult. I could be back next year. In any case, at the worst, I'll be back home in three years."

She shook her head obstinately.

"Maybe you don't know it, but me, I know that you will not come back."

"And why? Can you tell me?"

I was infuriated.

"You'll marry a Frenchman and you will stay," she predicted.

She cried softly. Her tears weakened my certainty. What if she were telling the truth? No, it wasn't possible; I had no reason to stay there. Besides, if I wanted, Ho would be there to bring me back, for he didn't want to lose me either.

I tried to convince my mother.

"Listen, my life is here. My memories are here. My family is here. I speak Vietnamese, and I'm a state employee. What reason would I have for not coming back home? Don't you understand that I would have nothing in common with a Frenchman?"

"Maybe you're right. I still have the feeling that I'm saying goodbye to you forever," she added, stubbornly.

I gave up on the discussion. I, too, was sad. Right now, this departure presented only disadvantages: my mother was desperate, and my sister, for whom I had portrayed an interesting life together with me, saw her hopes dashed outright. As for me, my stomach was tied up in knots from anxiety though I couldn't say why. As if this departure were going to be a definitive uprooting.

I felt in some vague way that my mother was not wrong, that I would be leaving forever. And I was afraid. Afraid of leaving my country and especially afraid of taking a leap into the unknown. France was a name for me, abstract images, a country associated with a hated father. If only I could back out. But how would I explain to the administration that I didn't want anything to do with the scholarship anymore? And for what reason?

Fortunately, the preparations occupied all my time. First of all, I needed warm clothes for the Parisian winter. Ho got himself a wool frock coat that cost the equivalent of several months' salary. I had two *aó dài* tunics made, a brown one and a black one, colors, I was advised, that were not likely to go out of style. And with that I discovered fashion.

We had always worn *aó dài*. The general form scarcely changed with the exception of a few details: every two or three years, the collar would go up or down a few inches or so. It was the same for the length of the panels and the width of the hems. But essentially it had stayed the same for generations. With the assimilation of that pleasant tyranny called "fashion," we had the feeling of taking a first step into the intimidating city that was going to welcome us: Paris.

The multiple steps necessary to put together the dossier, steps that we undertook in concert, had made my ties with Ho stronger. We went together to the Ministry, to the French Consulate, to the doctor's of-

fice. We were taken for a young engaged couple, and that impression
was justified by Ho's overly considerate attitude toward me. This misunderstanding irritated me, but I needed his strength to overcome my
fear. If it had been up to me, I believe that I wouldn't have gone anywhere. I would have pretended to be dead to the world, paralyzed by
my profound resistance to this trip. As a consequence, the scholarship
would have been taken away from me in order to let someone else take
advantage of it. I would have remained a teacher in Saigon.

Today I am taking the measure of my attachment to the land of
Viet Nam and to its culture. Through the years that have passed, as
time unwinds, I have noticed their deep imprint on my personality.
Viet Nam has shaped the core of my being.

I remember the feeling of terror and desperation that I experienced as the departure approached, a feeling similar to a child's, brutally snatched from its mother's breast. I remember as well my fear of
France, a blend of panic and repulsion, like when a virgin is thrown
into bed with an unknown man. France was the image of the father
who had abandoned me.

But life took it upon itself to refute my foreboding. For what Viet Nam
had refused me, France granted me: it welcomed and accepted me. All
things considered, I have not been disappointed. In France things seem
simple to me. If I say I'm Vietnamese, I'm taken as such; if I say I'm
French, I'm asked what my origins are, nothing more. Of course, I
know about the currents of racism directed toward the Maghrebi community and perhaps tomorrow toward the Asian communities, more
numerous by the day.[2] But isn't it comforting to observe that there are
also so many people against racism among the French? During the time
I lived in Viet Nam, I didn't encounter a single defender of the *métis*.
The most tolerant attitude consisted of pretending not to have noticed
their difference.

I am not accusing Viet Nam. It is a country that is dear to my
heart. I loved it with a kind of love that I never got in return. The mem-

_____

2. The Maghreb refers collectively to Morocco, Algeria, and Tunisia, former colonies of France.

ories of my childhood are impregnated with its climate, with its landscapes, with its odors, with the music of its language. I catch myself
sometimes humming old tunes that I believed buried in forgetfulness.
Viet Nam . . . it's the sweetness of my mother's face.

Today I love that land in another way, no longer as the wounded
child, but as an adult capable of taking into account what it gave to me
and what it refused me.

Already October was drawing to a close and most of the scholarship
holders had taken off for France. I was still hemming and hawing, hoping for who knows what—a last-minute illness or a catastrophe that
would have prevented me from taking the plane.

For several weeks, my mother and sisters had been living with me.
We were continually remembering past times, as if we were afraid of
not being able to say everything to each other before our separation.
Our chats took on a nostalgic tone, and my mother would cry. I tried to
be cheerful.

"Don't cry, Mother; I'm not dead!"

"A definitive separation is like death," she retorted.

I, too, had the premonition that we were going to leave each other
forever, all the while sincerely nourishing the intention of coming back.
I tried to soothe her pain.

"I'll write to you as soon as I arrive, and you will see that your fears
were unfounded."

"No, no . . . you will be among your own there, the people of your
race, and you will forget us."

"The people of my race. No one lets up talking about the people of
my race, but what race am I then?"

She wiped her tears, conciliatory. "Let's say no more about it. Let's
not make our last moments sad."

I left on the 28th of October, the final deadline for the stragglers.

In France, it was autumn—with its leaves and with All Souls' Day.

Beforehand, I had made my last visits to friends, acquaintances,
and benefactors. To all I promised a prompt return.

Of the last days spent in Saigon, I have retained the memory of constant anguish. I was living in a trance with the feeling of being attached to a wire whose other end led to the plane that was to take me away. At the time of departure, the wire would snap; everything would be over with.

It was a hot and humid night in Saigon. Sitting in the front seat of the car, I looked at the road without really seeing it.

We arrived at about seven in the evening at Tan Son Nhat Airport. There were not many people in the waiting room: a few individuals and our small group of scholarship holders accompanied by their families. We were the last to leave. To conclude this first phase of Franco-Vietnamese cultural collaboration, the Minister of Education honored us with his presence: there were speeches, congratulations, thank yous.

Everyone I loved was there: my mother; my sisters; Ma and his parents, who had loved me dearly like their own daughter; my dear friend An, my confidante since the Couvent des Oiseaux; and Bich with whom I kept up a friendship that was not very chatty, almost virile.

I tried to engrave their faces in my memory. I wanted to retain each trait.

My mother had ended up adopting the chignon of women from the South. Her hair was pulled back, exposing her beautiful face. How old was she? In her forties? She was thin and seemed as fragile and precious as a piece of porcelain. My sister Dzung, slightly taller, was standing back a bit. Her eyes were very stretched toward her temples like two widely split almonds. Ma was very near her.

Once the baggage was checked, we found ourselves at loose ends, not knowing what to do. The wait was long. The variety of the people who had come to be with me prevented any intimacy. Each remained silent, vaguely uncomfortable, looking off into space and sighing discreetly. From time to time someone would smile at me; I would smile back.

This lull put off the irreversible. I was still there, among my friends and family, on Vietnamese soil. What if I beat a retreat, leaving the airport and taking up my previous life? But I didn't move.

What suffering to bear, what struggles, and what a lot of patience it took to get to this point in my life. I had to pay dearly for what I had acquired. Since childhood I had continually endured scorn, rejection, and sometimes hate on the part of the people I considered my own. I was constantly reminded, against my will, of the humiliation of colonization and the arrogance of the white man. I was the impure fruit of the betrayal of my mother, a Vietnamese woman.

I had spent my life wanting to prove my innocence by conforming to all the rules of my society. But it was my very essence that was unacceptable. I had profoundly loved the country that had shaped me and I loved it all the more now that I was going to leave it behind. Now I had to say goodbye to it forever.

I looked away, hiding my pain. Ho helpfully drew all my mother's attention, preventing her from noticing my haggard look.

"My respects, Madame. My name is Ho. I'm a classmate of your daughter's. I am leaving, too."

In other circumstances, she would have met him with a distrustful coldness. But her pain had deadened her suspicion.

"I'm happy to meet you. Be a good older brother to her; take care of her."

She enveloped me with her tearful gaze.

There was nothing left to say.

The voice on the loudspeaker announced the immediate boarding.

"Write to me soon."

I said yes and turned away.

Our group moved away toward the departure gate. I was walking last in line.

I turned around: the familiar faces and the waving hands grew distant. I desperately tried to absorb these images as if they could save me. Soon I lost sight of them.

The plane was taking off. My throat was dry. And behind my closed eyelids, behind the veil of my tears, there were the bamboo hedges, the pond of my childhood, the beloved faces, and the satin-smooth back of the old wet nurse who was carrying me through the quiet streets of Hanoi, on a drizzly night . . .

GLOSSARY

áo dài: a long Vietnamese garment. Women's *áo dài* feature a fitted bodice and long skirt, split on both sides to the waist. Long trousers are worn underneath. In the original text, the word "tunic" is used to refer to the *áo dài*.

anh: older brother; pronoun meaning *I* or *you* if the person is male and older (up to roughly twenty years older) than the person spoken to or addressing him. May be used in third person with the word *ấy*.

Annamite/Annamese: considered by many to be pejorative, these words were derived from "Annam" or pacified south, the name China used to refer to its southern colony (111 BCE–939 AD). The terms were often used during the colonial period to refer to all Vietnamese.

bà: grandmother; pronoun meaning *I* or *you* if the person is female and much older (from roughly twenty years older and up). May be used in third person with the word *ấy*.

baccalauréat: diploma from secondary school or *lycée* in French; achievement examinations given at the end of the American equivalents of junior and senior years determine whether a student will receive the *bac*, as it is popularly known.

chị: elder sister; pronoun meaning *I* or *you* if the person is female and older (up to roughly twenty years older) than the person spoken to or addressing her. May be used in third person with the word *ấy*.

couvent: French for convent.

em: younger brother or sister; pronoun meaning *I* or *you* if the person is younger (up to roughly twenty years younger) than the person addressing her/him or speaking to her/him. May be used in third person with the word *ấy*.

métis/se: masculine/feminine adjective and noun. This French word has

267

no adequate equivalent in English. Suggested dictionary translations such as "mulatto," "half-caste," and "mixed-race" carry too many connotations, while "biracial," if more neutral, does not convey the idea of cloth woven (*tissé*) from two threads, linen and cotton.

nhà-quê: Vietnamese for *peasant*; often pejorative when used in French.

phở: noodle soup with beef or chicken, commonly eaten for breakfast, and often at other mealtimes, in Viet Nam.

ACKNOWLEDGEMENTS

I would like to thank my colleagues at Louisiana State University for their support and advice. Specifically, I wish to acknowledge Sylvie Dubois for helping me resolve some tricky translation problems, and for supporting (as chair of my department, along with Dean Gaines Foster in what was then known as the College of Arts and Sciences) my request for a sabbatical in Hanoi where I began this translation in 2009. This work was born there, in a sense, as was Kim. Thanks also to Dean Stacia Haynie, who took the reins from Dean Foster of what is now known as the College of Humanities and Social Sciences, who, along with my department chair John Protevi, generously supported a Fulbright teaching/research semester in Hanoi during spring 2016; to Emily Batinski for lending me her copy of R. Lattimore's translation of *The Trojan Women* by Euripides; to Michelle Massé for sharing her expertise on the intricacies of knitting; to Betsy Wing and Judith Miller for reading and commenting on an early draft of Chapter One; and finally, to Kate Jensen, John Protevi, Adrienne Moore, Jim Moore, Mark Schafer, Joey Zimmerman, and Sylvie Dubois for their friendship and support.

In addition, I would like to thank the friends and colleagues who, having read *Métisse blanche*, encouraged me in my goal of translating this memoir: Kate Jensen, Claire Longuet, Claire Malarte Feldman, Nathalie Nguyen, and Mary Jean Green all come to mind. They would join the students from my seminars that included *Métisse blanche* on the reading lists both at the University of Oregon and Louisiana State University and contributed their wisdom and insights to our class discussions.

My colleagues in Asian studies, having heard me use parts of this translation at the postcolonial studies conference focusing on sexualities at the University of London in 2011 and at the World History Association conference on Southeast Asia and its role in world history in

Siem Reap in 2012, expressed interest in using the book in their future courses. I would mention, too, the charmed encounter with Rachel Harrison, Tony Day, Ben Tran and Janit Feangfu at a panel I was asked to chair at the Association of Asian Studies meeting in 2011, and their abiding support of my work.

Thanks, too, to Pamela Kelley at the University of Hawai'i Press for her advice and sustained interest in this memoir, to her colleagues Debra Tang and Grace Wen for their work in production and marketing, and to Jennifer McIntyre for her excellent emendations and advice as copy editor. My gratitude, as well, to the outside readers of the manuscript, who provided many useful suggestions and signposts to guide me in my final revisions.

Finally, I would like to thank Kim Lefèvre for her generosity in clarifying certain textual ambiguities and answering questions about, particularly, her references in French to Viet Nam and its culture, an essential part of my own imaginary since I first walked into a Vietnamese language class nearly forty-five years ago.

Jack A. Yeager
Baton Rouge, Louisiana
August 2017

Born in Viet Nam in the 1930s, **Kim Lefèvre** is a memoirist, novelist, and translator who has lived in France since 1960. She is best known for *Métisse blanche* (1989), her memoir of growing up biracial in Indochina during the colonial period and after, and its sequel, *Retour à la Saison des Pluies* [Return to the Rainy Season] (1990), recounting her first return to Viet Nam since her departure thirty years before. Kim Lefèvre is also known for her translations from Vietnamese into French of the works of Nguyen Huy Thiep and Duong Thu Huong. She currently resides in Marseille.

Jack A. Yeager is professor of French studies and women's and gender studies at Louisiana State University in Baton Rouge. His research and publications focus primarily on the Vietnamese novel in French from Southeast Asia and on narrative texts by writers abroad with connections to Viet Nam. Yeager holds a PhD in French with a minor in Southeast Asian studies from the University of Wisconsin–Madison and has lived in Paris and Hanoi.